روهی متلُونه

Rohi Mataluna

PASHTO PROVERBS

روهی متلُونه

Rohi Mataluna

PASHTO PROVERBS

Revised and Expanded Edition
of the original work by
Mohammad Nawaz Tair & T.C. Edwards

Editors

Leonard N. Bartlotti
Raj Wali Shah Khattak

RESOURCE *Publications* • Eugene, Oregon

Resource Publications
A division of Wipf and Stock Publishers
199 W 8th Ave, Suite 3
Eugene, OR 97401

First Edition, 1982
Mohammad Nawaz Tair & T. C. Edwards
Pashto Academy, University of Peshawar, Pakastan

Rohi Mataluna: Pashto Proverbs
Revised and Expanded Edition, September 2006
Edited by Bartlotti, Leonard N. and Khattak, Raj Wali Shah
Published by InterLit Foundation, Peshawar, Pakistan
and Pashto Academy, University of Peshawar, Pakistan
Copyright (all additional material) © 2006 InterLit Foundation

ISBN 13: 978-1-60608-203-4
Publication Date: 3/3/2009

This limited edition licensed by special permission of InterLit Foundation

InterLit Foundation

INTRODUCTION
To the Second Edition
An Introduction to Pashto Proverbs

Over the last twenty years, my family and I have had the joy of living and working among one of the largest and most fascinating Muslim peoples in the world—the 27 million Pashtun of northwest Pakistan and southern and eastern Afghanistan. Between 1985 and 1999, we lived in the city of Peshawar at the foot of the Khyber Pass. I engaged in language study, cultural research, educational and consultancy work, including the founding of the InterLit Foundation, while my wife served in an ob/gyn hospital for Afghan refugee women, and my children grew up revelling in the vibrancy of life on the Afghan frontier.

In those years, we made many Afghan and Pakistani Pashtun friends and fell in love with this noble people and their language, oral literature, customs and culture. My Ph.D. in Islamic Studies involved extensive ethnographic research into Islam and honor in Pashtun culture, and focused on the meanings and usage of Pashto folklore, particularly the genre of proverbs, as a tool for understanding the construction and maintenance of ethnic identity among the Pashtun.[1]

The Pashtuns are men and women of faith and honor, and consider themselves the "true Afghans". Their pride, martial qualities, shrewdness and fierce independence are legendary. The Pashtuns have resisted invaders for centuries, and when outside enemies are in short supply, they fight among themselves.

The Pashto language is as rugged and beautiful as the people. Pashtuns themselves commonly affirm, with mischievous delight, "Pakhto is a hard (*sakht*) language". Like the jagged mountains, plains, and valleys of the Pashtun homelands of the Afghan borderlands, Pashto is full of jagged sounds, entertaining pleasantries, and unexpected depths of emotion and meaning.

For a Pashtun, the world is a dangerous place. Life and death and challenges to honor—loss of reputation and the threat of social death—are ever present. To negotiate such a world, a man or woman needs wise words. With the authority of tradition, Pashto proverbs provide critical lessons about faith and honor, human nature and relationships, friends and enemies, power and revenge, in short, how to negotiate life in a society that is at once fragrant with friendship, fraught with ambiguities, and seared by treachery.

Anthropologists and folklorists regard proverbs as an important ethnographic tool. The study of this apparently simple genre of oral literature in its sociocultural setting can give us insight into complex and varied aspects of a culture, for example, its sociological characteristics, underlying themes, patterns and values, ethics, religious concepts, interreligious relationships, gender relations and views of women, cultural and societal attitudes, views of everyday life and of death. So compressed is their meaning, so complex is the relation of metaphor to meaning in a flowing conversation, that linguists tell us that it takes more social knowledge to correctly use and understand proverbs than any other item of folk speech.

Among Pashtuns, proverbs are a highly valued expression of their folk life and identity. While the sayings of these frontier warriors may not sound "wise" to a Westerner, or applicable to life in a high-tech globalized world, they are prized pearls of wisdom in the towns, cities and tribal homelands of the Pashtun.

Proverbs are like "prisms". As a glass prism separates and disperses white light into a spectrum of colors, so proverbs display light on Pashtun culture, and enable us to see and understand a colorful spectrum of images, beliefs, values, behaviors and customs associated with this people and their way of life. In one sense, proverbs, like other genres of folklore or oral literature, can be said to "reflect", "express" or "embody" aspects of culture, for example, values, ways of thinking and speaking, categories and labels for dealing with people and situations.

Thus, one finds in proverbs concise "images" of the Pashtun and their world. While some of the notions expressed are common to the proverbial literature of other nations, the images are often distinctively Pashtun. For example, there are stereotypic representations of the mullah (152, 1029, 1275), *pir* (459, 653) and *qazi* (1038), and one-line commentaries about the proud (781), the poor (228, 657, 808), and the laborer (957). There are subtle word pictures of the Pashtun's pragmatic faith (650), his understanding of human nature (444, 854), and the inadequacies of religious performance not matched by a changed life (787, 927). Some proverbs point to a strong religious devotion (120), while others elevate *pakhto*, the "code of honor" (608).

A previous generation of paremiologists (proverb scholars) viewed proverbs as relics of the past, the verbal equivalent of archaeological specimens to be retrieved, collected and preserved lest they be lost. Others have presumed to find a "national character", national ideology or philosophy in proverbs. Scholars today are cautious about these approaches. Many texts have ambiguous origins or show evidence of borrowing or adaptation from the proverb corpus of neighboring peoples. Also, as is common in many cultures, there are apparent "contradictions" between texts, each of which represents not so much an alternative philosophy as another perspective on an issue, and another rhetorical strategy.

Thus, recent emphasis in folklore scholarship has turned our attention to the performance of proverbs, the ways they are actually used. Proverbs are a form of communication, and it is as communication that they must be studied if we are to understand their import and meaning for Pashtuns. In fact, the significance and fuller meaning(s) of a text emerge only as we study the dynamics of its *usage* by real people in the context of actual *situations* in daily life.

Proverbs are meant to be used. As paremiologists (proverb scholars) know, proverbs have little or no meaning apart from context. The "meaning" of a proverb is not purely "in the text", but "in the context", that is, how it is used and performed by a particular person with a particular intent in a particular situation before a particular audience who hear and understand it in diverse ways.

Accordingly, proverbs are not folkloric relics, verbal decorations, or collector's items. They are very much alive and play an important role in the speech of Pashtuns today. Pashto proverbs are found in textbooks, newspapers, and radio and television dramas, as well as in conversations in the bazaar and in homes, between and among men and women. They are heard in political speeches and political commentaries, in situations of social conflict, and in heated family arguments. This makes proverbs not only a clever form of verbal art, but also a potent tool of verbal combat!

Proverbs not only encapsulate wisdom, they are what literary critic Kenneth Burke calls "tools for living", rhetorical devices for dealing with social situations. As such, they provide a kind of ethnographic record of tensions and conflicts in a society. Proverbs identify recurring situations in a culture and give such situations a "name", a label indicating that such situations have occurred before, and have been handled in this or that way. Through the use of a proverb, the presumed wisdom of the past is invoked and made accessible to speakers and hearers in the present. The authority of tradition ("we say", "people say", "there is a *matal* [proverb] that says") can be used to propose a course of action, effect a change of attitude, or provoke a change in perspective. Proverbs are rhetorical tools to accomplish social or personal ends.

Proverb use is not a simple matter! For Pashtuns, proverbs also serve as rhetorical tools for negotiating the demands of *pakhtunwali*—the traditional code of honor that defines what it means to be Pashtun. In these pages the reader will find texts that give insight into what it means to "do *pakhto*", to live out the idiomatic values, ideals, ethos and behaviors associated with being a "true Pashtun". These pithy sayings can be dangerous and penetrating weapons in the verbal arena of interpersonal politics and everyday Pashtun life.

For many Muslim peoples, the worldly wisdom and authority of local (or national) proverbs serve as a moral guide and resource, alongside Islam, in the conduct of their everyday lives. This ethnographic reality "on the ground" is often overlooked by orientalists and others who peer into written (usually religious) "texts", and may fail to hear the voices that speak through oral literature in its various forms.

Rohi Mataluna: Pashto Proverbs is not only a contribution to the field of paremiology (the study of proverbs), it is a useful resource for the study of popular or everyday Islam, folklore in Islamic contexts, and the anthropology of Muslim societies.

For generations, Pashtuns inhabited the mountainous (*roh* means "mountain" in Pashto) margins between empires, and the borderlands between the Persian, Central and South Asian cultural spheres. Thus, a study of the proverbs (*matal*, pl. *mataluna*) of this rugged people is another facet of the proposed sub-field of

"Rohology" which the Pashto Academy defines as the study of the peoples and cultures found within this specific geographical area.

Hopefully, this collection of 1350 Pashto proverbs with English translations and annotations will help both Muslim and non-Muslim, westerner and non-westerner, move beyond facile stereotypes toward a more balanced and nuanced appreciation for Muslim peoples in general, and the infamous Pashtun in particular. The meanings associated with proverbs are linked to a worldview and way of life. These proverbs are not only windows *into* their world, they are windows that enable us to look *out* from their vantage point, and see the world through Pashtun eyes.

In his Introduction to the 1982 edition, Professor Tair affirmed, "Nothing in the entire Pakhtun culture has escaped the province of the proverb." He explained the background of the proverbs selected for this volume:

> Proverbs have been called the "molecules" of popular literature, for they provide the ingredients for the myths, the folk tales, the epics and folk poetry that express cultural identity ... Feelings and aspirations, reflections and revelations all are here in the popular sayings of ... Pashto speaking people. Some proverbs are the embryonic "punch lines" found in folk tales. Others teach and perpetuate customs and traditions that are an integral part of the Pakhtun way of life. Many more simply offer a mundane and often humorous observation on a fact of life....[F]or this volume we have selected representative examples from the rich storehouse available, adding an explanation when a proverb is ambiguous or is used in a particular way, and including the source story or folk tale where appropriate. Our aim has been to preserve some of the original flavor of a literature, largely oral, that reflects a culture now facing inevitable change.

This new edition of *Rohi Mataluna: Pashto Proverbs* has been completely updated, revised, and expanded with a considerable number of new annotations, while taking care to preserve and honor the original contribution of Mohammad Nawaz Tair and Thomas C. Edwards.

Rohi Mataluna: Pashto Proverbs is much more than a selection of exotic texts with English translations. There are several features that make this book unusual among such collections:
- Annotations that provide cultural background and contextual information.
- Explanations of key words and concepts.
- Examples of how certain texts are used in social situations.
- Observations on the form and structure of Pashto proverbs.
- Parallel and variant texts.
- Background stories and anecdotes.
- An Index of key words, persons and places used in the proverb texts and annotations.

One great value of the earlier work was that it was co-produced by a Pashtun, a local scholar and "insider" who drew upon a variety of local sources. Therefore, apart from minor changes to reflect contemporary spelling, the original Pashto texts have been faithfully reproduced, so as to preserve potentially important dialectical distinctives. Variants, alternative wording and parallel proverbs are sometimes noted; these we have enclosed in square brackets "[ ]".

Similarly, the original English glosses (translations) of the Pashto texts have been preserved, and the editors have not sought to produce new translations. Any minor changes made to an English translation for the sake of clarity are indicated by the use of square brackets "[ ]".

The editors have smoothed the language and phrasing of Tair and Edwards' English annotations (e.g. corrected spelling, improved grammar, etc.), while attempting to remain faithful to the original wording. Minor changes have not been noted; other editorial changes are indicated by the use of square brackets "[ ]".

New material contributed by the co-editors, particularly a host of cultural annotations, is enclosed in square brackets "[ ]", followed by the initials of the writer ("LNB" and/or "RWS").

Several other changes, additions, and distinctive features of this revised and expanded edition of *Rohi Mataluna: Pashto Proverbs* should be noted:

- *Alphabetization.* Proverbs in the original work were arranged alphabetically by first Pashto word. In part because some texts were out of order (e.g. due to miss-spellings, alternative spellings, etc.), we have re-alphabetized the proverbs following a contemporary dictionary arrangement by first Pashto word. Pashto readers will also note that, in accordance with current usage, we have divided words beginning alef+mad from the simple alef and made them into two separate alphabetical sections.

- *Pashtun/Pakhtun.* Throughout the book, where Tair and Edwards variously used the words "Pathan", "Pashtoon", "Pukhtoon" or "Pakhtoon" in an English translation or annotation, we have replaced and standardized it with the more widely accepted "Pakhtun" or "Pashtun". (Where "Pakhtun" occurs in the Pashto script, we have preserved this in the translation. In our notes, we usually, but not always, use the term Pashtun.)

- *Index.* Generally, when proverb collections are arranged alphabetically by first word (as herein), as opposed to the recommended paremiological order of first key word, it can be difficult to find and compare texts that contain or revolve around a particular word. (Consider the number of English proverbs that begin with the words "a" or "the"!) To overcome this difficulty and to facilitate further study, an Index was created based on key terms used in the English translations and/or in the annotations, e.g. "enemy", "faith", "friend", "God", "honor", "mullah", "women", etc.

The numbers in the Index refer to proverb (not page) numbers. In the Index we have used "see also" to refer to the occurrence of the word in the annotations, as opposed to the proverb text (English gloss) itself. Sometimes transliterated Pashto words are included in the Index (e.g. sub-headings for "friend" include "*ashnā*", "*dost*", "*mulgarey*", "*yār*"), however, the overall Index is based on English (not Pashto) words. "Persons", "Places" and varieties of "Animals" have also been indexed. In this way, readers and students can find a familiar text, and explore how a particular word is used or what Pashto proverbs say about a certain topic or theme.

- *Parallel proverbs, literary allusions and quotations.* To explain the meaning of a Pashto proverb, Tair and Edwards often use what appears to be a parallel English proverb, literary allusion or quotation from English literature (Shakespeare, the Holy Bible, poets, etc.). The annotations to the First Edition also are heavily seasoned with English idioms, proverbial expressions and sayings. However, we realize many students and local readers may not be familiar with these quotations and traditional or idiomatic English expressions. Therefore, where possible we have tried to identify the source and background, and in simplified English, to explain the meaning of potentially difficult words, English sayings, literary quotations, Biblical allusions, proverbs and idioms.

- *Poetry.* In Pashto, verses from classical as well as folk poetry (*tappas*) may convey wise advice and be used proverbially. The boundary between genres like proverbs (*mataluna*) and poetry is often less than clear, so these texts, too, can be associated with proverbs (see e.g. Index for "Abdur Rahman Baba" and "proverbs: folk poem: *tappa*"). Thus, variability of genre (whether a saying is considered to be a "proverb" or a "poem") and perception of proverbiality depend upon the "truth value", context, traditionality, and usage or performance of a given text, rather than purely structural differences. It also should be noted that Pashtun "quoting behavior" includes, in addition to proverbs, folk and classical poetry, Qur'anic verses, riddles and other oral forms.

- *Poetic Devices.* Like the proverb corpuses of other nations, Pashto proverbs contain many literary devices and "sound echoes" associated with poetry and other oral forms, including *rhyme* (similarity in the sound of word endings), *poetic language, rhythm* and/or *meter, repetition, assonance* (repetition of the same vowel sound), *alliteration* (repetition of the same initial consonant), *colliteration* (the clustering of similar consonant sounds), and *internal rhyme* (rhyming of the last word in a line with a word(s) inside the line). A given proverb may include one or more of these poetic devices, as in Proverbs 1006 and 1185. Though the constraints of space and the makeup of our audience have necessarily limited technical observations on the grammar, structure and poetics of Pashto proverbs, scholars and local readers of Pashto will delight in the pleasures of Pashtun verbal art.

- *Stories.* In many cultures, a proverb may be associated with one or more stories, anecdotes, myths or legends. In Pashto, a story may serve to explain the saying's alleged "origin" or purported "author", or alternatively, the proverb/saying may function as the springboard for a story, or the "moral", summary or logical conclusion of the narrative. One strength of Tair and Edwards' original work was its inclusion of many examples of stories associated with a variety of Pashto proverbs. Though these stories are too numerous to list separately, the reader may refer to Index entries for "story, fable, tale" and for "myth".

- *"Impolite" or "obscene" proverbs.* The proverb repertoires of many nations commonly contain texts that use what many would consider crude, suggestive or obscene language, or words with double meanings. Another common feature of proverbs is the use of circumlocution or word substitution to avoid these potentially offensive or "impolite" terms; (even then, the substituted word may still carry a double meaning, and both forms of the proverb may circulate side by side). Despite the use of indelicate terms and references, however, these proverbs are still considered wise sayings which may be socially useful. It is said that there are thousands of such proverbs in Pashto. Out of respect for the reading audience, only a few of these proverbs are included in the present collection. See Index entries for "proverbs:impolite" for illustrative texts.

- *Origin.* No judgment is made about the origin of the proverbs in this collection, whether from Persian, Arabic, Latin, English or other languages. Without textual evidence, it can be difficult to trace "international" proverbs to a single source or language. Sharing between languages is quite common (for example, many English proverbs are of Latin or Greek origin). Some Pashto proverbs are known in identical or nearly identical forms of expression in other Asian and/or European languages. For example, proverbs akin to "All five fingers are not equal" are found in 43 other languages in Southern and Eastern Europe and Asia, including Turkish, Kurdish, Tadjik, Hindustani, Sindhi, and Uzbek. We take the view herein that the acceptance, commonality and usage of a saying among Pashtuns, and its inclusion in this selection co-edited by a Pashtun, makes it a "Pashto proverb".

- *Variants.* Despite the common notion that proverbs have (or should have) a traditional "standard" or fixed form, actually they are quite variable and the same text may circulate in different forms in a given language. The variation may involve minor changes in verb forms (see e.g. Proverbs 22 and 31), or shifts in phrasing or vocabulary (see e.g. Proverbs 556 and 557) that may reflect regional, dialectical or historical changes in meaning, emphasis, politeness, audience, context or situational usage.

- *Structure*. For the sake of students and scholars of Pashto, we have also included occasional observations on proverb structure. For example, some Pashto proverbs have the form of an invocation or prayer, "Oh God! ..." (e.g. Proverbs 915 to 923). Other proverbs are in the form of blessings or curses (e.g. Proverbs 913, 1006, 1180), poetry (as noted above), or the statement and riposte structure of "dialogue proverbs" (e.g. Proverbs 85, 797, 957). However, since this is an introductory book aimed primarily at English readers, we have not attempted to undertake a meticulous literary or structural analysis of each text.

Rohi Mataluna: Pashto Proverbs will appeal to a broad audience of those interested in the peoples and cultures of Pakistan and Afghanistan in general, and the Pashtuns in particular.

- Students, development workers, scholars, tourists and other Western readers will appreciate the way this selection of colorful proverbs, with its succinct annotations and cultural explanations, provides insight into this multifaceted and complex culture.

- Local readers and students of Pashto and English in Pakistan and Afghanistan comprise another primary audience for *Rohi Mataluna: Pashto Proverbs*. For them, this revised and expanded new edition will be a source of instruction as well as enjoyment, and an affirmation of Pashtun heritage.

- For the large Pashtun diaspora in America, Europe, and other parts of the world—and their English-speaking children—*Rohi Mataluna: Pashto Proverbs* is a gift that will transport them to the rugged realities, sights and sounds, and ineffable romance of life in the Pashtun homelands.

I want to express our sincere gratitude to those who have helped make this book possible. Special appreciation is due the InterLit Foundation for its financial sponsorship and support of this project, in particular, Executive Director Susan Smith, for her assistance in the painstaking work of proof-reading, editing, and producing this book. It has been a long process, involving much painstaking labor and research, and the editors are indebted to Ms. Smith for her perseverance and gracious help in bringing this book to completion. I also want to express our deep appreciation to Mr. Geoff Smith, who has served for many years as InterLit's liason with the Pashto Academy, and the local staff of the InterLit Foundation, who have helped with additional research, proof-reading in Pashto and English, and other services.

It has been a privilege to collaborate on this project with my long-time friend and co-editor, Dr. Raj Wali Shah, who helped make this new edition a reality after years of patient work. His personal commitment has been a great encouragement to me.[3]

I want to express particular gratitude to the joint-publisher of this book, the Pashto Academy, Peshawar University. Since its founding in 1955, the Pashto Academy has been dedicated to the task of promoting, developing and preserving Pashto language and literature. The current Director, Dr. Salma Shaheen and other fine staff invariably have offered me a warm Pashtun welcome to the Academy, as well as hours of interesting interaction and academic assistance.

I would also like to honor my dear friend Prof. Mohammad Nawaz Tair, whose vision and patient scholarship led to the first edition of this book. The work that Dr. Raj Wali Shah and I have done is built upon the foundation laid by Prof. Tair, and is in part a tribute to him.

Finally, I remember the many Pashtun friends my family and I have known over the years—too numerous to mention by name, but whose faces shine in my memory—who opened their hearts, minds and homes to us, and helped me gain some insight not only into Pashtun culture, but into Pashtun hearts and the nature of friendship itself. This book, produced out of years of study and friendship and in collaboration with two local publishers, is a small gift in return for those who welcomed me and my family with such love and hospitality. It is my hope, my dream and my prayer that the revision and re-release of this book might serve to inform, entertain, refresh and enlighten a new generation with the wisdom of the Afghan frontier.[2]

Leonard N. (Len) Bartlotti, Ph.D.
La Mirada, California, USA

September, 2006

---

[1] *Negotiating Pakhto: Proverbs, Islam and the Construction of Identity among Pashtuns.* Unpublished Ph.D. thesis. University of Wales, 2000. Publication forthcoming.

[2] Some material in this Introduction has been adapted from my "Preface" [Introduction] to *Sound the Bells, O Moon Arise!: A Collection of Pashto Proverbs and Tappas* by Jens Enevoldsen (Peshawar: InterLit Foundation, 2000).

[3] This introduction is not identical in content to Dr. Raj Wali Shah's Pashto Introduction to the Second Edition.

PASHTO INTRODUCTION
TO THE SECOND EDITION

متلونه د يوې ژبې د اولسي ادب يوه ارزښتناكه اثاثه وي. د اولس و پوهي،
رواياتو، نفسياتو او د حس ظرافت (sense of humour) د معيار يو عکس هم په متل
کښې ښکاري. په پښتو ژبه کښې بې شمېره متلونه دي. په پښتني اولس کښې پوئ
او هوښيار سړے هغه بلل کېږي څوک چې څومره زيات په متلونو پوهېږي يا
څومره زيات متلونه ورته ياد وي. د پښتو متل د دانش يو عجيبه انداز لري. په
څرګنده يوه ساده خبره چې د متل حيثيت اختيار کړي نو د دانائي يو علامت
اوګرځي. متل په فوکلور کښې د ټپې په شان يو داسې اولسي صنف دے چې
ويونکے او جوړونکے ئې معلوم نۀ وي. يوه واقعه، توقه، پېښه، ماحول په يو
محصوص حالت کښې په غير ارادي توګه متل وزېږوي. ثقافتي روايتونه هم کله
کله په متل د پيدا کولو کښې اثر ولري. د ثقافتي ژوند په هر اړخ کښې داسې
حالات پېښېږي چې د خبرو په دې صنف متل کښې مستقل ځائے ونيسي. مړانه،
جرات، سخاوت، شجاوت، مېلمستيا، بنائست، تضادونه، ناشوني، ناسازي،
مينه محبت، پښتو او پښتونولي په انفرادي هم او اجتماعي توګه هم متلي رنګ
اختيار کړي. دا د عبرت د سبق، د ستائنې او غندنې په باب له د مثال په ډول
وړاندې کولے شي. ژوند يو مسلسل عمل دے په دې عمل کښې واقعات او پېښې
که هر څو د ماضي برخه کېږي ولې د حال د پاره د ماضي نه سبق اخستو يو
مئوثر سبب هم ګرځي. په هر موجود حال کښې ځينې واقعات د مستقبل د ژوند
دپاره د ژوند د رنګ د تسلسل په خاطر داسې ادبي او اولسي پنګه جوړوي چې
راتلونکے نسل پرې د خپل شناخت او د خپل ثقافت سره د روايت په تار خپل
تړون وساتي. او بيا په پښتو کښې خو شفاهي او زباني روايتونه لکه د ناليکلي

ائين پکارولے شي. د پښتونولۍ د عمل بنياد اکثر په روايت کلک وي. او روايت
خپل رنګ اکثر په متل کښې ښکاره کوي. نو متل کله کله د اولسي قانون حيثت
هم اوزومي. چې اکثر شخړې په يوۀ متل هوارولے شي.

د ثقافت د مفهوم د ابلاغ دپاره متل ډيره مئوثره زريعه ده. دغه سبب دے
چې د سلونو کالونو پخوا وئيلي شوي مکالمې د متل په رنګ کښې تر اوسه ژوندۍ
دي. کۀ دغه متلي رنګ په ځۀ شعر کښې موجود وو يا په سندره او ټپه کښې وو
نو هم داسې شعرونه، ټپې او د سندرو سرونه هم د متل په توګه وئيلے کېږي او د
مثال په ډول وراندې کولے شي. ولې اصل متل هغه مکالمه وي چې د دانائى يو
محصوص رنګ لري، د کاني د کرښې په شان يوه پخه خبره وي. د يو محصوص
حالت د مختصر تشريح خاصيت او حصوصيت لري. دا په خپل پس منظر کښې
يوه واقع لري خو ضروري نه ده چې دغه واقعه دې هر چا ته يا متل ويونکي ته
هم ياده وي. ځکه چې د متل خبره په رنګ کښې پوره مفهوم هم لري. په پښتو
کښې چې لکه څنګه ځيني شعرونو، ټپو او سندرو د متل حيثيت اختيار کړے
دے دغه شان ځيني مقولې د لويو خلقو وبنا وي او ځيني محاورې هم د متل په
حيثيت استعمالېږي ولې ټولې مقولې او محاورې متل نۀ وي. متل خپل مخصوص
رنګ او واقعاتي پس منظر او معنوي صورت لري ډير متلونه کۀ څۀ هم ځۀ خاص
واقعاتي پس منظر نۀ لري د يو وخت يو مخصوص تاثر د لاندى يوه خبره هم د
متل حيثيت اختيار کړي بيا د پوهې او دانائى د دليل پۀ توګه پکارولے شي.

"روهي متلونه" د پرفيسر محمد نواز طائر او بناغلي تهامس سي اېډوريز
شريک تاليف وو. چې د پښتو يو شمېر متلونه د انګرېزي ترجمې سره د پښتو
اکېديمي له خوا په کال ١٩٨٢ء کښې په کتابي صورت کښې شائع شوي وو. دا يو
ارزښتناک کتاب وو. او په لږه موده کښې د دې وروميې ايډيشن ختم شو. کله چې

د پښتو اکېډمي پېښور يونيورسټي او د انټرلټ فاونډيشن پېښور پخپلو کښې يو علمي ارتباط جوړ شو. نو د انټرلټ فاؤنډيشن يو فعال غړي ډاکټر لِن بارټلوټي د روحي متلونو د دوباره اشاعت تجويز پښتو اکيډمي ته وړاندې کړو. چي د دواړو ادارو له خوا د يو مشترک پبليکېشن په حېثيت شائع کړے شي. ډاکټر لِن د ډېر وخت راسې په پښتو فوکلو کار کوي. ډېر د پښتو متلونه ورته ياد هم دي. او د پښتو د متل په معنى او روح هم تر ډيره حده پوئ دے. ډاکټر موصوف ”روحي متلونه“ په تنقيدي نظر کتلې او مطالعه کړے وو. په انګريزي ترجمي کښې ئې ئيني غلطۍ په ګوته کړې وې. ورسره ئې د ترجمي ئيني حامي او کمي هم محسوس کړې وې. په پښتو متن کښې هم اکثر ځايه تېروتنې ښکارېدې. يو کار پکښې دا هم وو. چي د متل د معنى او مفهوم ځۀ ځايونو کښې مناسب نۀ ښکارېدو. بل خوا د دې کتاب دوباره شائع کولو د غوښتنو زور هم وو. نو ډاکټر لِن دا تجويز وړاندې کړو چي زۀ او هغه په شريکه دغه تېروتنې سمې کړو. د ترجمي خامي ترې اوباسو. نوے تدوين ئې اوکړو. په کوم ځايونو کښې چي د اصلاح ضرورت وي. هلته اصلاح وکړو. چرته چي متل د ورکړو معنىؤنه سيوا نورې معنې هم لري. هغه هم ورسره ځائے کړو. نو کتاب ”روحي متلونه“ به په يو نوي اهتمام د دواړو ادارو له خوا په بنۀ رنګ دوباره چاپ کړو. ماته دا تجويز غوره ښکاره شو. او کار مو پرې شروع کړو. اصل کتاب د پروفېسر محمد نواز طائر او اېډوردېز سي تهامس متن او ترجمه مو د اصلاح نه پس پخپل رنګ کښې هم هغه رنګ وساتل ځکه چي بنيادي کار د دغه دواړو بناغليو دے. البته چرته چي د متل د يو بله تشريح د [RWS] لۀ خوا ورکړې شوې ده. هغه زما يعنى د راج ولي شاه خټک له لوري شوې ده. دغه شان [LNB] مطلب لِن بارټلوټي دے. چي لوستونکي په دې پوئ شي. چي دغه اضافي زمونږ د دواړو دي. د پښتو زړه املا هم په نوي املا بدله کړے شوې ده.

د کتاب متن د انگریزي هم او د پښتو هم د سمونې کار مهربن مسز سوزن سمتھ (Mrs. Susan Smith) تر سره کړے دے. او رشتیا خبرا دا ده. چې دغه اهم کار دغه مهربنې ډیر په مینه شوق تر سره کړے دے. نو کتاب کښې د مهربن سوزن سمتھ برخه په هیڅ صورت زمونږ له واړو څخه کمه نۀ ده. بلکې کۀ دا اووئیلے شي. چې د کتاب د دوباره ترتیب تدوین او اشاعت کار ټول د دغه مهربنې دے. نو بې ځایه به نۀ وي.

د کتاب په دوباره ترتیب کښې بناغلي جیفري کار و زیار هم د ستائنې وړ دے. چې د انټرلټ فاؤنډیشن یو اهم غړے دے. ورسره د بناغلي محبت شاه خټک د ټائپست په حبث کار هم اهم دے. چې مونږ ئې مننه کوؤ. زۀ د دغه واړو بناغلیو ډېره مننه کوم. چې د هغوي په زیار د پښتو اکېډیمی دا اهم کتاب سر دوباره پۀ نوي رنگ کښې چاپ شو. ورسره د هغه ټولو اهلکارو شکریه هم ادا کوؤم چې دې منصوبه کښې ئې کار کړے دے.

پروفیسر ډاکټر راج ولي شاه خټک

Prof. Dr. Raj Wali Shah Khattak
Peshawar,
September 2006

INTRODUCTION
TO THE FIRST EDITION

Many mysteries surround the presence of proverbs in most of the literature of the world, past and present. In some cultures they are a rich part of everyday life, spoken trippingly and immediately understood. Yet among other people, such as the American Indians, they are a rarity. Their origin is obscure, often reaching far into the past, often seeming to derive from a story or a historical event, and sometimes apparently growing out of a simple unrehearsed happening. And even more curious is the existence, in widely different cultures and periods, of proverbs with identical meanings. This phenomenon has led to the intriguing suggestion that there may be everywhere an underlying universal wisdom, some elemental area common to all human thought. Before this theory can hope to gain widespread acceptance however, much more data is needed. The present collection offers one more source of raw material from which such a study may be advanced.

Proverbs have been called the "molecules" of popular literature, for they provide the ingredients for the myths, the folk tales, the epics and folk poetry that express cultural identity. This is especially true of the thousands of popular expressions that flow from the lips of the Pakhtuns[i], a proud tribal people living in Afghanistan and in the North West Frontier and Baluchistan Provinces of Pakistan. Feelings and aspirations, reflections and revelations all are here in the popular sayings of approximately 22 million Pashto speaking people. Some proverbs are the embryonic "punch lines" found in folk tales. Others teach and perpetuate customs and traditions that are an integral part of the Pakhtun way of life. Many more simply offer a mundane and often humorous observation on a fact of life. Nothing in the entire Pakhtun culture has escaped the province of the proverb.

In gathering the materials for this volume we have selected representative examples from the rich storehouse available, adding an explanation when a proverb is ambiguous or is used in a particular way, and including the source story or folk tale where appropriate. Our aim has been to preserve some of the original flavor of a literature, largely oral, that reflects a culture, now facing inevitable change. Already radio and television have made far-reaching inroads into tribal life, bringing with them political innovations and the ways of the west.

In another generation many of the accepted attitudes and conventions of those people [the previous generations] will have faded into the past. Recording a portion of the Pashto folk literature that is so much a part of their history should be an

---

[i] [Professors Edward and Tair originally used the words "Pathan", "Pashtoon" and "Pukhtoon" or "Pakhtoon" when describing the Pashto-speaking people. These terms have been changed throughout the book to "Pakhtun" or "Pashtun" as appropriate to reflect current word usage and spelling.]

invaluable service to those anthropologists, sociologists and students of folklore who may wish to understand the Pakhtuns.

No discussion of Pashto proverbs can omit the celebrated scholar and educator Maolana Abdul Qadir, founder and first director of the Pashto Academy at the University of Peshawar, for he initiated the collecting and study of Pashto literature in all its forms, particularly proverbs, folk tales and folk poetry. These materials have yet to be published, but the collection of proverbs has been studied and greatly augmented by Professor M. Nawaz Tair (now Director of the same Academy).

Professor Tair has published numerous works in Pashto, including an extensive collection of Pashto proverbs in two volumes, with matching translation in Urdu. The present volume satisfies his ambition to make them available also to English speaking readers.

A few years ago Professor Tair sent hundreds of these proverbs with rudimentary translations to Assistant Professor Thomas C. Edwards of the Humanities Department, College of Engineering at the University of Michigan. Rendering them into English proved impossible at such long range. Professor Tair consequently came to Michigan to work closely with Professor Edwards. The result is the present publication.

Since no scheme for categorizing these proverbs seemed satisfactory, we have simply presented them with matching numbers.

The introductions are identical in content.

Our gratitude extends to a number of individuals who assisted and encouraged us in our endeavor, but we are particularly grateful to the Pashto Academy and to the Vice-Chancellor of the University of Peshawar for permission to use the materials, as well as to the Asia Foundation for its generous financial support and encouragement. Mrs. Joanna Miloglav, Mr. William D. Evans and Mr. Richard Hendrickson of the foundation were especially kind.

We also owe a debt to Professor Thomas M. Sawyer, Mr. Paul Brown, Mr. Saleem Ataullah, Mr. Sayed Athar Naved Zaidi, Professor Alton L. Beeke, Mrs. Jane Edwards and the Department of Humanities in the College of Engineering, University of Michigan. The secretaries of the Humanities Department, Sharon Finton and Vicki West, could not have been more helpful and patient.

In the Pashto Academy we acknowledge, with thanks, the services of Mr. Purdil Khattak, Mr. Raj Wali Shah Khattak, Mr. Mohammad Ishaq, Mr. Lutfullah, Mr. Saifur Rahman Sayed, and Mss. Nizan Press. To these and others we extend our sincere thanks.

Thomas C. Edwards
M. Nawaz Khan Tair
Ann Arbor, Michigan, USA.
31st January, 1982

بسم الله الرحمن الرحيم

نحمده و نصلی علی رسوله الکریم،

پیژند ګلو

د دنیا په مخ هر چرته په پخوانی او اوسنی ادب کښې د متلونو زیرون همیش د پاره په راز کښې پاتي شوے دے. په ډیرو تمدنونو کښې متلونه د روزمره ژوند یوه اهمه برخه ده چې بې اختیاره ویلے کیږي. اؤ اوریدونکي پرې سمدستي پوهیږي. خو په ځینې اولسونو لکه د امریکي په هندي قبائلو کښې دا ډیر کم موندے شی.

د متلونو د رازبریدو عمل اکثر نامعلومه خو ډیر لرغونے دے. دا لکه چې زیات د کومې قیصې، تاریخي واقعې یا د څۀ خاصي تجربې په بنا پۀ وجود کښې راغلي وي. ولې زیاته ناشنا خبره پکښې دا ده چې ځینې متلونه په بیخي مختلفو معاشرو اؤ دورونو کښې یوه معنیٰ او یو شان استعمال لري. د دې توارد اؤ همرنګئ په بنا کله خو دا خیال ته راشی چې کېدے شي چې د کلهم انساني و ګري د پوهي مخزن یو وي. او د دوئ بنیادي فکرونه د یو ځایه را توکېدلي وي. خو د دې نظرئی د مقبولیت د پاره د ډیري زیاتي مطالعې حاجت دے اؤ دا مجموعه د دې قسم مطالعې د پاره د خام مواد د یوې برخې په توګه پیش کولے شي.

متلونو ته د اولسي ادب جوهر وائي ځکه چې دوئ کښې هم د اساطیرو آمېزش وي. او هم د اولسي قیصو او جنګونو د روادونو رنګ او هم دا د هغه شفاهي

سندرو اثر لري چي د يوې معاشري خاصه کنلرې کېږي. دا خبره په خاص طور
سره د هغه زرګونو وېناګانو پۀ حقله زياته صحيح ده کومي چي هره ګرۍ د
ننګيالو پښتنو قبائلو په خلۀ وي. دا قبيلي د پاکستان په قطبي قبلئيزه سيمه او په
افغانستان کښي اوسي. د خواؤشا درې کروره پښتنو عقائد، رواجونه، احساسات،
آرزوګانۍ،دلائل او پېش ګويي غرض دا چي هر څۀ چي د دوئ د ژوند سره تعلق
لري په دې وېناګانو کښي موندے کېږي.

څينې د پښتو متلونه په اولسي قيصو کښي اخښلي شوي مجرد تصورات دي.
بعضي پکښي د هغې رواجونو او رواياتو بنودنه کوي کوم چي د پښتو قبائلو د
اولسي ژوند او د دوئ د تمدن اهم جز وي. ډير پکښي د ژوند عامي مشاهدي او
تجربې دي. او د ژوند روزمره حقائق په ګوته کوي. لنډه دا چي په پښتنه معاشره
کښي متلونو د ژوند هر يو اړخ احاطه کړے دے. ځکه دا د پښتو د شفاهي ادب
يوه ډيره اهمه او په زرۀ پورې برخه ګڼلے کېږي.

د دې مجموعئ دپاره د مواد را جمع کولو په وخت د بې شماره متلونو نه څينې
نمائنده مثالونه غوره کړے شوي دي. او کوم څاے چي وضاحت پکار وو. هلته د
متل وضاحت شوے دے. او معنوي استعمال ئي په ګوته کړے شوے دے. چرته
چي د متل په شا کومه قيصه يا واقعه راغلي وه هغه ورسره راوړې شوی ده. د
دې نه زمونږ مقصد د هغې ادب د اصلي خوند تحفظ کول دي. چي اکثرو خلکو
ته زباني ياد وي ولې په ليک کښي نۀ وي راوستي شوي. دا د هغې پښتني ثقافت
څۀ لږ شان اظهار دے چي اوس عملاً په بد ليدو دے. د ريډيو او ټيليويژن له
مخه د دې قبائلو په اولسي ژوند کښي عظيم انقلاب را روان دے. مغربي تهذيب

- xvii -

هم د دوئ په معاشره كښې لاره موندي ده او پېرۍ نيمه پس به د دوئ اكثر پخواني روايات او اولسي انداز د دوئ نۀ پردے شي. او دا به د ماضي په تېرو كښې ورك شي. د دې د پاره د پښتو د شفاهي ادب د خۀ حصې د محفوظولو د ضرورت له مخه دا مجموعه تياره كړے شوه. دا د پښتو د فوكلوري ادب يوه معمولي شان نمونه ده. مونږ هيله لرو چې د انسانياتو سوشيالوجي او د شفاهي ادب دطالب علمانو د پاره به دا مجموعه د پښتون او پښتونوالي په پېژندو كښې لاس او كړي .

د پښتو متلونو د ذكر سره د نوموړي پوهاند مولانا عبدالقادر مرحوم، چې د پېښور يونورستۍ د پښتو اكيډيمي باني او وروميږ ډائركټر وو. يادګيرنه يوه لازمي خبره ده. ځكه چې هم هغۀ د پښتو ادبياتو د ټولو اقسامو د راجمع كولو او د هغې د مطالعې او اشاعت لاره روانه كړې ده. هغۀ په خاص طور سره د پښتو متلونو، عوامي قيصو او اولسي سندرو په را جمع كولو كښې دلچسپي لرله. هغه د دې په اهميت پوهه وو. او د دې ضرورت ئې محسوس كړے وو. دغه ټول مواد خو به لا شائع كښړي ولې د متلونو ذخيره ئې د پښتو اكيډيمي پروفيسر محمد نواز طائر (موجوده ډائركټر) بنۀ زياته كړې ده. او په بنۀ جوړله ئې د دې ذخيري مطالعه هم كړې ده. پروفيسر طائر په پښتو ادبياتو ډير كتابونه ليكلي دي. په دغو كښې د پښتو متلونو يوه مجموعه سره درنه د اردو ترجمې شامله ده. دا موجوده كتاب د هغۀ د هغې آرزو تكميل دے چې پښتو متلونه دې هغه چا ته هم اورسي څوك چې په انګريزۍ ژبه پوهېږي او لوستے ئ هم شي.

- xviii -

څو کاله کیږي چي پروفیسر طائر د پښتو متلونو یوه مجموعه د مسودې په شکل،
سره د ځۀ نیمگړي شان ترجمې اسستنت پروفیسر تهامس سي ایدوریز ته را
استولې وه (پروفیسر ایدوریز د میشیگن یونیورستی امریکې د انجنئرنگ کالج د
هیومینیتیز په شعبه کښي کار کوی) خو داسې د ورایه د ترجمې کار نه شو
کیدے. آخر پروفیسر طائر په خپله میشیگن یونیورستی ته راغے او د پروفیسر
ایدوریز سره ئي په شریکه د ترجمې په کار کوتې پورې کړې او دا مجموعه ئي
تیاره کړه.

هرکله چي د دې کتاب د ترتیب په لر کښي کوم خاص انداز قابل عمل نۀ وو. د
دې کبله د شمار ساده ترتیب غوره اوګنلے شو. او د ترجمې او اصل د پاره د پیش
لفظ هم یو شان او ساتلے شو. په میشیگن کښي د پښتو د کتابت د آسانتیا د
نیښتوالي د کبله د پښتو برخه پروفیسر طائر په خپله اولیکله. او دغه مسوده ئي د
اشاعت د پاره د ځان سره پاکستان ته یوړه. که ځۀ هم زمونږ دا خواهش وو. چي
دا کتاب ددې ځایه شائع کړے شي. ولې د فني او دفتري مشکلاتو له کبله داسې
او نۀ شوه. بیا هم زمونږ دا باور دے چي دا کتاب چي هرکله او هر چرته شائع
شي نو بین الاقوامي افادیت به ضرور لري. مونږ د ځینې هغې کسانو چا چي په
دې لر کښي زمونږ سره کومک او امداد کړے دے ډیر ممنون یو. په خصوصیت
سره د پیښور یونیورستی د پښتو اکیدیمي د مونږ ته ئي د دغې مواد نه د کار
اخستو موقع راکړې ده. بیا د ایشیا فاؤنډیشن چي زمونږ د دې کار ډیره بنه
پذیرائي ئي کړې ده او د هر قسم مالي امداد ئي راته راکړے دے. په تبره
مسزجین میلاګلاؤ، په پاکستان کښي د ایشیا فاؤنډیشن نمائیده بناغلے هندرک سن

او ښاغلے وليم ډي ايونز چې د پاکستان دپاره د ايشيافاؤنډېشن په صدر دفتر کښې کنټري ډائر کټر دے دا ټول زمونږ د خاص شکر ئي حقدار دي چې دوئ زمونږ په کار کښې د آسانتيا پيدا کولو باعث وو. مونږ د ښاغلي پروفيسر تهامس ايم سائر، ښاغلي پال براؤن، ښاغلي سليم عطاءالله، ميرمن جين ايډوردز، پروفيسر ايلټن ايل بيکر او سيد اطهر نويد زېدی د ميشيګن يونيورسټی د کالج آف انجينئرنګ د هيومينيټيز د شعبې او د دغې شعبې د سيکرټر يانوميرمن شيرون فينټن او پيغلې ويکي ويسټ او د نورو ملګرو د همکاري او تعاون ډيره مننه کؤؤ. ځکه چې د دوئ د اخلاص او عملي امداد نه بغير به دا کار غالباً چې سم نۀ وي ترسره شوی.

په پښتو اکيډيمي کښې مونږ په خصوصيت سره د ښاغلي پردل خټک، راج ولي شاه خټک، مولوي محمد اسحاق، لطف الله کاتب سيف الرحمن سيد او ميسرز نظام پريس تشکر کؤؤ، چې د دې کتاب په اشاعت کښې ئي په هره مرحله کښې پوره په اخلاص زيار ايستلے دے.

و ما توفيقی الا با لله

مؤلفين

ټامس - سی - ايډوردز

محمد نواز طائر

تاريخ ۳۱ - ۱ - ۸۲

- XX -

Transliteration
and Guide to Pronunciation

In 1815, Mountstuart Elphinstone, the first European writer on the Pashtuns, described Pashto as "rather rough … a manly language, and not unpleasing to an ear accustomed to Oriental tongues"[1]. Ethnographers like Grima (1993) and Lindholm (1982) and linguists like Penzl (1955) have employed differing transliteration schemes for Pashto, while a simple typewriter-based system (devised by Eugene Glassman of the Summer Institute of Linguistics for learning conversational Urdu and Persian, and modified for spoken Afghan (Eastern) Pashto by Randall Olson [1996]) proved to be adequate and practical for expatriate language learners and their local helpers. However, this system is unfamiliar to most academics. Thus, in this edition of *Rohi Mataluna* the system for transliteration of the Journal of Middle Eastern Studies has been adopted as a guide to pronunciation, with some modifications.

Transcriptions of certain words and phrases are provided to give language specialists and non-specialists alike some sense of the poetics of the Pashto language. Inasmuch as pronunciation varies considerably across Pashtun areas, the transcriptions should be viewed as a guide, not an exact representation. Each sound is generally represented by one Roman letter symbol; but the transcription makes no distinction between (Arabic) letters pronounced alike, such as /te/ and /twe/, rendering both as /t/, nor between the letters /se/ and /sin/, or /gaf/ and /ge/, or /ze/ and /zwad/ and /zwe/ which in northeastern Pashto are pronounced as /s/ and /g/ and /z/ respectively. Similarly, in the Peshawari dialect, the articulation of /khe/ and /khin/ is so close as to be indistinguishable from each other, and so these are rendered /kh/. The four retroflexes are represented by /ṭ/ /ḍ/ /ṇ/ /ṛ/. The consonant clusters /ch/, /ts/, /sh/, /dz/ and /zh/ are written as they would be in English, but generally following the Peshawari pronunciation.

In Pashto "vowels are much more liable to be influenced by neighboring sounds."[2] Therefore some of the following phonemes represent ranges of sounds. The vowel /a/ is like the sound in "ap*a*rt" (USA), whereas /ā/ indicates the longer sound as in "f*a*ther". The pronunciation of the long vowel /i/ is like the "i" in "litre" or the "ee" in "meek", but unstressed it varies according to dialect from the "i" of "pin" to the "e" of "pen". The mid-high front /e/ common in Nangarhari Pashto is similar to the vowel sound in words like "bait" and "eight" but without the glide. The /o/ sound is like the "o" in the American pronunciation of "rose" or "boat" or the British English pronunciation of "bow-tie". The vowel /u/ is similar to the sound in "boot", but in some unstressed syllables it will sound like the "oo" in "cook". The /ə/ or *shwa* sound represents a problem; this sound is similar to the American pronunciation of the "u" in "putty" or "us", or the "e" in "the" (as articulated before a consonant). The contrast between /a/ and /ə/ is often a matter of dialect, and serves as a reminder that the transcriptions are approximations.

There are five diphthongs. The diphthong /ay/ is close to that in "my"; /ey/ is close to the English diphthong in "day"; /əy/ is difficult to approximate in English but is based on the *shwa* sound; /oy/ is close to the English "boy" or "toy"; and /aw/ ranges from the diphthong sound found in words like "owe" to that in "now" and "ouch".

The following chart is a pronunciation guide for the Pashto vocalic system.

WRITTEN	PRONOUNCED	EXAMPLES IN PASHTO
Vowels		
ā	/a/ (very long), e.g. f*a*ther (UK), *ah*	*pāk, kitāb, halāl*
a	/a/ (short), e.g. ap*a*rt (USA)	*pashto, nawe, dushman*
ə	/u/ (short), the *schwa* sound, e.g. p*u*tty, *u*s	*stərga, tər, wayəl*
e	/a/ (long, not a dipthong) e.g. *ei*ght, b*ai*t	*ebādat, wraze, che*
i	covers a range from short /i/ to long /ee/, e.g. p*i*n, p*e*n, l*i*tre	*pir, imān*
o	/o/ (long), e.g. r*o*se, b*oa*t (USA), n*o*te	*tsok, khole, obə*
u	/oo/, as in f*oo*d, b*oo*t, r*u*le	*wukṛa, kum, hindu*
ey	/a/ (very long, open), e.g. th*ey*, d*a*y	*saṛey, malgərey, lidəley*
ay	e.g. m*y*, b*u*y, s*i*te; sometimes herein as /ai/	*mayen, ghayrat, khoday*
əy	---	*ḍodəy, maṛəy, kāfirəy*
oy	e.g. t*oy*	*zoy, soya, toyawəl*
aw	e.g. o*u*ch, o*w*e	*yaw, wāwra, dawlat*
Consonants		
t	dental /t/ (Pashto *te* and *twe*)	*tez, takht, bakhtawər*
s	(Pashto *se* and *sin*)	*saba, samdasti, korsəy*

g	(Pashto *gaf* and *ge*)	*gilās, gumanz*
z	(Pashto *ze, zawad* and *zwe*)	*zikər, zāmən, muzakar*
kh	Scottish lo*ch*, (Pashto *khe* and *khin*)	*khalaq, makhluq*
ṭ	the retroflex or hard /t/	*ṭāl, jaṭka, ṭamaṭər*
ḍ	the retroflex or hard /d/	*ḍāl, ḍālər, ḍānḍey*
ṇ	the retroflex or hard /n/	*pāṇa, kāṇey*
ṛ	the retroflex or hard /r/, similar to the ending of the name Ca*rl*	*məṛ, ṛund, maṛwand*
ch	e.g. *ch*ur*ch*	*chula, chokey, chāy*
ts	e.g. ha*ts*, ca*ts*	*tsə, tsinga, katsuṛa*
sh	e.g. *sh*eep	*shpa, māshum*
dz	often pronounced /z/	*mendz*
zh	--	--
gh	the gutteral voiced counterpart to the /kh/	*ghwag, mārghə*
j	e.g. *J*im, *j*oin	*jangla, bāja*
w	aspirated /w/, between /v/ and /w/	*wegən, wakil, mashwara*

---

[1] Elphinstone, Mountstuart. (1992 [1815]). *An Account of the Kingdom of Caubul.* Karachi: Indus Publications. Volume I, p.253.

[2] Morgenstierne, Georg. (1932). *Report on a Linguistic Mission to North Western India.* Cambridge: Harvard University Press. [Reprinted Karachi: Indus Publications, n.d.], p. 10.

آ تیرا کون سوزځه ، رب مې درنه بوځه ، نوم به دې وانخلم که راپورې وي دا پوزه.

1. *Oh Tirah, cursed be thy name. May God help me to leave thee. I will never utter thy name as long as I have this nose.*[ii]

The meaning is, as long as I have my good name, I will not utter the name of this cursed land. Nose and honor are synonymous in Pashto, much as in English a man's name or word is his bond. [*See* Proverb 853.] Tirah is the tribal area occupied by the Afridis and Orakzais. The proverb applies to anyone who has become bored with life in his native area.

[This expression is not used by a native living in Tirah, but is made by someone who has come to Tirah as a guest. *RWS*][iii]

[Cf. a traditional form of punishment involves cutting off the nose of the offending person, thus dishonoring them publicly. *LNB*]

آ خورې خورې خیال دې تا گوتې پردی.

2. *Oh, my darling sister! It is someone else's art that has made you attractive.*

Everyone should develop his own skill for creating artistic things.

[ii] [The exclamation "Oh" may here, and in Proverbs 2 through 4, also be translated "Ah" (the nuance of Pashto *alef-mad* exclamation, versus the usual *alef-yeh* "Oh") to convey a note of sadness or disappointment.]

[iii] [The editors have sought to honor and maintain the integrity of the original wording. Textual corrections, revisions and additions have been enclosed in square brackets [ ] to distinguish them from the 1st Edition. New annotations by the editors are indicated by their initials.]

- 1 -

آ خوري خوري سياله مي ئې مخې مي نۀ ئې.

3. *Oh, my sister! Thou art my rival, but not my equal in pedigree.*

When the two wives of one man quarrel among themselves, the one who is superior in breeding will use this proverb against her rival.

[The term *siyāl*, here translated "rival", connotes one's "equal". In general, the logic of honor involves a complementary tension between equality and rivalry. The quarreling among multiple wives is proverbial. *LNB*]

آ خوري وسواسي کله اسې کله داسي.

4. *Oh, sister melancholy, you haunt me now in one form, now in another.*

This proverb is applied to a person who worries overmuch. He is sometimes referred to as a "sister melancholia". Since a sister has the privilege of visiting the household at any time, the implication is that worry is likely to plague the individual at any time or in any form, preventing him or her from accomplishing anything.

آدم ته د جنت غنم بنۀ نۀ لکي.

5. *The wheat of Paradise sickens Adam.*

It is said of Adam, that he was driven from Paradise for eating the forbidden wheat. The proverb implies that something may possess excellent qualities, but may still be dangerous to the individual and may cause his downfall.

[This proverb is applied to the person who prefers low quality to high quality according to his nature. *RWS*]

[In the Islamic tradition Adam ate forbidden "wheat" when tempted by Satan. In the Judeo-Christian tradition Adam and Eve ate forbidden "fruit", proverbially identified as an "apple". *LNB*]

آدم خان دې په خیال ګوروان راغلے دے.

6. *Mistake not Adam Khan for a shepherd.*

The meaning is, "You have misjudged the true status of Adam Khan."

The proverb is used ironically to censure one who despises another.

Adam Khan is the hero of a romance known throughout the Pakhtun regions. He had gone to see his beloved, Durkhanai, while wearing a disguise and was forced to undergo many hardships. The English equivalent might be, "Don't mistake the prince for a pauper", or "You shouldn't judge a leopard by its spots."

آدم خان میرو پردي ورخونه نۀ خوري.

7. *Adam Khan and Mero never rely upon the resources of others.*

This is said of those who have great self-confidence. Adam Khan is the hero of a famous Pashto romance called "Adam Khan and Durkhanai." The plot is strikingly similar to that of "Romeo and Juliet", in which Mero parallels the character Mercutio.

آره آره یوم پغاړه.

8. *You still ask where the spade has gone when it is on your shoulder.*

When a farmer goes to the field he carries the spade on his shoulder until he reaches the site.

The proverb is generally applied to one who seeks something that he already has. It is similar to "You can't see your hand in front of your face."

آزار نه چا بازار موندلے نۀ دے.

9. *The tyrant finds no happiness.*

> The ill wishes of a tyrant's subjects, or those around him, prevent him from being happy. "Tyranny makes no friends."

آس آسان دے سنج ئي گران دے.

10. *Buying a horse is easy, feeding it is difficult.[iv]*

> Some things are easy to acquire but difficult to maintain.

آس به اوبو له بوځي. خو چي اوبۀ نۀ څښني نو څۀ به ئي کړې.

11. *You can take a horse to the trough [water], but you cannot force him to drink.*

> This is similar to the English proverb, "You can lead a horse to water, but you can't make it drink." [*See* Proverb 739.]

> [One cannot change the will. Literally, "... if he does not drink the water, what can you do?" *RWS, LNB*]

آس پردے سور پرې کماۍ.

12. *Although Kamalai rides like an owner, the horse belongs to another.*

> This proverb is used about someone who uses another's property while pretending it is his own.

---

iv [To be faithful to the original text, we have preserved both spellings of the Pashto word for horse, so that the *alef* occurs both with and without the *mad*.]

آس په خپل قابو ترپېږي.

13. *The horse gallops according to his strength.*

The meaning is, if a powerful man does the work, he will do it easily and confidently.

[A man will act according to his ability. *RWS*]

آس توبره په کار زياتوي.

14. *The more a horse works, the more grain he eats.*

This is similar to the British saying, "A laborer is worthy of his hire."

[The more one works the more one gets. *RWS*]

[The now proverbial British saying quoted above is from the Holy Bible,[1] and refers to the just rewards for one's work. In the 1st Edition, Tair and Edwards often used a parallel English proverb, literary allusion or quotation from English literature (for example, Shakespeare, or as here, the Bible, etc.) to explain the meaning of a Pashto proverb. Since some readers may not be familiar with these quotations, where possible we have tried to identify the source, background and meaning of these English expressions. *LNB*]

آس چي په ميدان ورځي نو د سوارۀ په زور ورځي.

15. *The horse is in the race because his master [rider] desires it.*

The implication is that a subordinate, or a young person, would not take the initiative to do something unless it met with the approval and the encouragement of his superiors or his elders. It is also used of one who does something remarkable, implying that he has some driving force behind him.

[Literally, "… he goes because of the power (or skill) of the rider." Thus, the subordinate should not be blamed for something beyond his control. *LNB*]

آس چِي خدائے خواروي نوم ئِي يابو کړي.

16. *When the horse loses his place in the animal hierarchy, he is treated as a mule.*

آس د بله، غمچينه د خُنګله، چِي دے ئِي نۀ زغلوي نو به ئِي څوک زغلوي.

17. *Who will refrain from racing the borrowed horse or from using a riding crop obtained from the jungle?*

    Put another way, no one refrains from thumping [beating] a borrowed horse. No man respects another's property.

آس د خرو په ډله خر شی.

18. *When a horse lives with donkeys, he becomes a donkey.*

    Man changes his habits with his company.

آس د سوارۀ کوناتي پيژني.

19. *The horse recognizes the rider by the feel of his buttocks.*

آس د موبړي په زور تربکي وهي.

20. *The horse gains his courage from his master.*

    [The aggression of a man shows the force behind him. This proverb could also be translated, "A horse jumps because he knows he is tied to a hitch." That is, the horse is fastened to a stake driven into the ground. *RWS*]

آس دے خو د خر نه پاس دے.

21. *True it is a horse, but it is a bit better than a donkey.*

The man of prominent class should behave according to his social status.

[Sometimes a man belongs to a high class but his actions put him closer to a lower class. *RWS*]

آس دې وي په لس دې وي.

22. *Let there be a horse, but let it cost only ten rupees.*

The implication is that the wish is unrealistic. A good thing cannot be purchased at a low price. [*See* Proverb 31.]

[The *rupee* is the basic monetary unit in Pakistan. The *paisa* is a small fraction of a *rupee. LNB*]

آس شیشني خر رائي، غاتر نورې بلا وائي.

23. *The horse whinnies, the donkey brays, and the mule neighs some other nonsense.*

Each man speaks of his own interests in his own way. Analogous to "Every one to his own taste" ["To each his own"], or "Every one blows his own horn [trumpet]."

آس بۀ دے کۀ متروکه. لعنت شه په دواړه توکه؟

24. *Which is more useful, the horse or the whip? Cursed be both.*

When one is dissatisfied with two things, he will reply, "Cursed be both", if asked which is more useful.

آس کهٔ تېکنے دے میدان لنډ دے.

25. *The horse may be obstinate, but the distance is not long.*

Used to encourage a man who, though unable to perform a task, is
still urged to try.

[A man may not be well qualified, but if the job is easy he can be
recommended for it. *RWS*]

آس که د وښو سره یاري وکړي نو خوري به څهٔ.

26. *If the horse pities and spares the grass, what else will he eat.*

[Literally, "If the horse makes friends with the grass ..." While
making friends, one should keep one's own interests in mind. *LNB,
RWS*]

آس لره په دست لره.

27. *Keep a horse, but stay in the saddle.*

This is similar to the English saying, "Be master of your own
house."

[Tair and Edwards refer to an English legal proverb with parallels in
many European languages, "Every man is master in his own house."
The meaning of the Pashto text is that of all the places a man lives
and works, he should at least retain control of his own home. *LNB*]

آس مې در کړو خو سورید‌ې به پرې نه.

28. *I have given you a horse, but you must not ride it.*

This proverb is said of a man who, pretending to give a gift,
prevents the recipient from using it.

[This refers to a gift given unwillingly. *RWS*]

آس نه راکوز په خرهٔ سور.

29.   *Down off the horse and up on the donkey.*

   The reference is to one who accepts an inferior position after having enjoyed a higher status.

آس نه راکوز شه آس زما دے.

30.   *Get down from that horse, it is mine.*

   The aggressor may say this to the actual owner.

   [One should not boast of another's property or deeds. *RWS*]

آس هم غواړې په لس ئې هم غواړې.

31.   *You want to buy a horse, and you want it for ten rupees.*

   One must pay a proper price for an expensive object. Precious commodities cannot be had cheaply.

   [One should desire according to his status. *RWS*]

   [This proverb is a variant of Proverb 22. Despite the common notion that proverbs have a traditional "standard" or fixed form, actually they are quite variable and the same text may circulate in variant forms. The variation may involve minor changes in verb forms (as with Proverbs 22 and 31), or shifts in vocabulary or phrasing reflecting regional, dialectical or historical changes in meaning, emphasis, politeness, context or usage. *LNB*]

آس ئې په خرهٔ بار کړو خر ئې پرې مردار کړو.

32.   *The poor donkey was killed when they placed a horse on his back for him to carry.*

   People of limited means cannot shoulder great responsibilities.

آس ئې په سوو کتي مېړونه ئې په خولو کتي.

33. *A horse earns his tray with his hooves, a man earns his bread with his sweat.*

Each earns his living in his own way.

آس ئې و هغو ته ورکړو چې د تانګ د تړلو ئې نۀ وو.

34. *Horses were given to those who did not know how to saddle them.*

The proverb is applied to a man who is unworthy of the position given to him.

آسانه کلیمه په هندو ګرانه.

35. *Though the "kalima" is easy to recite, the Hindu cannot do so.*

The *kalima* (the declaration [or creed] of a Muslim that he believes in one God and his Prophet Mohammad (PBUH)) is easy to recite. The Hindu cannot do so.

The message of the scriptures cannot be appreciated without faith. Hence, the Hindu, an unbeliever, cannot read it properly

If someone accepts a relatively simple job unwillingly, he will probably fail at it.

[Recitation of the *kalima* is the first of the five pillars of Islam (*see* note to Proverb 291 and "creed" in the Index). Even an easy task is difficult for a Hindu; therefore, it is difficult for a Hindu to recite the *kalima*. *RWS, LNB*]

[In Pashto proverbs, the Hindu is stereotyped as weak, impotent and incapable of performing anything with the strength and capability of the proverbial manly Pashtun. *See* Proverb 340. *LNB*]

آسره په وينو سره.

36. *To be beholden is to be besmeared with blood.*

This proverb is applied to a friend who is dependent upon the promises made by someone who has failed to keep his word. This has resulted in annoyance and dissatisfaction.

[Longing or hoping always has some bad effects. *RWS*]

آسمان به ولاړ وي. لات به مردار وي.

37. *The heavens will remain as they are, but the foreign rulers will be gone.*

آسمان په ډوزو مۀ وله.

38. *Don't throw stones towards the sky.*

Do not boast of doing something beyond your capabilities.

آسمان په ستورو او جينۍ په خالونو ښائسته ده.

39. *As the sky is beautiful with stars, so the maidens are beautiful with khāls.*

The *khāl* is an artificial mole or beauty mark popular with some Pakhtun tribes.

آسمان په لته نشي وهلے کېدے.

40. *Nobody on earth can kick the heavens.*

No one's reach is unlimited.

آسمان ته لاړې مهٔ توکه په خپل مخ به دې راپرېوځي.

41. *Don't spit at the sky, you will get it back in the eyes [face].*

This is similar to the English proverb, "Don't spit into the wind".

[The proverb appears in other languages and in variant forms, for example, "Don't spit upwards, for it will fall back in your own face" (or, "nose" or "eyes"); "Never spit into the wind (against the wind)"; "He who spits against the wind spits in his own face." *LNB*]

آسمان ته منجیله مهٔ تړه.

42. *Don't set your turban [pad] to carry skies.*

Do not shoulder a heavy responsibility that you are not capable of fulfilling.

[When carrying a heavy load on one's head, the *manjilə*, a cloth, rope, grass or wood pad, (here losely translated "turban") is used as a cushion against the weight of the load. *LNB*]

آسمان چې تنېږي دومره نهٔ وربرېږي.

43. *Thunder does not necessarily mean a downpour.*

Equivalent to the English proverb, "Barking dogs seldom bite" [Or, "A barking dog never bites." *See* Proverbs 511, 685 and 1226.]

آسمان چې وریځي خوروي باران به وکي.
کونډه چې سترګې توروي مېړهٔ به وکي.

44. *When the clouds darken the sky, they may rain. When the widow blackens her eyes, she may find a husband.*

For every action there is a cause. [*See* Proverb 209.]

آسمان د سترگو په ککۍ کښې لیدے شي.

45. *The whole sky is mirrored in the pupil of an eye.*

This proverb cautions that great people should not look down upon the insignificant man or even upon small things, as they may eventually prove to be great.

آسمان کښې چې وریځې ګرځي باران به وشي.

46. *When clouds drift in, it will eventually rain.*

[Everything that happens has its signs. *RWS*]

آسمان لرې مزکه سخته.

47. *The heavens are far above and the earth is so hard.*

The heavens will not hide me, nor will the earth swallow me.

The proverb refers to the wish to hide in shame or embarrassment, as in the English expression, "He prayed that the earth would open up and swallow him."

[In addition to being an image of embarrassment, "Oh, if only the ground would open and swallow me", the "open ground" "earth swallowing" idiom is also related to Divine judgment or a curse, "(May) the ground open her mouth, and swallow him" For the latter, *See* Proverb 341. *LNB*]

آسونه ئې نالول. چونګبنو هم پښې پورته کړې.

48. *When the horses were being shod, the frogs lifted up their feet too.*

The frogs also wished to have iron shoes [horseshoes].

[This proverb refers to one who vainly desires for something greater than his ability. *RWS*]

آسیاوان چې تسپي اړوي ژرنده کرے خطا کوي.

49.   When the āsiyāwān *turns his beads he is actually trying to cheat the simple miller.*

In Afghanistan, the *āsiyāwān* is a Persian-speaking mill owner who [in this text], while showing false piety, is trying to cheat the other fellow. The cunning man always tries to make a good impression by his outward appearance.

[The word *āsiyāwān* is the Persian term (also used in Afghan Pashto) for a "miller". Prayer "beads" (*tasbəy*) are used by pious Muslims to recite the names of God; they may be perceived by some others as merely an outward sign of religiosity (as in this proverb) or used as "worry beads". *LNB*]

آشمن د خداے دشمن.

50.   *The rich man is the enemy of God.*

Rich people seldom follow what God ordains, as their wealth diverts their attention to other pursuits.

ابا اوبو يوړو وئيل ئي ابا څۀ كوې چي غاړي غرونه ئي يوړل.

51. *"Help" he cried. "Father has been carried away in the flood." But his brother replied, "What to speak of father, when the very mountains and dales have been washed away."*

The implication is that in times of great catastrophe, those losses that would normally seem disastrous are relatively inconsequential.

[The proverb also refers to those who deliberately ignore the urgent and avoid duty by lame excuses. *RWS*]

ابا حلال ډرے نۀ حلال.

52. *Slaughter my father, but not my lamb.*

It is a Pakhtun custom to keep animals and poultry in the name of the children. Each child knows which animal belongs to him, but sometimes it is necessary to sell or slaughter the animal. When the young owner weeps, it is assumed that the lost beast or fowl meant more to him than does his family.

The implication is that one's personal property is the most precious thing in the world.

ابا مۀ ګوره خورجين ئي ګوره.

53. *Pay no attention to the father, but keep an eye on his purse.*

This proverb is applied to the person who is concerned with his own welfare regardless of that of his elders.

[It is wealth that gives value to the relationship. *RWS*]

ابا ولاړ دم ئې لاړ.

54. *Father died while standing.*

This is said about an accident that causes a loss, but also laughter.

For example, if flour were placed in a bin, children might climb in to press it down. Their weight bursts the bin—and the children roll onto the ground covered with flour. [Such an "accident" causes loss and laughter, and the use of this proverb.]

The proverb stems from an Islamic legend. King Solomon (*Bacha Suliman*) had employed the *jinn* and giants to build the temple of Jerusalem for him. When he realized he would not live long enough to see it completed, he prayed to God to conceal his death from them so they would not relinquish their work when relieved of the fear he engendered with his presence. The prayer was answered and King Solomon died while leaning on his staff. He remained in this position for a year without his death being suspected, until white ants (or a worm) ate away the staff and the corpse fell to the ground. The temple was completed before the *jinn* and giants realized that they had been duped.

A reference to this legend appears in the Holy Qur'an "And when We decreed death for him, nothing showed his death to them save a creeping creature of the earth which gnawed away his staff and when he fell the *jinn* saw clearly how, if they had known the unseen, they would not have continued in despised toil."[2]

[This proverb can be said when something unusual or unexpected happens. *RWS*]

اباسین هم چې په کاسو شي نو اوچ به شي.

55. *Even the mighty Indus would dry up if all men were permitted to take water from it in their bowls.*

Even abundant wealth will not satisfy the needs of numberless persons. [*See* Proverb 583.]

[This is said about the lavish distribution of something. *RWS*]

ابۍ ابۍ په کوم تاخ کښې اگۍ واچوم.

56. *Oh mother, on which ledge shall I lay my egg?*

In the Pakhtun household the poultry have free run of the house and do not care where they lay their eggs. The proverb is directed at someone who makes lame excuses for laziness.

[It is also used when everything is in a state of disorder and the place for doing something specific is not clear. *RWS*]

ابۍ ابۍ ځاے دې دینگولی.

57. *Oh mother, you are tied to your sink.*

Used to chide someone who busies himself with his daily chores and menial tasks without trying to better his lot.

[Used also when someone doesn't progress or is incapable of adapting to a situation. *RWS*]

ابۍ پۀ سمه کډه ئې پۀ سوات.

58. *Mother on the plains and her luggage in Swat.*

This proverb applies to the person who lives in one place, while his possessions are in another. It stems from the annual migration of the Yousafzais in times past from the Mardan plains to the Swat hills. It refers especially to the woman who has been left behind while the caravan carrying her luggage has gone ahead to the hills.

[Another version of the same text says, "... her spinning wheel (*tsarkha*) is in Swat." The actual meaning of this expression cannot be written, that is, it may be suggestive. The proverb is used as well about one's actual place of honor, in comparison with a place of temporary abode. *See* note on Proverb 104. *RWS, LNB*]

ابی پی پخپله وخبنل او پردی پیشو په پتو کښې زغلوی.

59.   *The mother drank the milk herself then chased the neighbor's cat.*

One does a bad deed himself and passes on the blame to another.

ابی چې د زړۀ کوي نو په څمخي کښې تبی کوي.

60.   *If the mother wishes, she may mix fat even in a spoon.*

The proverb refers to someone who, when she wants to do you a favor, will pour butter oil into your spoon, if not the whole [butter oil] dish into your kettle. This is about someone who wishes to help another in an unaffected way.

[This proverb describes favoritism being shown in an unobjectionable manner. *RWS*]

ابی خو په څار څار ګوره په ورکړه ئې زړۀ چوي.

61.   *Listen to the kind words of the mother, though when you ask for something, she becomes angry and her kindness vanishes.*

There is a world of difference between sweet words and actual deeds.

ابی مړه شوه تبه ئې وشلېده.

62.   *The fever has passed away, but so has the mother.*

Spoken when a trouble, while vanishing, causes more trouble.

ابی مې لیونۍ شوه په ژمي باتینګنړ غواړي.

63.   *Mother has gone mad, she wants* brinjal *in winter.*

The reference is to asking for something out of season or impossible to obtain.

[In some of the Pashtun tribes, tomatoes are also called *bātinguṇ*, here translated "*brinjal*' or eggplant. In the old days tomatoes were not available during the winter. *RWS*]

اتفاق ته غرونه څۀ دي.

64.   *United efforts move mountains.*

When people unite, even the largest obstacles can be overcome.

اتلس شلي ورځي دولس مياشتي دي د کال، ګنده ئي پشکال.

65.   *There are 360 days or 12 months in the year, but the most terrible are those of* Pashakal.

The *Pashakal* covers the days from mid-July through September, the hottest and most humid period of the year when the temperature may reach 110 degrees Fahrenheit in the shade.

[This proverb seems to originate from the plains of the Peshawar Valley, because it is there that these summer months, especially August, are most severe. *RWS*]

اتڼ په دوۀ ګوتي تودېږي.

66.   *A dance can be started with the snap of a finger.*

An insignificant action can set great things in motion.

[Enjoyment and jubilation need no great preparation. *RWS*]

اتڼ په يو لاس نۀ كېږي.

67.   *ataṇ cannot be danced with one hand.*

    ataṇ is a folk dance of the Pakhtuns that includes much clapping. We would say, "It takes two to quarrel" [or "It takes two to tango" *LNB*]. It implies also that it takes two to woo.

[In *ataṇ* both hands are used for clapping. If a person is using one hand for something else, he is unable to participate. It also takes two to accomplish certain tasks. There is blessing in cooperation and unity. *LNB, RWS*]

اتڼ وران سهي چې امرالدين لا لا ناري وهي.

68.   *Let the dancers stop when Amruddin Lala calls.*

    This proverb is used when a newcomer, interested in other things, interrupts the work in progress. It is used ironically when force is employed to stop the work.

اتي په ډمامو نۀ وېرېږي.

69.   *An elephant is not afraid of the beat of drums.*

    Small things will not affect a strong man.

اتي تېر دے خو لكۍ ئې پاتې ده.

70.   *He has swallowed the elephant, but the tail remains behind.*

    He has devoured everything except a small portion.

    [The elephant has passed, but its tail has not: it is still there. *RWS*]

اتي چي مړ شي قيمت ئې زيات شي.

71.   *When the elephant dies, its value increases.*

The ivory has no value as long as the elephant is alive. Many men are also worth more dead than alive.

[A living elephant costs one *lāk* (100,000) *rupees*, but a dead one is worth two *lāk. RWS*]

اجل په علاج نۀ ستنبړي.

72.   *Death cannot be avoided by care.*

[The term *ajal*, translated "death" here and in Proverbs 73 and 74, refers to the hour of death, more specifically "the appointed time of death" as ordained by God. Thus, it cannot be avoided even with the best *elāj*, a term that refers to medical care, a cure or remedy. Life and death are in God's hands. *See* Proverb 94. *LNB*]

اجل په نېټه دے.

73.   *Death comes at its appointed time.*

In this fatalistic view, one should not fear danger, because he will not die before his appointed time.

اجل نه اګاهو مۀ مره.

74.   *Do not die before your death.*

One should not lose heart when it [death] is foreordained.

احتیاط ښهٔ دے په هر کار کښی تلوار مهٔ کړه.

75. *It is better to be cautious in everything than to be hasty.*

The meaning is similar to the saying, "Haste makes waste."

[This expression in Pashto seems to be a line of verse. *RWS*]

[The warning to be cautious and the well known rhyming proverb, "Haste makes waste", remind us of other proverbs asserting the opposite truth, as in the English saying, "The early bird catches the worm" and the Pashto saying, "The Pakhtuns are very much in love with short cuts" (Proverb 340). Contradictory proverbs are a well known feature of the proverb repetoires of many nations. They remind us that proverbs do not embody a strict philosophy of life, so much as function as rhetorical tools to be used as the occasion demands, viz. in some cases haste and in others, caution. *See* Proverbs 320 and 321. *LNB*]

اختر پټ میړهٔ نهٔ دے.

76. *The* Eid *is not a secret husband.*

"Truth will out!" The well-publicized and eagerly anticipated *Eid*, a festival that follows Ramazan (the month of fasting), can never come as a surprise. *Eid* is celebrated by all. It is not a secret thing.

If someone doubts another's veracity, or if one is falsely accused, he uses this proverb in his defense. Also, one who has nothing to hide will use this proverb.

[The truth has to come out ultimately, so one should not try to conceal it. *RWS*]

اختر چې تیر شي نکریزې په دیوال وتپه.

77. *After* Eid, *of what use is henna? Paint the walls with it.*

Women use henna as a form of cosmetic to decorate their hands and feet. It is used specially at celebrations such as *Eid* and weddings. The proverb expresses a kind of complaint against help that comes too late. It parallels the American expressions "Too little too late" and "Why shut the barn door after the horse is gone?"

[Everything has value at its proper time. After that time it becomes valueless. *RWS*]

اختر د يوهٔ سړي نهٔ دے.

78. *The* Eid *is not for one man alone.*

Celebrations such as *Eids,* the Muslim days of thanksgiving, are for all persons alike.

اختر هم نهٔ شو اؤ ږيره مې هم وخرئيله.

79. *Foolishly did I shave, as the* Eid *did not take place.*

The speaker has prepared himself [literally "shaved my beard"] for a special occasion that has not materialized.

اخ رنګه په دوه رنګه.

80. *A good quality with two shades.*

This refers firstly to clothes. The shades indicate price and quality. The quality should be high, the price low and the quantity great. Secondly the proverb also is used to refer to anything one wishes to obtain with the same characteristics.

[That is, something that may look good, but also has some other hidden (possibly bad) quality. *RWS, LNB*]

اخر عمر د خوارۍ دے.

81. *Old age is a time of wretchedness.*

اخره زمانه شوه د چرګانو يارانه شوه.

82.   *The world is coming to an end, the cocks [roosters] are friends.*

Since cocks [roosters] will fight with one another to the bitter end,
it would be a sign of doomsday if they became friendly. This proverb
is used when two bitter enemies are seen together in a friendly mood.

[Many Pashto proverbs warn of the dangers of trusting an enemy's
soft words or smile. *LNB*]

اخبنلي در بخبنلي خو چي اوچ مي لامدهٔ نهٔ کړي.

83.   *Keep the dough; leave me the dry flour.*

This means, What's done is done, but don't go any further.

The proverb stems from a story about a woman who went to a
neighbor's house and started kneading flour for herself without
permission from the mistress of the house. The mistress was much
annoyed by this act, but could do nothing about it. She could only
say, "Let the moistened flour be yours, but do not make my dry flour
wet." It is used when someone does something stupid.

[It can also be used when someone is being stopped, in an inoffensive
way, from doing further damage. *RWS*]

[In many cultures, a proverb may be associated with one or more
stories. The story serves to explain the saying's "origin" or purported
"author", or alternatively, the proverb / saying may function as the
"moral" of the story. *See* Index entries for "story, fable, tale" and for
"myth", and note to Proverb 1193. *LNB*]

اخبنې چي روپۍ شيندي د کلي ټولي جونه ئي خدمت کوي.

84.   *If the brother-in-law is generous toward his sister-in-law, he will be
served cordially by all the damsels in the community.*

اخون صاحبه غوړي دي! غږ مۀ لره سړي دي!
دا نور دي په لاس کښې څۀ دي؟ نغن دے. څۀ عجب
ئي خوند دے.

85. "Oh, Akhund, I have brought fat (a gift) for you."
     "Quiet! There are others here. What else have you brought?"
     "Wheat bread."
     "Oh, how tasty!"

This proverb is applied to those who receive an unexpected gift
and selfishly do not want to share it with others.

The story is told that someone visited an Akhund and said, "I have
brought fat for you." The Akhund (*ākhund*) replied, "Be quiet so that
others may not hear you." Then the Akhund quickly continued,
"What else is in your hand?" The reply was, "It is wheat bread." The
Akhund in pleased anticipation cried, "It has a pleasant taste."

The appellation Akhund or teacher carries the connotation of
pundit.

[The Akhund is supposed to teach generosity to the people, but when
it comes to himself, he is miserly. The proverb is about the hypocrisy
of mullahs. *RWS*]

[This proverb, and others like it, present a common stereotype of the
mullah or religious teacher as a greedy lover of food, quite in contrast
with the Pashtun ideal of generosity. The quadripartite statement and
riposte structure is typical of what are called "dialogue proverbs" and
appears in other proverbs about "mullahs" (roughly equal with
Akhunds in many areas). *See* Proverb 89. *LNB*]

اخوند ګرمولم زۀ نۀ ګرمېدم.

86. *The Akhund accused me, but I was innocent.*

The implication is that anyone blamed for a fault will not accept
the verdict of his judges. Convinced of his innocence, he will try to
justify his actions.

[The verb *grəmawəl* means to warn, accuse or implicate someone of
guilt. *RWS*]

[The proverb describes the proverbial audacity of the Pashtun who will, for the sake of pride, reject even a religiously motivated accusation or challenge to his autonomy. *LNB*]

اخوند له بنوروا هم بس ده.

87.   *For the Akhund soup is sufficient.*

A poor man is satisfied with ordinary things.

اخوند موړ شو پاتې ئې کور شو.

88.   *Though the Akhund has had his full, his family is hungry.*

Even if replete, a greedy man will not be satisfied until his dependents are provided for as well.

اخونه ربنتیا مۀ وایه په کلي کښې به دې خاۍ ورک شي.

89.   *Oh, Akhund! Do not speak the truth, otherwise you will lose your place in the village.*

An Akhund is a teacher of religion. The meaning is caught in [the Latin, and now common English saying,] "When in Rome, do as the Romans do." [*See* Proverbs 631, 885 and 1255.]

[Telling the truth is the job of the strong. The weak person who tells the truth will suffer. *RWS*]

[As the Akhund or mullah is paid by the village, he is in a somewhat tenuous position inasmuch as his verdict on an issue (for example, a feud or religious question) could cost him his job. *LNB*]

اخونه اخونه مار دے! د ښو ځوانانو کار دے.

اخونه اخونه تربل دے يو زۀ يم يو مي ځوے دے.

اؤ يو ملا اکبر دے!

90. *"Oh, Akhund! Here is a snake to be killed."*
"Oh, but that is the work of brave young men."
"Oh, Akhund! Here is a dinner for you."
"Ah, but there are three of us; myself, my son and Mullah Akbar."

This proverb implies that a cowardly man shrinks from danger, but when good things are distributed he always rushes forward and claims his full share.

[This dialogue proverb plays on the stereotype of the mullah. *See* Proverbs 85 and 89. *LNB*]

ادب له بې ادبه زده کيږي.

91. *Manners can be learned from the manner-less.*

A story is told of the philosopher Luqman, who was once asked, "From whom have you learned your good manners?" Luqman replied, "From the ill mannered ones." He was asked, "How can this be?" Luqman replied, "I learned from them what actions were evil, [and these] I did not wish to do."

[The term *adab* ("manners") refers to "proper behavior". *See* Proverb 92. Luqman, who is called "Luqman the Wise", is mentioned in the Holy Qur'an in *Sura* 31 known as "Luqman". "We bestowed (in the past) wisdom upon Luqman....For Allah is Exalted in power, full of wisdom."[3] This *Sura* includes admonitions regarding the true worship of God and other wise sayings. As Maududi comments, "It is as if to say, 'O people: In your own country there has lived a wise man, named Luqman, whose wisdom has been well known among you, whose proverbs and wise sayings are cited in your daily conversation and who is often quoted by your poets and orators. Now you should see for yourselves what creed and what morals he used to teach.'" Commentators have various views regarding Luqman's background, but he may have been an Arabic-speaking black African. *LNB*]

ادب له زخمه اخستل کیږي.

92. *Only with a beating can manners be taught.*

This is similar to the saying, "Spare the rod and spoil the child." [*See* note to Proverb 310.]

[*adab* (manners, proper behavior) can only be taught by discipline (including physical punishment). Another well-known variant of this text uses alliteration: "Manners (*adab*) can only be learned by a beating (*ḍab*)." The proverb refers not just to a beating, but also to any rebuke or discipline, expressing the general principle that the community (in the form of parents, a boss, elders or those in authority) can enforce morality or compliance with its customs and expectations. *LNB*]

ادته بلا په بسم الله نۀ اوري.

93. *The habitual mischief-monger cannot be discouraged by one's reading holy prayers.*

A chronic nuisance needs to be dealt with firmly.

[A bad "habit" of any kind will not go away just by saying "*bismillah*" (In the Name of Allah). *See* Proverb 160. *LNB*]

ادې به وروستو ایمانداره بولم. که حُنکدن ئې په خبر تبر کړو.

94. *Only when she dies in peace will I know that mother was faithful.*

It is said that at the time of death [literally, *zankadan*, "the last breath of life"; cf. Index entries for "death", *ajal*, the "hour of death". *LNB*] one reviews his whole life, good deeds as well as bad. If the list of good deeds is greater than the list of bad, then he or she will die in peace. Otherwise he or she will die in torment. The implication is that a man cannot be considered loyal and trustworthy until he is subjected to the final test.

[It is believed among the Pashtun that the agony of sinners is very hard and difficult. *RWS*]

ادې په سوات بابا په باجوړ.

95. *The mother remains in Swat, but the father lives in Bajaur.*

Though the proverb may be used to suggest the unnatural separation of married couples, it is also used to ridicule the laborer who arrives without his tools, as does the proverbial American plumber.

ادې ته د مرګ کلیمه مۀ وایه.

96. *Do not recite the prayers of death before mother.*

Even if one wishes to praise a man, one should not speak of any subject that makes him fearful. The proverb is sometimes used on the occasion of the circumcision of a boy.

ادې چې زورروه وه د بابا د زوره وه.

97. *If the mother dominated the family, it was because of the father, who patronized her.*

ادې خدای ښۀ دے کۀ سخې.

98. *Oh, mother! Which is more precious, God or calf?*

In the mountains, children make echoes by shouting this sentence. The echo, of course, replies "calf". When the echo replies, the children laugh to hear nature confirm their belief that one's personal property is the most precious thing.

ادې زۀ صبرناک یم ماته ئې په دې زمکه راواچوه.

99. *Oh, mother! I am not in a hurry, but put it on the ground for me.*

This is said of the man who blames others for his own greed and impatience.

ادې که ئې د زړۀ کا اوګرې ته تبے وکا.

100. *If mother wishes, she may even mix fat with the porridge.*

ادې ګوره خپلې پښې ګوره.

101. *Watch mother and lift your feet.*

If the mother is angry, the child should run without delay.

ادی مې غم تسوی ویر ګرمومي.

102. *The mother cares not for the mourning of others, she merely fulfills the obligation to add to the mourners.*

She wants to increase the tempo of mourning.

[The Pashtun concept of *ghəm* (here translated "mourning") is associated with suffering, tragedy and feelings of sorrow. *ghəm* is a common theme in Pashto folklore, including poetry, music and drama, and appears in a number of proverbs in this book. Pashtuns, both men and women, commonly visit each other at *ghəm* events (for example, illnesses, deaths and times of loss), as in this proverb. The word *ghəm* has also been variously rendered in this book as "sorrow", "grief", "trouble", "burden" and "worry", and each of these words appears in the Index. For convenience, we have also combined all references to *ghəm* as a separate Index entry. *LNB*]

ادې هم د کور مبرمن شوه.

103. *The mother has become the master [owner] of the home.*

Used ironically when an insignificant person assumes authority.

[In other versions of this text, the "guest" (*melma*) or "neighbor" becomes the master of the house. This proverb implies that the rightful owner did not have the courage, resources or character needed to assert leadership as he should have. *LNB*]

اډوکي دې خوړو د کوني مبچ دې نۀ کوو.

104. *Before you swallowed the bone, why didn't you measure your anus.*

This proverb is applied to a person who assumes a responsibility beyond his capabilities. It is similar to the English expression, "He has bitten off more than he can chew."

[This is an example of an "impolite" or "obscene" proverb. The proverb repertoires of many nations commonly contain texts that use crude, suggestive or obscene language, words with double meanings, or circumlocution and word substitution to avoid the direct use of impolite terminology. Despite the use of indelicate terms and references, these proverbs are still considered wise sayings which may be socially useful. It is said that there are thousands of such proverbs in Pashto, though out of respect for the reading audience, only a few have been included in the present collection. *See* Index entries for "proverbs:impolite". *LNB*]

ارزان بې علته نۀ وي. گران بې حکمته نۀ وی.

105. *The cheap has flaws and the costly is flawless.*

Things of quality are expensive and inferior things are cheap.

[Literally, "... the expensive is not without wisdom," here meaning it is perfect or "flawless". For example, if a farmer buys cheap insecticide for his crop he may need to spray twice, because the cheap variety is not of high quality. If he buys the expensive insecticide he would pay more, but would only have to spray once. It is sometimes worth spending the extra money to buy something of quality. *LNB*]

ارمان ارمان د دادا کوره. د پکه شکوره په چاپیره ګرخُبدمه.

106. *Alas! Alas! For the home of father where I used to go around the basket full of bread.*

This proverb refers to a girl who has recently been married and is suffering at the hands of her mother-in-law. She weeps for the days in her father's home, where everything was plentiful. This is a *landəy* or *tappa* , but it is frequently used as a proverb.

[The *tappa* (also known as *landəy* or *misra*) is a metered folk song (a folk poem which may be written, spoken or sung) with 9 syllables in the first line, 13 in the second and always ending with the Pashto letter *heh* (the sound "*a*"). The *tappa* is usually anonymous and is the most popular, widely circulated and well-known form of Pashto verse. Though often said to be composed by women, they may simply represent a woman's point of view, expressing emotions like love, hatred, grief and, as in the above text, sorrow. *tappas* usually involve the use of a primary poetic image, for example, flowers, moon, the joy of reunion, laughter and kissing, heart and eyes, honor, sword, etc.

It is said that proverbs are the wisdom of the Pashtun, and that *tappas* express Pashtun emotions. However, the *tappa* and other verses of classical or folk poetry may also convey wise advice and be used proverbially (*see* Index for "*tappa*"); variability of genre (that is, whether a text is considered to be a "proverb" or "poem") depends upon context and usage or performance. Pashtun "quoting behavior" includes, in addition to proverbs and *tappas*, Qur'anic verses, classical poetry (*see* Index for "Abdur Rahman Baba"), riddles and other oral forms. *LNB*]

ارمان به وکړې وخت به تېر وي.

107. *You will repent, but too late.*

This well-known proverb relates to [the English proverbs] "Time and tide wait for no man", and "Act in haste, repent at leisure." [*See* Proverbs 195 and 1131.]

ارمان به کړې هلکه بيا به نۀ مومې ادکه.

108. *Oh, young man! You will repent when your mother is gone.*

ارمان! پس له زواله وي.

109. *Repentance comes only after a downfall.*

ارمان روسته عقل وړمبے وے!

110. *Repentance comes after; wisdom, before!*

[Alas, the wisdom that came too late, should have been there first.
After making a foolish mistake, a person wishes that he had known at
the start what he now knows, so that he could have acted with greater
wisdom. *RWS, LNB*]

ارمان دے خپله لاسه. چې څومره خورې هومره اوباسه!

111. *Ah, my hand! Help yourself to as much as you desire!*

A man's desire can be fulfilled only by his own hand.

اړ سترګې نۀ لري.

112. *He who is stubborn has no eyes.*

Men sometimes become so selfish that they have no regard for
others.

اره په اره خلاصيږي.

113. *Only a bowlful of food repays a bowlful of food*

> This is similar to the English expression, "One good deed deserves another."

[Reciprocity or exchange, especially in matters of hospitality and gift giving, is an important Pashtun practice. *See* Proverbs 247 and 283, and Index entries for "exchange, reciprocate". *LNB*]

ازمائيلي څوک نۀ ازمائي.

114. *Test not the tested.*

> The implication is that once a man has had the chance to distinguish himself, and has proved either loyal or disloyal, he should not be required to prove himself again.

ازميښت اول په کال اؤ تلين وو. اوس دم په دم دے.

115. *A tested man was once reliable for a year, now he must prove himself daily.*

> This proverb is predicated on the assumption that dishonesty and unfaithfulness are now rampant and no one can be trusted for very long.

[Suspicion, intrigue and distrust are endemic in Pashtun culture and relationships. Despite the air of bravery and courage, the Pashtun world is filled with rivalry and threats to honor, including the risk of being betrayed by a friend. *LNB*]

ازوګل ئي ګټي مازوګل ئي بائيلي.

116. *Azo Gul earns it and Mazo Gul spends [loses] it.*

> The earnings of one are shared by his dependents.

[The word translated "spends" indicates a profligate or wasteful way of using money, hence the alternative translation "loses". *RWS, LNB*]

اسپه کښنې د زرو روپو بچے وي.

ولې څوک ترې خبر قدرې هم نۀ وي.

چرګه کښنې د یوې پیسې اګۍ نۀ وي.

اؤ ټول کور ئې په سر اخستے وي.

117. *The mare foals a thousand rupee colt secretly. The hen wakes the household with an egg worth a paisa.*

The implication is that while a man of breeding performs good works quietly, the lowborn man boasts of insignificant achievements.

استاذ د پلار په ځاے وي.

118. *The teacher takes the place of a father.*

Before his students, the teacher should be given the same respect as a father.

[The teacher is considered to be a spiritual father. *RWS*]

استعاره له مستعیره، لکه سپے چې ډوډۍ غواړي له فقیره.

119. *Begging from a beggar is like a dog demanding bread from a* faqir.

A *faqir* is a holy man dedicated to a vow of poverty who lives on gifts of food from others. Hence, the proverb instructs us not to ask for something from a person in need.

[Alternative translation: "Borrowing the already borrowed thing is like a dog demanding bread from a beggar." That is, the beggar has already "borrowed" that which the dog now tries to get from him. *RWS*]

اسلام تر توري لاندي دے.

120.   *It is the sword that protects Islam.*

[Literally, "Islam is under the sword", which is generally understood to mean, "Islam is by / with force." This proverb may be based on a *Hadith* (saying of the Prophet) from al-Bukhari that "Paradise is under the shades [that is, the shadow] of swords,"[4] a saying intended to inspire the Prophet's followers for a battle with a clan of infidels and assure them of Paradise should they be slain. While the Pashto proverb above can refer to the sword of *jihad* as divinely justified war, it can also be used to legitimize any coercion or action employed to enforce community values. *LNB*]

اسو چرته خو به دې وكسو.

121.   *Oh, month of* Asu*! We shall see [you] again, sometime.*

In September the flour bins begin to get empty, the people tire of the heat, and the farmers sigh this proverb.

اسو و دې سو.

122.   *Oh, month of* Asu*, you have burnt us.*

In the month of *Asu*, a period in August and September, the rains cease, the skies clear and the sun blazes down. In the fields the farmers become sunburned. When weary of their work in the fields, they use this proverb. Not only the farmers, all the people use this proverb.

اسواره ده اسو كټه ده.

123.   *In autumn the foundation is laid.*

In autumn the crops are harvested and the land is prepared for sowing the new crop.

اسي بسي بلا مې درته نيسي.

124. *For no reason at all, I want to pick a fight with you.*

This proverb is uttered by a man who is being teased in imitation of his oppressor. The meaning is, of course, just the reverse: for no reason at all you want to pick a fight with me.

[I don't want to fight you, but something makes me want to confront you. *RWS*]

اشنا پيش کېدو نه ناشنا غلېدو نه.

125. *No friend speaks up, and I cannot bluff the stranger.*

Spoken when a person in need has no friend to rescue him and he is not clever enough to bluff [deceive] a stranger.

اشنا د کوڅې تبر کړه بيا ئې هېر کړه.

126. *Be happy with your friend, take him to the end of the street and forget him.*

[Accompany the friend to the end of the street and then forget him. This proverb is about the unfaithfulness of friendship. *RWS*]

اشنا، راغلے نه دے ناشنا ټګلے نشي.

127. *The friend has not come, and the stranger I cannot cheat.*

People can easily cheat friends who trust them, but not strangers who are cautious.

[This proverb has something in common with Proverb 125. Though I have the habit of cheating, at the moment there is no one for me to cheat, because I don't have a friend and strangers are too cautious. *RWS*]

اشنا ښه دے که خوړونکے سپے وي.

128. *A friend is good, although he may be a vicious dog.*

It is better, in other words, to live among quarrelsome friends than among strangers.

[Though a friend may be like a biting and vicious dog, still to have a friend is good. *RWS*]

اشنا! غر چې نۀ خورې بیا بد پرې مه وایۀ.

129. *Oh my friend, if you are unable to benefit from the mountain, don't curse it.*

[Alternatively, if the Pashto words *ashnā* (friend) + *ghar* (mountain) are written / spoken as one word *ashnāghar*, referring to a people and a location: "If you don't benefit from Ashnaghar (a Pashtun tribe from Charsadda) don't curse or say anything bad against it / them." *RWS, LNB*]

اشنا مې کړې د ځان بلا مې کړې.

130. *I made you my friend and made trouble for myself.*

اشنا نیسه کور ئې کسه.

131. *Before making a friend, see his home.*

If you wish to befriend a person, first look into his status and his pedigree.

اشنائې په اصل ښه ده نۀ په بې اصل.

132. *Seek a noble, not a base, friend.*

- 38 -

اشنائي د مُلا تر سبقه پوري ده.

133. *The teacher's influence on the student lasts only while the pupil is in the school room.*

    The student respects his teacher [literally, "mullah"] as long as he is capable of teaching. After this, he does not care for the teacher.

اشه اشه بابا اشه! قاضی غلام غوندې مربي لري!

134. *Get going, get going, donkey! You have a master as good as Qazi Ghulam!*

    This proverb is used ironically to chide an unkind man who boasts of his kindness to his subordinates.

    [Or, "Get away, get away, *bābā* ("old man" or "grandfather"), get away! You have a protector like Qazi Ghulam!" *RWS*]

اشه ببه ده که کله، مۀ یوه وینه مۀ بله.

135. *Which is better: to have to drive a pack of donkeys, or a herd of cattle? May you have to drive neither.*

    Spoken when one is faced with making a decision between two unpleasant and monotonous duties.

اصل به جفا نۀ وکي کم اصل به وفا.

136. *A gentleman from a good family will never cheat, while a rogue is never loyal.*

اصل یا په علم پټېږي یا په مال.

137. *One's birth can either be hidden by knowledge or wealth.*

Even if a man is of low birth, society will accept him if he has either knowledge or riches.

اصیل ته اشاره کم اصل ته لوړ.

138. *For the noble, a signal [hint]; for the mean, a club.*

This is similar to the English expression, "A word for the wise, a rod for the fool."

[In Pashto proverbs, a man of good character can be called *asil,* which can be translated "noble (man)", "gentleman", "man of breeding" or "well-bred man." *See* Proverbs 139 to 144, and individual headings in the Index for descriptions of various types of people, for example, "brave man", "greedy man", "honorable man", etc. The Pashto proverb echoes other international proverbs, including the Latin saying, "A word to the wise is sufficient" (*verbum sat sapienti*), the Arabic saying, "A nod for a wise man, and a rod for a fool," and the ancient Hebrew proverbs, "On the lips of one who has understanding wisdom is found, but a rod is for the back of one who lacks sense" and "A whip for the horse, a bridle for the ass, and a rod for the back of fools."[5] *LNB*]

اصیل بها نۀ لري.

139. *The character of a blue-blooded man is priceless.*

اصیل په سپېرۀ خُل کېنې ښائسته دے.

140. *A gentleman looks good even in shabby clothes.*

اصيل په ګډله کښې کم اصل په ګزبره کښې.

141. *The well-bred man now wears shabby clothes while the ill-bred fellow wears silken clothes.*

[This proverb is a sad comment about the tragic way in which times have changed. *RWS*]

اصيل سړے غبر غماز وهي کم اصل سړے پير استاذ وهي.

142. *The man of breeding will fight against the wicked; the rogues fight with their teacher and spiritual guides.*

اصيل کول ګران، ساتل ئي آسان،

کم اصل کول آسان، ساتل ئي ګران.

143. *To train a man is difficult, to keep him is easy (once he is trained). To spoil a man is easy, to keep him is difficult (once he is spoiled).*

[The reference is to "training" a man in good character, to behave as a well-bred man (*asil*). While this proverb advises training in good character, a common Pashtun notion is that the character of a man or woman is inherited or related to one's family background and thus, is relatively unchanging (*see* Proverb 145). Character training is a difficult, but valuable exercise. *LNB*]

اصيل کسه سپے تری نيسه.

144. *Look to a man's upbringing and keep the dog from him.*

One should show respect for the man of good family, but discourage the rogue.

[Or, "Keep the man of honor away from 'dogs' (rogues)." *RWS*]

اغزے چي تبرۀ وي له کومه ځايه وي؟

145. *Where is the origin of the sharpness of a thorn?*

The character of a man is inherited.

[*See* Proverb 143]

اغونده کډله خو له پوره ځخه ځغله.

146. *It is better to wear shabby clothes than to borrow from others.*

اغه ځۀ قبر وي چي درز دروز پکښي نۀ وي.

147. *What kind of grave would it be without lively beating and torture [or, where there is no sound of beating]?*

When a person is buried, he expects to have two angels descend and question him about his religious beliefs. If he gives the correct replies, he will remain at peace till doomsday, but if he gives the wrong answers, he is beaten and tortured until the end of time. So says the mullah to the people in the Pakhtun lands.

[The sense is that every place should have its proper identity and characteristics. Beating and torture of the wicked are associated with the grave. *RWS*]

اکا چي ځۀ رنگ وي هغسي به دې ژاړم.

148. *Oh, my husband! As much as you have loved me in life, as much shall I weep for you.*

The implication is that repayment will be made in the same coin, [as in the now proverbial quote from the Old Testament law], "An eye for an eye."[6]

[I shall weep at your death according to your behavior with me in life. *RWS*]

[In Pashtun custom it is one's womenfolk (wife, daughters, sisters) who openly express their grief with wailing and weeping. The absence of tears would signal dishonor and be a public "payback". The Pashto word *akā* (here and in Proverb 149) literally refers to a paternal "uncle." *See* Proverb 1310. *LNB*]

اکا دا هغه سر نۀ دے، چي به ستا په توره پرې شي.

149. *Oh, young man! This is not the type of head that your sword can sever.*

The brave man's head cannot easily be cut off.

اکبر باچا اکبر پوره جوړه کړه، غلو ورته جبه جوړه کړه.

150. *The Emperor Akbar founded the village of Akbar Pura and thieves occupied the marshes around it.*

[The second half of the proverb can be translated literally, "... thieves made the village of Jabba." The Mughal Emperor Akbar founded the village Akbar Pura on the main road to Peshawar and robbers established the village of "Jabba" opposite to it, which is commonly known as Taro Jabba. This proverb is spoken when the government, or another agency, does something for the welfare of the people or improves a particular thing or situation, but criminals or opponents find a way of sabotaging it. *RWS*]

الا بلا به وکړې د کالۀ زړګي به بنۀ کړې،

د ګور سوال جواب به څۀ کړې.

151. *Your antics may amuse your neighbors, but what will you do when you must account for them to your family?*

Never do extra favors for your neighbors.

[Alternatively, "Your antics may amuse your family, but what will you do when you must account for them in the grave." *RWS*]

[The *RWS* translation is preferred; the earlier Tair and Edwards' version is based on a typing mistake: "*da kor*" ("family") should be "*da gur*" ("grave"), that is, the answer or accounting you give in the grave (*see* comments concerning Proverbs 31 and 103). Thus, the proverb is a warning about the consequences of bad behavior. *LNB*]

الا بلا به گردن مُلا.

152.   *All responsibility lies on the shoulders of the mullah.*

Literally, "on the neck". The proverb refers to passing responsibility onto someone else. The mullah is one skilled in religious doctrine and is often the head of a mosque. A tale is told of a man who asked a mullah about the propriety of wearing polluted clothing at prayer. The man was doubtful, but the mullah allowed him to say his prayers. Before praying, the man muttered, "May all responsibility lie on the neck of the mullah."

[It is spoken when someone else is made responsible for the information that the teller passes on. *RWS*]

[This is a Persian proverb commonly used in Pashto. *LNB*]

الا وه که بلا وه د لالي د سر قضا وه.

153.   *Whether it was peaceful or destructive, it has taken away my beloved from me.*

To others an action may mean nothing, but to a certain individual it may be an irreparable loss.

[Alternatively, "Whether it was something more or less fatal, it still took the life of my beloved." An action may not be important or dangerous to some people, but to others it can prove serious or even fatal. *RWS*]

الف وئيلے نه ، لام خْيرلے.

154.   *You haven't learned the first letter of the alphabet, yet you are trying to read the third lesson.*

[This advice is similar to the English proverb,] "You are trying to run before you have learned to walk" [or, "You have to crawl before you can walk, and you have to walk before you can run." *LNB*]

[Literally, "You can't say *alef* and yet you are trying to read *lām*." *alef* is the first letter of the Pashto (and Arabic and Persian) alphabet, *lām* is the 33rd letter. Ambition (such as "trying to read the third lesson") is good, but one must acquire the proper skills before attempting something difficult; begin with the basics. *LNB*]

الف هيڅ نۀ لري.

155. *The letter "A" has no dots.*

This is said of one who is devoid of worldly possessions and without responsibility. The English equivalent would be, "He has nothing to lose."

[The first letter of the alphabet in Pashto is a straight, vertical line without dots. It appears to stand alone at the beginning. *RWS*]

الوتي مرغۍ په لاس نۀ راځي.

156. *A bird that has flown from the hand will not return.*

"Don't cry over spilt milk" is an English equivalent. [*See* Proverb 189.]

[Meaning, a lost opportunity hardly ever comes again. *RWS*]

الله رازق دے، مگر شولې په اوبو کېږي.

157. *God gives man his living, but rice still needs water.*

Do not be fatalistic, use effort and means [to achieve your goal].

[The first half of the proverb affirms, God is the Bestower of Daily Bread, the Provider or Sustainer (*al-Razaq*). The reference is not to cooking rice, but to the necessity of watering a crop of rice in a field. On the need to use effort and not presume on God, *see* Proverbs 650 and 905, and Index entries for "effort". *LNB*]

الله هم پاک دربار ئي هم پاک.

158. *God is clean and so is his court.*

This proverb is used to indicate the absence of possessions. As the British might say, "Poor as a church mouse", or "Poor as Job."

[The proverbial "church mouse" lives a lean life, because people do not eat in church and there is no kitchen and no food. The idiom "Poor as Job" refers to the Prophet Job, who through one trying period of his life, was stripped by Satan of all his possessions: Job has come to personify poverty and patience. *See* Proverb 379. *LNB*]

امبرسری غوائي تش رنگ خرڅوي.

159. *You sell your appearance like a cow from Amritsar.*

Though you may be an Apollo [Greek god of the sun, renowned for his youthful beauty], you lack all other qualities.

It suggests the expression, "Looks are not everything."

[Amritsar, is a city in the Indian state of Punjab. The cow may be a reference to Nandi, the white bull of Lord Shiva, who used it as a means of transport. The bull (cow) represents strength and virility, and its image is usually placed at the entrance of a Shiva temple where devotees can touch it as they enter. *LNB*]

اموخته بلا په بسم الله نۀ اوړي.

160. *Evil habits are not erased by reading the Holy Creed.*

The implication, not necessarily religious, is that "Bad [Old] habits die hard." [*See* Proverbs 1146 and 1301.]

[The proverb is spoken when some action is required because mere words will not suffice. *See* Proverb 93, and cf. note to Proverb 291. *RWS*]

اموخته خور بلا خور.

161.   *The scrounger takes more than his due.*

اموخته خور بنهٔ دے کهٔ میراث خور؟ وئیل ئي اموخته خور.

162.   *Who is better, an habitual scrounger or one who waits for a dead man's heritage. The answer, "A scrounger."*

It is better to make use of what is available now. An analogous English proverb is, "A bird in the hand is worth two in the bush." [*See* Proverbs 433 and 434.]

[The term "one who waits for a dead man's heritage" refers to *mirās khur*, an undesirable legal heir. *RWS*]

امیر چې ظلم کار وي، اور بل په ټول دیار وي.

163.   *When a ruler is cruel, his whole country burns.*

امیر سړے کهٔ خر وی هم هوښیار دے.

ما غریب سړے هوښیار لیدلے نهٔ دے.

164.   *A rich man, although he may be an ass, is considered wise. I have not seen a poor man who is called wise.*

[This "proverb" appears to be more of a comic parody of a verse commonly attributed to the poet Abdur Rahman Baba (*see* Index) ("Every man has a purpose in friendship; I have not seen a man who was a friend for God alone") which has a similar structure and phrasing. See Proverbs 643 and 1331. *RWS, LNB*]

امیرۍ ورکې شوې. وینځې ملکې شوې.

165. *Princesses have disappeared, and maidservants have occupied their places.*

[The proverb bemoans the changes in time and culture. The lowbred or ignoble have taken the place of the highbred. *RWS*]

انتظار له قتله بد دے.

166. *The wait is worse than being killed.*

[Waiting to be killed is worse than the killing itself. *RWS*]

انسان تر کاڼي سخت تر گل نازک دے.

167. *Man is hard as a rock, yet soft as the petal of a flower.*

["Man" here means a person or human being. *RWS*]

انسان د انسان شیطان دے.

انسان د انسان رحمان دے.

168. *Man is a devil to his species (mankind), yet he is also a god to him.*

[This rhyming proverb contrasts the *shaytān* (devilish, mischief-making) side of man's character with the *rahmān* (merciful, kind, Godly) qualities that he / she may also display. *LNB*]

انصاف د باچا په کور کښې هم نشته.

169. *Even a king's court has no justice.*

[There is no justice to be found anywhere, even in the court (literally "house") of a king. *LNB*]

انگور دانه دانه ، توت کپه کپه.

170. *Grapes should be eaten individually, and mulberries in clumps.*

[Grapes are expensive, that is why they are eaten one by one, whereas mulberries are considered to be cheap and found in abundance, and can be eaten in bunches or handfuls. *RWS*]

انگی مل دې څوک ؟ د ټولو وروستو!

171. *"Oh, Echo! Echo! Who is your partner?" Reply, "The last of all."*

This refers to the man for whom opportunities always come late in life. The expression is also a shout used in the Pakhtun game of *angay* (meaning "echo"). [*angay* is the first word in the Pashto text. *LNB*]

[The term *angay* here refers to each member in the game of *angay*. The proverb is therefore about the person who is always left behind whenever there is an opportunity. It is not so much about fate, as the lassitude or laziness of the person. *RWS*]

اُوباز یم خو بې ګودره نۀ ګډیږم.

172. *Though I can swim well, I won't swim in water of unknown depth.*

[Alternatively, "Though I am a swimmer, I won't jump into water of unknown depth." *RWS*]

اوبو سره دې بدن صفا کړو زړۀ دې په څۀ صفا کړو؟

173. *You cleaned your body with water, but how could you clean your heart?*

Though the enemy is outwardly cordial, he is never to be trusted. [This is similar to the English saying,] "Appearances can be deceptive," [or "Appearances are deceiving" or "… are deceptive."]

[Interpreted more practically, one should not only wash the body to be clean for prayers, one should also clean one's heart by having a pure intention. *RWS*]

[A number of proverbs warn of the difference between the outward and the inward, *see* e.g. Proverbs 384, 401 and 444. The reference to having a clean heart and pure intentions, not just a clean body, reminds one of King David's prayer, "You desire truth in the inward being … wash me, and I shall be whiter than snow … Create in me a clean heart, Oh God."[7] *LNB*]

اوبو په اوبو وريږي.

174.   *Water flows to him who has water.*

In the Frontier water, like money, is a symbol of prosperity. Crops depend on the limited water supply. The proverb is similar to, "Money begets money."

[An alternative explanation: When something occurs in a place where it is not needed, it is a useless occurrence. Showering more water on a watered place is useless, compared to showering water on dry land. *RWS*]

اوبو ورے هر بوټي ته لاس اچوي.

175.   *A drowning man catches at a straw.*

[Literally, the proverb says, "A drowning man catches at every (or "any") plant" in order to save himself. *LNB*]

اوبۀ پنډي کړه باجرې غوندي کړه.

176.   *Dam the water in your fields and you will have a plentiful harvest [of maize].*

The meaning is equivalent to the English expression, "Make hay while the sun shines", but the metaphor itself is naturally reversed, because in Pashtun country there is sun in abundance, while water is scarce and crops must be irrigated.

[An alternative meaning is that while the harvest is being collected the water is stopped in an irrigated field, otherwise one is unable to cut the crop. *RWS*]

اوبهٔ اوڅښنه د لندۍ چې پرهار دې وکنډۍ.

177.   *Drink of the water of Landi, and your wounds will be healed.*

The River Landi (or Landai) begins in Afghanistan as the Kabul
River and flows eastward through the heart of the mountainous north
of Pakistan until it joins the Indus. It is therefore a favored river of the
Pakhtuns, and hence its water is the sweetest.

[The River Kabul is called "Landai" in District Nowshera, northern
Pakistan. It has been praised by Khushal Khan Khattak, the 17th
century Pashtun warrior poet, as comparable to the waters of the
Indian rivers and is associated with Pashtun homeland and identity.
RWS, LNB]

اوبهٔ په اوبو شودهٔ په شودو.

178.   *Water for water, milk for milk.*

Good comes out of good, bad from bad.

[The proverb refers to the practice of diluting milk with water; the
purchaser wants to pay for pure or real milk. It is used to indicate that
everything has its own proper value. *RWS*]

اوبهٔ په پیچون بیایه که لاړي لاړي که نه ښکته ئې لار ده.

179.   *Try to make water run uphill. If you succeed, well and good. If not,
the water will find its own downward course.*

[Let matters run their course. *RWS*]

اوبهٔ په ښکته زور کوي.

180.   *Water always seeks a lower level.*

[Alternative translation, "Water tends to flow downwards." *RWS*]

اوبهٔ په غاړه اوبهٔ غواړه.

181. *Water is at your side, yet you ask for it.*

This proverb covers the common momentary loss of something close at hand, such as when the butcher with a knife in his mouth asks if any one has seen it. A fitting response might be [the idiomatic English expression], "If it were a snake it would bite you."

اوبهٔ په ډانګ نهٔ بېلیږی.

182. *Water cannot be separated with a club.*

Cf. the proverb, "Blood is thicker than water." Water cannot be partitioned [cut] with a cudgel.

In Pashto, blood has a different connotation from that in English. In the latter, blood may connote a relationship or an inheritance, as in "blood brothers", "flesh of my flesh, blood of my blood", "blood lines" and "of royal blood". The same connotation in Pashto is expressed in terms of water. Hence, the meaning expressed here is much the same as in the English expression [from a German saying], "Blood is thicker than water." [*See* Proverbs 858 and 875.]

اوبهٔ په اوبو اودرېږی ولې غم په غم نه اودرېږي.

183. *Water becomes stagnant in a pond, but one's sorrow is a river.*

Sorrow spreads to others.

[The picture is of water that comes to a pond and stops. But grief added to grief does not stop. *See* Proverb 102. RWS]

اوبهٔ په نري ځاے ماتېږی.

184. *Water breaks through a weak dike.*

Water always breaks through a weak place.

اوبهٔ تیرﻲ شﻲ کاڼﻲ پاتﻲ شﻲ.

185.   *The water flows on but the stones remain.*

Ephemeral things pass, permanent things last.

اوبهٔ چﻲ اودرﯦږﻲ نو بوئین کوﻲ.

186.   *Stagnant water gives off a stench.*

Standing water becomes putrid.

اوبهٔ چﻲ په ځﺎﮮ اودرﯦږﻲ سخا شﻲ.

187.   *When water stands too long, it becomes stagnant and putrid.*

اوبهٔ چﻲ تر سره واوړﻲ څهٔ یو ګز څهٔ دوه ګزه.

188.   *When water flows over one's head, what matter whether it is one or two yards deep?*

What does it matter if the water is one or two yards above your head? [*See* Proverb 190.]

اوبهٔ چﻲ د ورخه تﺑرﻲ شﻲ بیا نهٔ راګرځﻲ.

189.   *Once water has passed through the sluice it never returns.*

This is another way of saying, "There is no use crying over spilt milk", or "It is water over the dam." [Cf. other related English proverbs, "Water gone over a dam never returns." or "It is water under the bridge." You can't undo the past. *LNB*]

- 53 -

اوبهٔ ځهٔ تر نامه ځهٔ تر زنګانهٔ.

190. *It matters not whether the water rises to the knees or to the navel.*

اوبهٔ خړوي ماهيان پکښ نيسي.

191. *He muddies the water to fish in it.*

This is said of someone who stirs up a quarrel in order to profit from it. That is, "Fishing in troubled waters."

["Fishing in troubled waters" refers to the story of the fisherman who beat the water in order to make the fish run into his net, but in the process muddied the water for others who wished to drink from the same stream. The full text of the proverb, well-known in Latin and other languages, is, "It is good fishing in troubled (muddy) waters." *LNB*]

اوبهٔ د پاسه خړېږي.

192. *The water can be made muddy from upstream.*

One must find a weakness before exploiting it. (The cause of a trouble may be somewhere else.)

[A proper excuse for causing trouble should be sought after. A weak or lame excuse cannot be the cause of a quarrel. *RWS*]

اوبهٔ د سيلي نغن د مروت.

193. *The water of the Sali and the bread of the Marwats.*

This is an exclamation of delight or amazement. The water of the Sali River is renowned for its pristine clearness and taste, and the wheat bread of the Marwat tribe is famous for its quality.

اوبهٔ د کاڼي خوله ماتوي.

194. *Water breaks the stone.*

Through constant flowing, water wears away even the hardest rock. That is, constant struggle can remove mountains.

اوبهٔ راځي له پاسه ښکته په ژړا ژاړی له فراقته.
چې لاړو لاړو بیا به رانهٔ شو ارمان ارمان تېره ساعته!

195. *The stream descending from the hills flows on immutably.*
    It weeps, laments that it cannot stay. I have gone and will not return.
    Alas! Alas! Oh, time that is past. Time is lost irrevocably.

The water that passes beneath the mill is gone and will not return.

[This saying has the form of a poetic couplet. *RWS*]

[The "proverb" is a reflection on "time", a common theme in the wisdom sayings of many nations; cf. the English proverb, "Time and tide wait for no man", "Time lost cannot be recalled", "Time wasted is time lost." (*See* e.g. Proverb 519.) The American poet and author Stephen Vincent Benét (1898-1943) said, "Life is not lost by dying; life is lost minute by minute, day by dragging day, in all the thousand small uncaring ways." For this reason, the Roman poet Horace (65-8 BC) encourages making the most of the present, in his famous axiom "*Carpe Diem*", commonly translated "Seize the day."[8] The tone of the Pashto text is grief over the passing of life. *LNB*]

اوبهٔ راغلي په ورخونه، اوبهٔ د هغو دي چې زیات وی په مېړونه.

196. *The water passing through the canal [or sluices] belongs to the largest tribe.*

The meaning is similar to the English proverb, "Might makes right." [*See* Proverbs 560, 665 and 695.]

[The word translated "canal" can also refer to the metal sluice gates or mud and stone dams that control which field receives water.

Therefore, this rhyming proverb can be translated, "The water reaching the irrigation sluices (*warkhunǝ*) belongs to the tribe with the largest number of males (*meṛunǝ*)." *LNB, RWS*]

اوبهٔ کهٔ برِي دي تر پلهٔ لري دي.

197.   *Though the water level is high, it is still below the bridge.*

اوبهٔ که گرمِي دي اور به مړ کړی.

198.   *Though the water may be hot, it can still extinguish the fire.*

[Though a man may be weak, he is still able to compete. The word "extinguish" (kill) functions metaphorically as in the English idiom, "Kill the lights," but with overtones of threat against potential rivals. *RWS, LNB*]

اوبهٔ هله څښنه چي شربت شي،

مړی هله خوره چي نعمت شي.

199.   *Drink water only when it has become syrup, eat your meal only when it gives you full satisfaction.*

[Everything should be done at the proper or appropriate time. The word for "satisfaction" (*nemat*) is elsewhere translated as "blessing" or "bounty", referring to the gracious favors and benefits received from God. *RWS, LNB*]

اوچاوده غوزه تري پيدا شوه پوندانه.

200.   *The pod burst open and out came the cotton.*

This proverb is said of the plain mother who gives birth to attractive children.

اوچ توت پسې ترکاڼ سيند ته دانګلي دي.

201. *To retrieve the dried trunk of the valued mulberry the carpenter leaped into the river.*

The mulberry is so precious that a carpenter will never pass it by, even if he drowns in his effort to rescue it.

اوچو سره لامدهٔ هم سوزي.

202. *Along with the dry the wet also burns.*

When the dry tinder flames, the wet wood is soon ignited. Used to imply that the wickedness of one involves all. This is similar to the English saying, "One rotten apple spoils the whole barrel." [*See* Proverb 588.]

[The poor, innocent and weak in this world suffer the consequences of the actions of the few and the strong. *LNB*]

اوچو کوهيانو ته اوښان مهٔ چو کوه.

203. *Never lead camels to dry wells.*

اوچه دې نهٔ تېرېده درلوندهٔ ئې کړه.

204. *You could not eat the dried bread until it was made wet for you.*

The story is told of how one day a guest arrived at a friend's door and asked the housewife to give him something to eat. She brought him only dry bread without anything to moisten it. He demanded some liquid to go with the bread, but she told him she had nothing else available at the moment. The man inquired, pointing to a cow in the corner, "Doesn't she have any milk?" "If you think you can milk her", the housewife replied, "go ahead and try."

Thinking that any man can milk a cow, he approached the animal with bowl in hand and tried to get some milk. But the cow was in no mood to cooperate and promptly kicked him hard with her hind leg. He fell down nearby and the cow began to prod him with its horns.

Seeing this, the housewife approached with a club to drive away the cow, but the man exclaimed, "Don't drive away the cow, for it was I who could not swallow the dry bread until it was made wet for me."

This proverb said of any person, not just a wife, who allows such a man to milk his cow.

اوخوره اؤ اونغره کښینې فرق دے.

205. *There is a difference between eating and swallowing.*

Eating requires good table manners, while even animals can swallow.

[Alternatively, "There is a difference between 'please eat' and 'take and swallow'." This expression is about the style of an invitation, or the way in which something is offered to others. That is, one's words count more than the thing being offered. *RWS*]

اودهٔ مزرے اودهٔ ښهٔ دے.

206. *Let a sleeping lion sleep.*

This is similar to the proverb, "Let sleeping dogs lie", [as in Proverb 208; cf. Proverbs 680 and 702], or "Don't upset the apple cart."

[The meaning is, don't challenge the status quo, or don't make someone angry who could cause you trouble. Cf. other English proverbs, "Don't wake a sleeping lion" and "A sleeping dog never bites." *LNB*]

اودهٔ به ویښ کړي، خو چې ویښ ځان اودهٔ کړي نو څهٔ به ئې کړي.

207. *One who is asleep can be awakened, but one who pretends to be asleep is difficult to wake.*

اودهٔ سپي په خان پسې مهٔ ويښنوه.

208. *Do not wake the sleeping dogs.*

This is very similar to the well-known English proverb, "Let sleeping dogs lie."

[This proverb is a variant of Proverb 206, (*see* Proverbs 680 and 702). It means, do not invite trouble for yourself, and is used when someone disturbs a situation or unnecessarily asks for trouble. *LNB, RWS*]

اودې وهلم څهٔ چې لا دې ګرندے کړم.

209. *It was your pounding on me that made me run faster.*

[This is an example of the now axiomatic principle,] "Every action has a reaction."

[The Tair and Edwards quote is based on Newton's third law of physics that, "For every action, there is an equal and opposite reaction." More specifically, the Pashto text suggests that provocation (beating) is suitable and necessary to get something done. *RWS, LNB*]

اور اوبهٔ سره شریک دي، خو نه له هندوانو.

210. *Water and fire are common to all, except among the Hindus.*

The reference is to the Hindu caste system, which forbids the privileged class from touching a commoner's cooking and drinking vessels. The proverb also reflects the Muslim's distrust of the Hindu, who is believed to be uncooperative.

[At one time in the culture, when water and fire were shared by the whole village, Hindus would have their own separate water and fire. In railway stations in India separate Muslim and Hindu water taps can still be seen. *RWS*]

اور اوبۀ نۀ سره يوځاے کېږي.

211. *You can't mix fire and water.*

People of opposite nature cannot cooperate.

اور په داسې تبغنې شه پورې چې مخ ئې اوم وي شوندې ئې تورې.

212. *Cursed be the grate that burns the bread at the edges and leaves it unbaked in the center.*

اور په غرۀ لګېدو، حاتمے په دامان ژړېدو.

213. *Though the forests were burning on the mountain, Hatemai was weeping on the plains.*

Though the calamity is distant, men fear that they too will suffer damage.

[This is said about one who unnecessarily fears calamity. "Hatemai" is the Pashto form of "Hatem", a common name. *RWS*]

اور ته چې نږدې کېږي، خو آخر به سوزېږي.

214. *He who stands near the fire is bound to be scorched.*

If one is to dare, he must be willing to risk hurt, pain and criticism.

The proverb could also be a warning to the intrepid not to approach danger without caution.

اور ته خپل او پردي يو دي.

215. *The fire burns both the friend and the stranger alike.*

Death makes no distinction between one man and another.

اور له بخري لګي.

216.   *The fire breaks out with a tiny spark.*

A tiny spark sets a fire ablaze.

[One should not underestimate a calamity even if it seems small. *RWS*]

[The proverb, "A little spark kindles a great fire" is found in the proverb collections of many languages, including German, Italian, Spanish and English, and in other forms for example, "Behold what a fire a little matter kindles." A similar thought is expressed in the Biblical observation, "How great a forest is set ablaze by a small fire,"[9] a warning about the dangers of the tongue. That is, careless talk can cause enormous problems. Cf. Proverbs 804, 882, 889, 1027, 1120 and 1257. *LNB*]

اور هغه ځای سوزوي، چې کوم ځای بليږي.

217.   *The fire heats only the place where it burns.*

Only the one who is in trouble understands the extent of his difficulty.

اوربشي ځۀ په زمکه ځۀ په جوال کښې.

218.   *What does it matter if the barley lies on the ground or is in the bag?*

This is said of anything that is not valuable enough to be treasured.

اوربشي غله نۀ ده خر ځاروے نۀ دے.

219.   *Barley is not grain, and a donkey is not an animal.*

Barley is more commonplace than other grains, and the donkey is considered to be below other animals. This proverb is applied to people who are not readily accepted by society.

اوربشِي که د روپۍ سل منه شي، د خرۀ خو لپه وي.

220. *Though a hundred* mans *of barley cost only one rupee, the donkey will still get but two handfuls.*

Times may change, but the poor are always with us.

[One *man* is approximately 40 kilos (eighty pounds), though the weight of a *man* in Afghanistan varies considerably. *LNB*]

اورۀ بيزو اوخوارۀ اؤ لاس ئې د وري په مخ راکښل.

221. *The monkey having eaten the flour, rubbed some on the mouth of the innocent lamb which then received the blame.*

The clever criminal finds a scapegoat for his crime.

اورۀ په اورۀ منت ئې په څۀ.

222. *When flour is exchanged for flour, why should one feel any obligation?*

When a thing is given in exchange for a similar thing, why should one feel obliged to the other?

اورۀ چي خمبيره شي، هر څوک ګوتې پکښي وهي.

223. *When the dough is ready, everyone fingers it.*

When one appears to be guilty, everyone points a finger at him.

اورۀ د مېچنې زوے د خچنې.

224. *The flour of the hand mill and the son of Khachana.*

"Khachana" is the nickname for a dirty and uncouth woman. The son of Khachana can never eat the flour of the hand mill because his lazy mother does not even have time to keep herself clean, much less time to grind flour by hand.

["Khachana" can also be the name of a Pashtun woman. "Khachana" here means a poor woman whose son usually performs well. The proverb refers to the comparative praise given to the flour of the hand mill versus the son of a poor woman. *RWS*]

اوٌخه ننوٌخه د گنجي بده وربوزه.

225.   *Oh ugly face of the scurvy-headed one, you merely come and go [go in and go out].*

This is said as a taunt to a man who wastes his time for nothing. [*See* Proverb 920.]

اوږدي چارې په اوږدو لاسو کېږي.

226.   *Great work requires strong hands.*

When hands become weak, the work ceases. Great resources are needed to accomplish great tasks. No important work can be completed without ample support.

[Alternatively, not "strong hands" but "long hands", meaning those who have access. That is, difficult tasks require access and a means of approach to those with power, influence or resources. *RWS*]

اوږي ته په تبخي هم لرې ده.

227.   *Bread is a long way from a hungry man even though it is already on the griddle.*

A needy person cannot tolerate even a short delay in fulfilling his needs.

اوړي ته ئي وې دوه اؤ دوه څو کېږي وئيل ئي څلور ډوډۍ

228. *Someone said to the hungry man, "How much is two times [plus] two?" "Four loaves of bread," he replied.*

اوړي د ډوډۍ تپارے اوري.

229. *A hungry person listens for the sound of baking bread.*

A hungry man can smell meat from a distance.

[This proverb refers to the sound of bread being made by hand, (slapping the dough), before it is put on the griddle. *RWS*]

اوږے د زوى سږے خوري.

230. *The hungry man eats the lungs of his son.*

A hungry man will stop at nothing.

اوړۍ ګېډه بلا ده.

231. *A hungry stomach is a calamity.*

The belly has no ears.

[The Pashto saying reminds one of the Latin proverb (well-known in Dutch, French, German, Italian and English), "A hungry belly has no ears," that is, it is futile to reason with a desperately hungry man, though the emphasis in the Pashto is on the misfortune of hunger itself. Three Pashto words are used for "stomach" (or "belly"): *gedə*, *nas* or *kheṭə*. *nas* is also translated as "womb" in Proverb 538 and as "heart" in Proverb 865. *LNB*]

اوس به دود دود اؤ پانی به پانی شي.

232. *Milk will be milk, water will be water.*

This is similar to the English proverb, "Truth will out."

[The meaning is, "Time brings truth to light." *See* Proverbs 76 and 1318. *LNB*]

اوس خبره په اباسین ورګډه ده.

233. *The matter has now been carried away by the Abasin.*

The matter is now out of one's control.

The Abasin River [literally, "Father of Rivers"], known to the rest of the world as the Indus, flows east of the North West Frontier Province of Pakistan. It has great bearing on the culture and traditions of the Pakhtuns.

[Alternatively, "The matter has now jumped into the Abasin." Meaning, a secret is no longer a secret, but has become public knowledge. The Pashto word *khabəra* (here translated "matter") refers to something said, talked about or discussed. *RWS, LNB*]

اوسپنه په اوسپنه ماتیږي.

234. *Iron breaks iron.*

This is similar to the English proverb, "Diamond cuts diamond."

[The proverb appears in English as, "Iron cuts iron". The Pashto proverb is used of proud men or men with strong characters, meaning it takes a person of greater pride or strength to defeat them. *See* Proverb 406, "There is always a head above a head" and Proverb 1187, "Though the mountain is high it still has a path across its peak". Someone who is proud can only be broken by someone prouder. *LNB*]

اوسپنه چې توده شي نو اوږده شي.

235. *When iron is hot it is moldable.*

If iron is not heated, it cannot be shaped. That is, difficult tasks need methodical handling.

[There are similar English proverbs, for example "When the iron is hot, it is time to strike" and "Strike while the iron is hot"; the emphasis in these texts, however, is on the need for opportune, judicious and timely action. *LNB*]

اوبۀ اوبۀ په خپله څبني خو شپيلک ئي مدور دے.

236. *The camel can drink the water himself, but whistling shows hospitality.*

One can help oneself, but a show of hospitality [or caring] adds to his pleasure.

[This seems to refer to a traditional practice in Pashtun areas: when the camels are given water for drinking, their owner whistles during the whole process. In rural Afghanistan, herdsmen whistle while their cows, sheep or goats drink water. *RWS*]

اوبښ په بروزه نۀ درنبړي.

237. *A camel cannot be overloaded by a blade of grass.*

If one can bear many hardships, the addition of one more would make little difference.

[Another common version of this text refers to the addition of a colander or sieve instead of grass. *RWS*]

اوبښ په کاسيره دے. چي کاسيره نۀ وي. نو څۀ به ئي کړي.

238. *Though the camel was worth only a quarter of a* pice, *there was not even that much. So what can be done?*

[For a poor person, it doesn't matter if something is cheap or expensive, he cannot afford it. A *pice* is a coin worth very little. The Pashto text uses the word *kāsirə* (translated *pice*), which is also an old coin of little value; it could be rendered in English as a "penny". *RWS, LNB*]

اوبښ ته چا وئیل چې لوړه بنۀ ده کۀ ژوره. وئیل ئې لعنت په دواړو.

239. *Someone asked a camel, "Is ascending better than descending?" He replied, "May both be cursed."*

اوبښ چې د لېژد په وخت مونده شي، ورک نۀ دے.

240. *When the camel is found at the time of loading it should not be called lost.*

Any man who is present when there is work to be done cannot be considered a shirker.

[To be available at the proper time is like actually being present. *RWS*]

[The "time of loading," literally, "time of departure" or "leaving", refers to the time when the caravan sets out on the next stage of its journey. *LNB*]

اوبښان په خپلو متيازو کښې ښوئيږي.

241. *The camels slip in their own urine.*

One's own action can lead to his downfall.

[Great people commit great blunders. *RWS*]

اوبښانو نۀ ژړل بورو ژړل.

242. *The camels did not weep, but their loads did.*

This proverb is used to refer to one who gets into difficulty by helping another. It is not he who complains, yet the recipient is unhappy.

[The helper does not complain, but the recipient is unhappy. *LNB*]

اوبښه! څه دې سم دي، چي پاتي ورمين؟

243. *Oh camel, what is in proportion about you that you should complain about your neck?*

This is said of a person who, although he has many defects, complains about only one of them.

[Though the most apparent and visible faults are pointed out, in fact the whole body is out of proportion. *RWS*]

[This humorous proverb paints a picture of the gangly, ungainly camel, whose every body part seems bent and misshapen. Cruder versions of this text also exist. Why complain about one thing when everything has gone wrong. *LNB*]

اوګره اؤ شېدهٔ يو شے دے.

244. *Porridge and butter [milk] are one and the same.*

This is similar to the English proverb, "Six of one, half-a-dozen of the other." [*See* Proverb 532.]

[This may refer to two things that are indispensable to each other, like porridge and milk (or butter). *RWS*]

اوګره دې وي. توده دې وي.

245. *Let us have porridge, but let it be hot.*

The implication is that although there is little to offer, it should be presented with grace and sincerity.

اوګره که بنه وے په بازار کښي به خرڅيده.

246. *Had the porridge been good, it could have been sold in the market.*

To have value, an object must be well made.

اوګوره! پښتون سل کاله پس بدل واخست ، وئيل ئي چي زر ئي واخست.

247. *See! After a hundred years a Pakhtun takes his revenge, and he says, "Still I have taken it quickly."*

This is similar to the sayings, "It is never too late to mend" or "Better late than never." A Pakhtun always considers revenge justifiable. [*See* Proverb 600.]

[In Pashtun culture, revenge in some cases is considered to be positive. *RWS*]

[The term *badal* refers broadly to the "exchange of gifts, hospitality, visits, or as here in this proverb, the exchange of violence or "revenge". The Pashtun code of honor requires a "payback" to the offender sooner or later, and in the Pashtun world view, "Better late than never" so as to preserve honor. Challenges to honor must be met with a retaliatory maneuver. *See* Proverb 282. *LNB*]

اول وخوره د ځان غوښي ، بيا وخوره د ښکار غوښي.

248. *First eat your own meat, then the meat of the hunt.*

If one desires the fresh meat of the hunt, he must exert an effort to get it. That is, first deserve, then desire.

[Achievement requires hard work. Hunting is a tedious game or job and entails thorough searching. One who wants to enjoy the meat of the hunt will have to search hard to find it. Also, struggle bears fruit. *RWS*]

اول ځان دے پسي جهان دے.

249. *First self, then others.*

[Literally, "First (my)self, then the world," that is, the other people in the world. One Pashtun expressed this notion humorously, "You first—after me!" *LNB*]

اول خوند وي بيا شخوند وي.

250. *First taste and then chew.*

At first there is pleasure and satisfaction, but even a joyful thing can also become monotonous.

اول دې نوک ځاے شي ، بيا دې سُوک ځاے شي.

251. *First let there be a hole big enough for a nail, then for a fist.*

This is similar to the French and English proverb, "Give him an inch and he will take a mile."

[Cf. the Chinese proverb, "The journey of a thousand miles starts with a single step." To begin a large task, start with a small first step. The "nail" refered to here is a "fingernail" (*nuk*). RWS, LNB]

اول زده کړه بيا کوژده کړه.

252. *First learn, then strive.*

That is, deserve before you desire.

[The Pashto translated "... then strive" is literally "... then make the engagement (get engaged)." That is, first "learn" the formalities of the engagement ceremony, after that "get engaged". LNB, RWS]

اول ستر سپي غپيږي پسې کم.

253. *The old dogs bark first, then the pups.*

The implication is that the elders usually initiate disputes and disturbances.

اول طعام بیا کلام.

254. *Food first, discussion later.*

This is part of the Pakhtun code of hospitality. Guests must always be treated with courtesy.

[Discussion and debates start after the meal, because they can lead to bitterness, which can spoil the feast. *RWS*]

اول کوه احتیاط ستري مه کوه پسات.

255. *First be careful, then don't quarrel later.*

[Alternatively, "First be careful; then don't boast." Boasting will lead to a disturbance. *RWS*]

اول ملګري بیا لار غواړه.

256. *First find a helpful companion and then the road.*

[If you think that you are in the right, first find the witnesses to justify your argument, and after that start the case. *RWS*]

اول ئي وبره څیروه، بیا ئي مبره څیروه.

257. *First judge the flock, then the master.*

Before befriending a man, look at his financial status and then judge his character.

[Alternatively, "First look at the hedge of the farm, then its owner." *RWS*]

اولاد د زړۀ د سره پيسه د زړۀ د بره.

258. *A child may be most dearly loved, but money is even more desirable (to some people).*

[Alternatively, "Children are an important part of the heart, but money is the force of the heart, or what drives people." *RWS*]

اوله ورځ بادشاه، بله ورځ وزير او بله ورځ د خاورو خمير.

259. *The first day, a king; the second, a minister; the third, death.*

The cycle of life is joy, worry and death. A youth is considered free of worry and free to enjoy himself, such as a king should be. The mature man, like a Prime Minister, has the responsibilities and worries attendant upon administering a country.

[Alternatively, it is about the untrustworthiness and changing scenarios of life. *RWS*]

[The idiom used for death is literally "the yeast (leaven) of dirt" (*khāwro khamir*). When Pashtuns make bread (*nān*), they leaven it by adding a little bit of yeast (*khamir*) kept back from the previous batch. In the picturesque language of this rhyming proverb, even the mighty king and *wazir* (prime minister) become *khamir* (yeast) that is added to the earth as part of the cycle of life. *LNB*]

اومره مې زوے نۀ ئې چې په دانو وتلے نۀ ئ.

260. *Until you have had smallpox you are not my son.*

Smallpox was once so common and fatal that a mother would not take her child for granted until it had survived this disease.

اومې نيوله خپله پوزه او پرې مې کړه دا تا والا.

261. *I caught hold of my own nose, but cut off yours.*

This proverb refers to a person who, though clearly guilty and deserving of punishment, has cunningly shifted the guilt to another.

اووه سیندونه پوري خپله برخه ده راپوري.

262. *If I cross the seven seas, my luck will still be with me.*

Whatever the trials and tribulations, a man will certainly get what is destined for him.

اوئي ایلی ورکوي. او سترګي نر پتوي.

263. *The duck lays the eggs, but the drake shuts his eyes.*

Although the duck performs the act of laying the egg, the drake pretends that he laid it. This proverb is said of a person who pretends to bear the troubles of another.

[Also, this may be about the sense of shame associated with an act. RWS]

اے په شیش محل کښي ناسته بل په کاڼو مۀ وله.

264. *Oh sitter in the glass house: Don't throw stones at others.*

This is similar to the well-known English proverb, "People in glass houses shouldn't throw stones."

ایسار ګیدړ د منزري سره جنګیږي.

265. *A jackal, when cornered, will fight with the lion.*

Even a coward will fight for survival. [*See* Proverb 291.]

ايمو غوړه خلوصه ، د وينځي غوړه نيولي.

266. *May I be free, but may the slave girl be strangled.*

    This proverb is applied to a person who lays blame or responsibility on his or her subordinates and takes advantage of his or her superior position.

[Normally the servants bring information to the master. The notion is, if there is some misinformation, may I not be caught, but let someone else (the maidservant, a woman) be held responsible and punished. *RWS*]

بابا چي غلا کوله اول به ئي له مُلا کوله.

267. *When father wished to commit a theft, he would steal from the mullah first.*

[The mullah is considered to be a sacred person. When a person starts to commit pre-meditated crimes, he will not worry about any kind of damnation or consequences, even though the mullah may issue an edict against him. *RWS*]

بابر لاندي غوږه باندي.

268. *Though Babar is defeated, he still blows his trumpet.*

This refers to any man who, though defeated, still continues to boast of his prowess.

Babar is one of the Pakhtun tribes.

[Alternatively, the proverb is about the greed of the Babars. *RWS*]

بادشاه به څۀ کړي چي طمع ورته نۀ کړي.

269. *What care you for a king if you ask nothing from him.*

بار باردار وړے دے، زور زوردار وړے دے.

270. *He who carries the load is born to do so, while he who commands is qualified to command.*

Every man for his own task.

[There is a difference between the strength needed to lift a load and the strength required in fighting. *RWS*]

بار ئې سپک خاوند ئې ملک.

271. *The load is light and its owner is called the mal_ək.*

The man with the lightest burden leads the caravan because he has the least worry.

[Those that have a light load to carry have the sort of qualifications for enjoying leadership. mal_ək is the title given to a leading personality, elsewhere translated "lord" or "*Khan*". *See* Proverbs 542 and 838. *RWS*]

باران نه تښتيدو د ناوې لاندې ئې شپه شوه.

272. *He ran out of the rain and spent the night under the gutter [rain spout].*

The same thought is expressed in the English proverb, "Out of the frying pan into the fire." [*See* Proverb 324.]

باړه دې لا ليدلې نۀ ده او پرتوګ ورته د دې ځايه وباسې.

273. *You have not even seen the Bara River and already you are removing your trousers.*

This is similar to the English proverb, "Don't cross your bridges until you come to them," [that is, don't worry about things before they happen. *LNB*]

باغ که باغوان لري. نو چغال هم خداے لري.

274. *If the orchard has its gardener, the jackal has his God.*

The jackal has other means of feeding himself if the gardener keeps him from the fruit.

بالا مانۍ دې خلاصه وي په نوم د اکبر خان.

275. *Let Bala Manrai be set free for the sake of Akbar Khan.*

Mohammad Akbar Khan was a noble and outstanding Orakzai Khan. When the British first arrived in the Peshawar region, they decided to destroy the village of Bala Manrai (Maṇai). But Mohammad Akbar Khan went to the Resident Commissioner and requested that the village not be destroyed. As a result of his intercession, Bala Manrai was spared. [Today Bala Manrai is an area within Peshawar lying between the Cantonment and the Old City. *LNB*]

When one person pardons another at the request of a responsible man, this proverb is quoted. It is mostly used in the villages surrounding Peshawar.

This proverb is the first line of a *chārbayta*.

[The *chārbayta*, which literally means "four couplets" and always includes a distinctive refrain, is a famous form of Pashto folk poetry which may be written and / or sung, and the subject matter often involves love, war or politics. Some common proverbs are taken from the lines of this form of verse. *RWS, LNB*]

بخت په تڼده دے نۀ په منډه.

276. *Good fortune is predestined, effort is of no avail.*

The implication is that man cannot change the inevitable. [Success comes slowly, step by step, not by "running" or human effort. *See* Proverb 322 and other Proverbs under the subject of "fate" and "fortune, luck". *LNB*]

بخت یا په پتي دے یا کوتی دے.

277. *Good fortune is either in wealth [fields, farm], or in a lucky forehead.*

بد بانګي زما، کمزورے د باچا.

278. *The strong rooster is mine, the weak one belongs to the king.*

The meaning is that a man wants the best for himself even though his partner may be of superior status.

This proverb is usually used by children who, when watching a quarrel, wish to stir up the combatants.

[In Pashtun culture, certain sayings are famous for being spoken during certain types of games like gambling. This seems to be one such saying. *RWS*]

بد بور په بد خائے کښي ګېرېږي.

279. *Even the dangerous wolf can be caught in a clever trap.*

[Alternatively, "The dangerous wolf is always caught in a terrible trap." Though an enemy may be strong, he can ultimately be caught. *RWS*]

بد په خولۀ خوږ په نیت.

280. *A foul mouth but a good intention.*

The expression, "His bark is worse than his bite" expresses much the same idea.

[A man may use foul language, but his intentions may be good. *RWS*]

بد د خپل ښانک نګولۍ دے.

281.   *One's own wicked deeds are the soup on his dinner table.*

One cannot escape the consequences of one's own wicked deeds.

بد مذهبي له خړ مذهبے.

282.   *For a perverted man, there should always be a mischievous man.*

[Literally, the terms used in Pashto refer to a bad way of life or mode of living. This proverb is similar in meaning to the English saying, "Send a thief to catch a thief." Both sayings mean that in order to deal with a "perverted" (*bad*) man, it takes a man even more "mischievous" and "perverted" (*khar*) than the first. (The adjective *khar* means "dark brown" and is used to describe someone who is full of deceit.) *LNB*]

[A similar proverb in Pashto says, "*ghee* cannot be pulled out with straight fingers." That is, the only way a normally good man can deal with a bad man is to act in an equally bad way, because that is the only thing the perverted man understands. *RWS*]

بدل په بدل خلاصيږي.

283.   *Tit for tat.*

[Literally, *badal* ends with *badal*, that is, "Tit for tat," meaning an action elicits or demands an equivalent response. The Pashto word *badal* meaning "exchange" or "reciprocate" is used in both a positive and a negative sense. When someone owes something to another person, this "debt" is also called *badal*. That is, there is also *badal* for gifts or visits, or for bad words, insults, slights or any other action. For example, one can send his daughter as a bride, or pay money, to finish an enmity (*badal*). One can give a gift at the birth of a baby and expect a gift in return (*badal*) when a baby is born in one's own household. One can give help to a traveler arriving back from a long journey, and expect the same care when he returns from a journey. *badal* is also used when brides are exchanged between families. *See* Proverb 247. *RWS, LNB*]

بدي چې نۀ کړي بدي چاري، بدي به چا واړۀ په لاري.

284. *Had Badi not been guilty of so many wicked deeds, he would not*
have been killed on the highway.

Neki (representing good) and Badi (the bad), are popular characters
in Pakhtun folklore, both sons of the same mother. As they played
beside the road, a traveler came by. Neki saluted him politely, while
Badi teased him by poking a finger into his back, an act that is
considered to be highly insulting. Surprisingly the man then gave him
a penny for his mischief.

Seeing this, another man asked why the traveler had done so and
received the reply, "You will understand the reason later."

Sometime afterwards Badi was found dead on the road. When the
traveler came by again the same man asked him why the boy was
dead. He replied, "By giving him a penny I encouraged him to
continue his mischief until he was ultimately stabbed by one who
would not accept such mischief." The questioner then said, "Had Badi
not been guilty of so many wicked deeds, he would not have been
killed on the highway."

"As you sow, so shall you reap." [*See* Proverb 645 and 800.]

برخه کومه بده ده، چې ورښکاره ئې کړې او ور ئې نۀ کړې؟

285. *Which is worse, not knowing about a share of something or being*
promised a share and then not receiving it?

برخې ټولې ازلي دي، نۀ په زور نۀ په سیالۍ دي.

286. *Everyone's share is predestined; it is obtained neither by force nor*
by competition.

برېند د لاري اوړي اوبے نۀ اوړي.

287. *The naked man leaves the path, but the hungry [man] never turns away.*

Hunger is a greater evil than nudity.

بربنډه مې اولیده زړۀ مې ورته اوشو.

288. *I saw her naked and felt desire for her.*

This is said of one who desires to take advantage of another's weakness.

[Alternatively, "You saw me naked and felt desire for me." *RWS*]

برېښوه ئې که برېښوی ئې چې بده تر کمره پریوځی بیا ئې څه له برېښوی.

289. *Light up the clouds in the distance, oh lightning! Of what use to me will you be if Badi falls over the cliff?*

Once a violent storm destroyed the crops of a poor, old woman who had a son named Badi. The following season it appeared again and threatened their crops. (Bolts of lightning, according to myth, are said to be the arms of the angels that push the clouds about.) Seeing the storm approach, Badi drew his sword and ran through the dark night toward the nearby cliff, shouting, "I won't allow you angels to bring the clouds closer and destroy our crops."

The mother, fearing that her son would rush over the cliff, prayed, "Light up the clouds in the distance, oh lightning! Of what use to me will you be if Badi falls over the cliff?"

بساط لږ ارواحان ډېر.

290. *Provisions are few and souls are many.*

There are scant provisions to feed many people.

بسم الله وئیل ثواب لري خو نۀ د ګیدړ د ښکار د پاره.

291. *It is profitable to recite the* kalima, *but not when hunting jackal.*

Another reference to the jackal as a coward. [*See* Proverb 265.]

[The *kalima* or Muslim creed is recited before starting a difficult task, or at the beginning of any undertaking. However, there is no reward for reciting the *kalima* before doing something forbidden or for a bad purpose (cf. eating the meat of jackals is forbidden). *RWS, LNB*]

[In the common understanding the *bismillah* ("In the Name of God") in the Pashto text can be understood to be a part of the *kalima* (creed), whose confession distinguishes one as a Muslim.

[In Islam, one gains spiritual reward or profit (*sawāb*) from religious practices, including (as here) the recitation of the *kalima* (*see* Proverb 35) and, in imitation of the Prophet, eating dates (*see* Proverb 945).

[In popular or everyday Islam, Muslims use the *kalima* or *bismillah* to invoke blessing, protection and spiritual power. Chanting of the *kalima* is also an important aspect of the Sufi (Muslim mystic) practice of *dhikr* (*zikər*), "the remembrance of God", wherein the devotee meditates on and repeats (out loud or silently) certain formulas, in particular the "Ninety Nine Most Beautiful Names" and attributes of God, and seeks an emotional union with Him and a release of power (*see* Proverbs 93 and 160). *LNB*]

بل ته ګوته ښه ښي ځان ته نۀ ښي.

292. *One can point at others more easily than at himself.*

This proverb refers to our reluctance to apply self-criticism.

بلا په مخ وهلے کېږي نه په شا.

293. *A calamity should be met face-to-face, not struck in her back.*

[Alternatively, "Calamity can be turned away if it is struck on the face." *RWS*]

بلا وه بركت ئي نهٔ وو.

294. *Though a calamity, it did not last long.*

[That is, "It was a calamity, but it had no influence (literally, *barakat*)." Spoken when a difficult time has passed without causing loss. The word *barakat* (blessing) is used to communicate that although there was trouble, it didn't greatly affect me. *RWS, LNB*]

بليا لژه وه بركت ئي ډېر وو.

295. *The calamity was minor, the losses were great.*

[This is the opposite of the previous proverb. The word blessing (*barakat*) is used with sarcasm, as the person has experienced a great deal of trouble and loss (*barakat*) from something small. *See* Proverb 294. *LNB*]

بنده اريان خدا ے مهربان.

296. *Kind God removes man's difficulty.*

[Man is worried about his needs, but God is very kind and provides him some cause for fulfillment. *RWS*]

بنده بې وزرو مارغهٔ د ے.

297. *Man is a bird without wings.*

Man can achieve any objective. He can even "fly" without having wings.

[Crossing many obstacles and reaching everywhere, man is like a bird without wings. *RWS*]

بنده په غُلو گنده.

298. *Man is a filthy creature.*

[Man has weaknesses, therefore he should not boast. This blunt and crude saying states that, "Man is dirty with excreta." Though the proverb uses an impolite word, the proverb itself has a wise meaning. *See* note to Proverb 104 and Index entries for "impolite proverbs". *RWS, LNB*]

بنده د بنده رحمان دے، بنده د بنده شيطان دے.

299. *Man is man's Rahman, and man is man's Satan.*

Man has the capacity to do good or evil.

This is sometimes used in the popular sense of, "You can tell a man by the company he keeps."

[This rhyming proverb contrasts *rahmān* with *shaytān*. A man can lead you to the good path and teach or show you how to do right like *Rahman* (the Most Gracious, Merciful God). However, a man can also lead you to the wrong path and teach you to do evil like Satan. *RWS*]

بنده د خطا دے.

300. *To err is human.*

[People make mistakes. The possibilty of human error is contrasted with the Godly response in the English proverb, "To err is human; to forgive, divine." The proverb is about the possibility of human error. *LNB, RWS*]

بنده دې حركت وكړي، نو خداے به بركت وكړي.

301. *Man shall work and God will bless.*

[This is a rhyming proverb that advises, if a man does not work, literally "act, move" (*harakat*), for something, how can he expect God's blessing (*barakat*). *See* Proverb 906. *RWS, LNB*]

بنده راشه د خدائے مل شه لکه په ځان ئې داسې په بل شه.

302.   *Oh man, come and be a friend to God; do unto others as you would have them do unto you.*

[The sentiment of the second line is identical to the so-called "Golden Rule" of Jesus Christ which is now proverbial in English; "Do to others as you would have them do to you,"[10] since loving God and loving others are the two greatest commandments. In this Pashto proverb, to "Treat others the way you want to be treated" is an expression of one's reverence for and friendship with God, who is kind to all. *See* Proverbs 886 and 1171. *LNB*]

بنده یو څۀ کوي، خدائے بل څۀ کوي.

303.   *[Man does one thing, God does another.]*

This is similar to the adage, "Man proposes; God disposes."

[Man has his choice, and God has his. *See* Proverbs 399 and 495. *LNB*]

بنده یو نُور جامه ئې دوه نوره.

304.   *The dignity of a man is one advantage and dress makes it double.*

A man's dignity is enhanced by proper dress.

بنو! ویه ډولونه ، جوار دې تش وتلي دینه.

305. *Beat your drums, Oh Bannuchis! Your millet has no ears on it.*

A Khattak tribesman, having never seen Indian corn before he visited the Bannu district, was surprised to see that the tall crop, which he took for millet, had no ears on the tips of the plants. When he entered the town, the people were celebrating their fine corn crop with music and drums. The simple Khattak, seeing this and considering the people to be fools, shouted, "Beat your drums, Bannuchis! Your millet has no ears on it."

[Satire and sarcastic remarks are common in Pashtun culture. This proverb can also be used when one is ignorant about his fields and crops and is busy making merry instead of being about his work. *RWS*]

[Names of various Pashtun tribes appear in Pashto proverbs, for example, Afridi, Bannuchi, Buniri, Yousafzai ; *see* Index for "Pakhtun tribes". Some proverbs praise one's own tribe (*see* Proverbs 661 and 890) and / or mock neighbouring tribes (as in this text). Proverb repertoires vary between tribes. Proverbial references to tribes and inter-tribal "slurs", as well as variant renderings of texts, are subjects for future study. *LNB*]

بوډۍ اسپې ته ترېکي مۀ ښایه.

306. *Don't teach an old mare to gallop.*

An experienced person needs no advice.

بوس راوړه شوملې وړه، د ماما کور دې خپل دے.

307. *Bring hay and take buttermilk in return, this is your maternal uncle's home.*

A proverb, usually ironic, meaning that a person in need of anything must give something in return.

- 86 -

بویه چې راورې زویه.

308. *It will take a long time to have a son.*

This proverb is used to suggest that one will probably not succeed
in his objective, even though his hopes are high, or an objective is
achieved only after a long struggle.

[It is also used when someone becomes pessimistic about something
or gives up hope. *RWS*]

بهر بروا په کور څوبارې چلوي.

309. *He is a coward outside, a bully at home.*

[A coward or a man of weak character can only beat the weak. *RWS*]

بې ادبي له خمسورتیا نه ولاړېږي.

310. *Spoiling a child leads to rude manners.*

The meaning is analogous to, "Spare the rod and spoil the child,"
[a now proverbial English saying based on King Solomon's (*Bacha
Suliman*) words in the Old Testament, "Those who spare the rod hate
their children, but those who love them are diligent to discipline
them."[11] *LNB*]

[A child learns rudeness from bad company. *RWS*]

بې اُمیده شیطان دے.

311. *It is only Satan who is without hope.*

[Hopelessness is a calamity and a great evil that crushes the human
spirit. Believers live in hope of Paradise, but there is no hope for
Satan who is "hopeless". *LNB*]

بې د خپلو څوک سر ته نۀ رسي.

312.   *One cannot achieve anything without the support of his relatives.*

That is, unity is strength.

[This proverb underlines the importance of the extended family in Pashtun society. One's relatives are the primary source of strength, help and resources in time of need and throughout one's life. *LNB*]

بې زما نه به ئې شل نۀ کړي.

313.   *You won't make it twenty without me.*

You won't complete your work without me, or, as in the internationally known proverb, "Many hands make light work."

[To "make twenty" is a common idiom in Pashto. It points toward the indispensable nature of the person who is needed to complete the task. *RWS*]

بې کارو له شيطان کار پيدا کوي.

314.   *Satan produces work for the idle ones.*

"The idler's brain is the devil's workshop," [more commonly known in the form, "An idle brain is the devil's workshop" or "An empty brain is the devil's workshop." *RWS, LNB*]

بې کوره سړے بنۀ دے نۀ په کور کښې هميش جنګ.

315.   *It is better to live single than to reside with a quarrelsome family.*

[It is better to be homeless (*be-kora*) than to live in a home (*kor*) where there is always quarreling (*jang*). *RWS*]

[One is reminded of King Solomon's (*Bacha Suliman*) wry wit in the Old Testament, "Better to live on a corner of the roof than share a house with a quarrelsome wife," and "Better a dry crust with peace and quiet than a house full of feasting with strife."[12] *LNB*]

بې مزده چار د هیچا نۀ زده.

316. *No one works without wages.*

بې نصیبه خوارۀ گران دي.

317. *Without luck it is difficult to prosper.*

[Without luck it is difficult to have food. *RWS*]

[The word for "luck" here is *nasib*, which refers to one's appointed share, portion or fate. In this case the reference is to the luckless (*be nasib*) person who receives an insignificant or lesser portion. *LNB*]

بې وخته میلمه د آسمان چرق دے.

318. *An untimely guest is a thunderbolt.*

The untimely guest causes the host great inconvenience.

[Though Pakhtun hospitality is legendary, and a visit from a guest honors the host, proverbs like this attest to the behind-the-scenes consternation that can be caused by the untimely or unexpected ("thunderbolt") visitor. The requirements of honor demand from even the poorest family generous provision of food, entertainment and the meeting of the guest's every need. A Pakhtun will borrow money to care for his guest. *LNB*]

بیربوتی د میلمنو قوتي یو پروس کالي راغلے وو یو سخ کال بل راغے.

319. *Barbotai is teeming with guests; one guest came last year and one has come this year.*

This is an obvious irony.

بيږه سپي کړي وه، چي ړانده کوتري ئي راوړۀ.

320. *The bitch made such haste, that she gave birth to blind pups.*

   The meaning is similar to the saying, "Haste makes waste." [*See* Proverbs 75 and 321.]

بيږه کونه ويږه.

321. *Haste uncovers the anus.*

   "Haste makes waste," and leads to shame.

   [This is another example of an impolite proverb that uses a crude term to make a wise point. *See* Proverb 104. *LNB*]

بيړۍ په بخت چليږي.

322. *A boat sails with good luck.*

   Success in life depends on good luck. "Fortune rules men's lives."

   [Tair here is referring to a Latin proverb from Cicero (106-43 BC), "Fortune, not wisdom, rules men's lives (*Vitam regit fortuna, non sapienta*)."[13] *LNB*]

بيړۍ هم تياره ده او ډوډۍ هم تياره ده.

323. *The boat is ready to sail, but the food is ready to eat.*

   This is said of one who has to decide between two alternatives and is uncertain which to choose. "He is caught between the devil and the deep blue sea." [*See* proverb 762.]

   It is also said of a miserly host who tells his guest that "though the food is ready, the boat is also ready to sail." That is, if he wants to go, he may.

بیزه د مرگه پټېده د قصاب کره ئې شپه شوه.

324. *The goat, hiding from death, passed the night in the home of the butcher.*

This is similar to the saying, "Out of the frying pan and into the fire."

[One can avoid a minor calamity and end up facing a bigger one. *See* Proverb 272. *RWS*]

بیل وطن بیل ئې دستور.

325. *Different countries have different customs.*

[*See* Proverb 1316 and Index entries for "custom, tradition".]

پاکه وار کوی ناپاکه گزار کوی.

326. *The virtuous waits, the unvirtuous strikes.*

پټ غل باچا دے.

327. *An unknown thief is a king.*

The proverb is said of a thief who escapes detection, that is, one who cannot be identified.

پټکے چې په اوږو تم شي، پرېوتی ئې مۀ گڼه.

328. *When the turban falls from the head but remains on the shoulders, do not consider it fallen.*

This refers to a man who, robbed of authority, still retains authority and respect in some other form. He has not suffered complete disgrace.

[The falling down of a turban is considered high humiliation in Pashtun culture. *RWS*]

[The turban is a traditional symbol of honor and authority. Thomas Hughes comments, "It is in the peculiar method of tying on, and of arranging this head-dress, that not only tribal and religious distinctions are seen, but even peculiarities of disposition. The humility or pride, the virtue or vice, as well as the social standing of the individual, is supposed to be indicated in this method of binding the turban on his head."[14] *See* Index entry for "turban". *LNB*]

پرتوگ مې هم واچاوهٔ او تحصیلدار هم رانغے.

329.   *Although I put on my* salwar, *the* tehsildar *did not arrive.*

In spite of careful preparations, nothing happened. (The *salwār* are
the trousers, and the *tehsildār* is the revenue officer.)

[This proverb refers to the Marwat tribe, where the *lungi* is worn
instead of *shalwār* (*salwār*) in the extreme heat of summer. RWS]

پردي کور کښې سل مېلمانهٔ څهٔ دي.

330.   *What are a hundred guests in another's home.*

A large number of guests are no problem if they are in someone
else's house. [*See* Proverb 318 for a similar sentiment, and Proverb
1154 for another reference to "a hundred (invited) guests". LNB]

پردے اس به دې پلے کړي.

331.   *A borrowed horse will cause you to walk.*

Things borrowed do not remain with the borrower for long.

پردے جنګ نیم اختر دے.

332.   *Hearing others quarrel is nearly as exciting as the* Eid.

This proverb is said about spectators who are watching and
enjoying a fight.

[There are two major *Eids* (Pashto, *akhtar*) celebrations in a year: *Eid-
ul-fitr*, "The Feast of Fast Breaking", which occurs following the
fasting month of Ramazan, and *Eid-ul-adha* (*azha*), "The Feast of
Sacrifice", which occurs about 70 days later (during the pilrimage (*al-
Hajj*), commemorating the Prophet Abraham's obedience to God in
offering his son and the sacrifice of a ram provided in his place. Both
are comparable to Christmas in their social significance, and
commonly involve gift-giving, buying new clothes, special foods,

family gatherings, and visiting friends and relatives. This proverb indicates that hearing someone else's quarrels is as exciting as an *Eid* celebration and certainly is better than quarreling in one's own home. *LNB*]

پردے غم د واورو سوړ وي.

333. *Another's trouble is colder than ice.*

We do not feel the trouble of others.

پردے غم نيم اختر وي.

334. *Another's trouble is half an* Eid.

Another's difficulties [literally, *ghəm* (*see* Proverb 102)] are amusing to us.

[The sentiment is similar to that expressed in Proverb 332 where one takes perverse joy in the sorrows, quarrels or difficulties of others. *LNB*]

پردے کار د ايمان په رڼا کېږي.

335. *Another's work is done only through the light of faith.*

پردے کټ د نيمي شپې وي.

336. *Another's bed is always available for only half the night.*

A borrowed article is always returnable at short notice.

[That is, it refers to the untrustworthiness of borrowed things. *RWS*]

پرون جولا شوې نن نچې پتوې.

337. *Only yesterday you became a weaver, today you steal the bobbins.*

This proverb is said of a man who, though a novice, claims after a short period to be a master of his trade.

[Alternatively, "... today you hide or cover the bobbins." *RWS*]

پریږده قمره! غوښت هم لا دانه ده.

338. *Leave it, Oh Qamer! Can millet even be considered a food?*

This proverb refers to a man or an object not comparable to another, superior one.

[The saying can refer to something that lacks value. *RWS*]

پړسو بابا دپره دوډۍ مۀ خوره، بدبېرو [بدبېرۍ] له به خو.

339. *Oh fat man! Do not stuff yourself with too much food, we are going to eat large jujube berries.*

One should not be greedy for inferior things when they are to be followed by superior commodities.

[Alternately, the Pashto could be rendered, "... we are going to the village of Badabera (a village near Peshawar)," meaning, over-eating causes trouble in walking. *RWS, LNB*]

پښتانۀ په لنډۍ لار مرۀ دي.

340. *The Pakhtuns are very much in love with short cuts.*

Even when it is dangerous, the Pakhtuns always take a short cut. [*See* Proverb 342 which expresses a similar truth.]

[This is one of a number of proverbs that present a picture or stereotype of the "typical", "ideal" or "true Pashtun". *See* Proverb 341, 342 and Index entries for "Pashtun"; *see* also Proverb 608.

Proverbial autostereotypes (sterotypes or caricatures of one's own group) are neither hostile slurs nor an always-accurate picture of reality. However, they do portray traditional views of the Pashtun's character. As such, they are socially useful in explaining or prescribing, with proverbial authority, behaviors and qualities that are in line with Pashtun values, the traditional code of *pashtunwali*, and the ethos of a man of faith and honor. *LNB*]

پښتون چې پښتو نۀ لري زمکه دې پرې ډکه شي.

341. *When a Pakhtun has no* pakhto *(that is, code of honor), may he fill the hollows of the earth.*

The Pakhtun must follow a strong code of honor, that is, family and tribal traditions.

[*Pakhto* or *pashto* (the same word as the language), also known as *pakhtunwali*, is a traditional code embodying Pashtun understandings of "honor", and covers every aspect of personal, family and tribal life. To keep the code is called "doing *pakhto*". *Pakhtunwali / pakhto* may best be viewed as a composite notion that embraces the customs and behaviour, morality, ethos, and notion of ancestral heritage associated with "being Pashtun". This proverb asserts that honor and *pashtunwali* are bound up with the very essence of "Pashtunness" and Pashtun identity—without the spirit of *pakhto*, one might as well be "swallowed up by the earth", i.e. dead. *See* Index for "*pakhtunwali*, *pakhto*"; cf. note on Proverb 608. *LNB*]

پښتون زوئ او ورور لنده حيله کوله تر کمره پرېوتل.

342. *The Pakhtun brother and son were so impatient that they took a short cut and fell off a cliff.*

This proverb shows the reckless nature of the Pakhtun. When he takes a short cut, he usually comes to grief.

پښتون سوال نۀ کوي، او چي کوي ئې نو خور ته هم اودريږي.

343. *The Pakhtun seldom begs from anyone, but when he does, he will even stand before (beg from) his sister.*

پښتون ښۀ ته هم کافر وائي.

344. *The Pakhtun will call anything that is good a "kafir".*

This is ironic, for the phrase is couched in opposite or unpopular terms. The *kāfir* is a non-believer in the true faith.

[*kāfir* here is a poetic term meaning the "faith-breaking" beauty of anything that is of extremely high quality. *RWS*]

پښتون نۀ دے چي د نوک جواب په سُوک نۀ ورکوي.

345. *He is not a Pakhtun who does not strike a blow if pinched.*

[Provocation of a Pakhtun is always harmful. *RWS*]

پښتون وړوکے بار نۀ وړي.

346. *The Pakhtun does not carry a small burden.*

He takes full advantage of his opportunities even if doing so endangers his life. Or, alternatively, he is fond and capable of shouldering heavy responsibilities. He does not like petty things.

پښه مې دي پاس وي، که په خرۀ وي که په اس وي.

347. *My foot should be high, whether I mount a donkey or a horse.*

This proverb is said of a man who wants to become prominent by any means, fair or foul.

پښې ئې پرېښنودې په سر روان شو.

348. *Instead of his feet, he began to walk on his head.*

This proverb is said of the man who abandons the dull routine of everyday life to satisfy his true desires.

It also means that he started to do the unusual and became hot-headed.

[This is about the nontraditional person that adopts uncommon or unconventional ways. *RWS*]

پکی (گنجی) د خان کره ډوډئ اوخوړه په لاري سمه نۀ تله.

349. *The pock-marked woman ate bread [dined] at the home of the Khan and then started strutting about.*

This proverb is said of a person who, being of little importance, shows great pride when patronized by someone.

پکے په لاس ننوځه او نالی په سر راوځه.

350. *Get inside the room when you need the fan, come out with the quilt.*

The reference is to the season. One should sleep outside in early spring and should go inside when the dew begins to appear in hot weather.

[Literally, "Get inside with fan in hand, get outside with quilt on your head." The proverb is a comment about the unreliable weather in some months of the year. It is used metaphorically about fast-changing circumstances. Nothing is stable in this life. *RWS, LNB*]

پلار ئې پېدا نۀ وو اؤ زوئ ئې په لښکر تلے وو.

351. *The father was not yet born and already his son had joined the army.*

Some people hope to use an object that they have no means of acquiring.

[The proverb speaks about claiming great deeds ahead of time or inappropriately. *RWS*]

پنبه کړه په جبت چي سرے شي پکبني سپت.

352.   *Sow cotton in the month of May and you will become wealthy.*

That is to say, sow it at the most appropriate time.

[Although other crops are not mentioned, this proverb is about all of the sowing seasons. *RWS*]

پور د بدو برخه ده.

353.   *Debt is a misfortune.*

[Alternatively, "Debt is a kind of vice." *RWS*]

پور د بدیِ تخم دے.

354.   *Debt is the seed of enmity.*

پور د مينِي لور.

355.   *Debt is the sickle of love.*

Debt breaks off a friendship.

پوره! ورک دې کړۀ دوه کوره.

356.   *Oh debt, you have destroyed two houses.*

In other words, debt destroys many people and families.

پوزے دے کہ پوزی خو ودیږي داؤدزی۔

357. *Though the dowry of the Daudzai maiden is only a mat, she certainly is to be married.*

An ironic expression applied to a poor couple who insist on having their daughter married.

[The proverb plays with the fact that the pronunciation of Pashto words may vary according to region or dialect: Whether you call the "mat" *puzay* or *puzai*, the Daudzai is going to marry. That is, no matter what the dowry is, the real purpose is marriage. *RWS, LNB*]

په اوبو کښې ډوب اوبهٔ نهٔ ویني.

358. *The drowned man cannot see the sea.*

He "can't see the wood for the trees."

[The well-known saying that, you "can't see the wood for the trees," cited by the English dramatist, poet and writer John Heywood (1497-1580),[15] and found also in many different European languages, communicates that a person is so involved in the details of something that he can no longer remember the real purpose or importance of the thing as a whole. *LNB*]

په اوړي خیته غومبر نهٔ کیږي.

359. *One cannot make merry with an empty stomach.*

Poor people are denied the comforts of life.

[Poor people cannot spare time for merry making. *See* Proverb 231. *RWS*]

په بنی کښې ئې یو موټے اوړهٔ نشته او لافې د دولتمند کوي.

360. *His leather bag contains not even a handful of flour, yet he boasts of his wealth.*

په ببړي (بوړي – توپک) ئې ګټم او په ببړي ئې خورم.

361. *I earn by my gun and spend for my gun.*

I live by force and spend my money for survival.

This Waziri proverb describes the only way of survival for the mountain Pakhtun. It means that I earn like a hero [a courageous and brave-hearted man] and spend like a hero.

[*boṛay* in the Waziri dialect is *beṛay*, the .303 rifle. The .303 was the standard issue rifle for the British colonial army and was much coveted by tribal Pashtun. *RWS, LNB*]

په پردۍ ژرنده کښې وار نيسي.

362. *He demands his turn in another man's mill.*

This proverb is said of someone who makes unwarranted demands of others.

[Or, "He is booking his turn in another man's mill." *RWS*]

په پردي لاس غل تانې ته مۀ بیایه.

363. *Don't rely on a stranger to take the thief to the police station.*

When you wish to do something, do it yourself without entrusting it to others.

[Don't trust others even in doing petty things. *RWS*]

په پردي لاس مار مۀ وژنه.

364. *Don't kill a snake by another's hands.*

Don't rely on others to do your work, [even work in which there may be a common interest *RWS*].

په پریوتي هر سرے دانګي.

365. *Everyone jumps upon a fallen man.*

په پوښتنه پوښتنه سرے کابل ته رسي.

366. *By inquiring, a man can reach Kabul.*

A determined man will surely reach his destination by exploiting all means.

[Nothing is beyond reach if one adopts a proper way. *RWS*]

په پښو اخبل دي په دیوال تپل دي.

367. *One must knead with his feet and plaster on the wall.*

When a man who must live under uncongenial conditions in a boring society is asked, "How are you getting on?", he may reply with this proverb.

[Dough is usually mixed with the hands, not the feet; it is stuck on the side of a *tandoor* (*tandur*), not a wall. The meaning is, with a sense of resignation, "People are kneading dough with their feet and plastering it on the wall and I can't do anything about it." One is reminded of the way women plaster cakes of manure on the wall to dry, so they can be used as fuel for the fire. *LNB*]

په پیینډه کښبي دي هم سجن اوسه.

368. *Even in a gathering of guests around the table there should be one of your friends.*

At no time should one be without a friend.

په تا مي وس نۀ رسي مر به دې پلار کړم.

369. *I can't hurt you, but I'll kill your father.*

The reference is to the coward who, unable to take revenge on his enemy, seeks out someone weaker.

[Alternatively, "I am unable to apprehend you, but …" *RWS*]

په تشه قوتۍ مېل کوي.

370. *No game of marbles can be played in an empty ring.*

That is, no business can be started without capital.

[The proverb is about a bad loser in the game of marbles. "Though the hole is empty, he is again crying 'foul'." *RWS*]

په تلۀ په راتلۀ نۀ شي چي څو درز د څتې نۀ شي.

371. *It (the work) will not be done until the falling of the gunny bag.*

The job is not completed until the share of the crop has been received. Or, mere running about the fields means nothing, it is the bag full of grain that counts.

په تود جنګ کښې اسونه نۀ څربېږي.

372. *Horses cannot be fattened in the thick of battle.*

Make the most of your time, or choose the proper time to do things.

په تبر واده سندري وائي.

373. *They sing about a marriage that has already been consummated.*

The song is too late for the celebration. The proverb refers to happiness that does not suit the occasion.

په تکواړه کښې خراڅ سوزي.

374. *Larks are burnt in Takwara.*

Takwara, noted for its extreme heat and lack of water, is a village in Kulachi Tehsil in the Dera Ismail Khan Division.

په ټوپک ويشتلے بنۀ دے، په خبره ملامت شرمنده دے.

375. *It is better to be shot by a bullet than to be disgraced by words.*

[Contrary to popular stereotypes, most tribal people spend more time fighting with words than with bullets. Honor and shame are as much dependent upon words—including accusations and verbal interpretations of one's behavior—as they are upon fighting or physical prowess, and hospitality or generosity. Words can destroy a man's honor, his public image or reputation, and taunts, insults and scornful words (*peghor*) are not easily forgotten *See* Proverb 1254. LNB]

په جنت کښې خرۀ تړلے نشي.

376. *Donkeys are not tied in Paradise.*

Men of low degree are not called to an important gathering.

په جنگ پسې کروئ ګرځوي.

377. *He visits a quarrel with payment.*

This proverb is said of one who is always picking a quarrel with others.

په چا غم په چا ښادي.

378. *Some are joyful, some in grief.*

People of different status lead different lives.

[The proverb contrasts not only the two extremes of human emotion, but the two types of events and rituals that mark Pashtun life, viz. events characterised by sorrow (*ghəm*), for example sickness, death, and those characterised by happiness (*khādi*), for example, births, engagements, weddings. *See* Proverb 102. *LNB*]

په څرمن کښې ئې يوه کوړۍ هم نيشته.

379. *He does not carry a single shell on his body.*

That is, he is hopelessly poor, as in the proverbial English phrase, "Poor as a church mouse."

په ځاے ډکيږي په ځاے تشيږي.

380. *He fills and relieves himself in the same place.*

This proverb is said of the man who earns his living without the slightest effort; a human parasite.

[With crude connotations, but without using impolite terms, this proverb pictures one who eats, drinks and relieves himself in the same place. *LNB*]

په حرامه راغلې وه په حرامه لاړه.

381. *Unlawfully earned and unlawfully spent.*

    Ill gotten; ill spent.

[The Arabic word *harām* used here is an important Islamic term. It refers to that which is "forbidden" or "taboo", "proscribed" or "reprehensible", and thus a threat to sanctity; cf. *halāl*, Proverb 562. *LNB*]

په خپل کور کښې خو مږے هم زورآور وي.

382. *Even an ant is brave in his own home.*

    This proverb applies to one who, confident of support from his relatives, is aggressive even though he is basically cowardly.

په خُلۀ توبه له بدو په زړۀ حمله په بدو.

383. *His tongue repents of evil, his heart yearns for it.*

[This proverb describes a person's duplicity. *RWS*]

په خُلۀ مسلمان په زړۀ کافر.

384. *A Muslim's mouth, a* kafir's *heart.*

    The reference is to a hypocrite.

[Alternatively, "A Muslim by mouth and a *kāfir* by heart." *See* Proverb 173 and 444. *RWS*]

په خوږه خُله ښار خوړلے شي.

385. *A sweet tongue can rule over a city.*

Love can rule a kingdom without a sword. [*See* Proverbs 418 and 1166.]

په دا وړوکي خُله څۀ غواړې.

386.   *What do you want, you of the small mouth.*

Don't ask for things beyond your reach. This proverb is applied to social climbers.

[Alternatively, "… you with such a small mouth." *RWS*]

په دې خُله سرے لُور خور ورکوي.

387.   *By this very word a man gives his daughter or sister (in marriage).*

The Pakhtun's promise is a sacred bond. Once he has given his word he will honor it, even if it means giving away his daughter or sister in marriage.

[In *pakhtunwali* one's word is honored like a written agreement. This is one reason why *pakhtunwali* is called an unwritten constitution. *RWS*]

په دې قبر شکرې نيشته.

388.   *There is no sugar on this grave.*

Not every man shows kindness to the needy.

[This proverb is about useless or unmet expectations. *RWS*]

په دنيا کښې خو يا نشې دي يا تماشې دي.

389.   *The world has only intoxicants and merry making.*

The happy life calls for wine, women and song. It is the hedonistic view expressed in the saying, "Eat, drink and be merry."

[The now proverbial "Eat, drink and be merry ..." is based on an ancient saying of the Egyptians who, at their banquets, exhibited a skeleton to the guests to remind them of death and encourage them to enjoy life: "Gaze here, and drink and be merry; for when you die, such will you be."[16] The Prophet Isaiah used similar words, "Let us eat and drink, for tomorrow we shall die,"[17] to describe and rebuke the mentality of people who lived a life of pleasure without repentance and fear of God. *See* Proverbs 694 and 999. *LNB*]

په دنيا کښې مويزي بې خلي نۀ وي.

390.   *In this world there is not a raisin without a straw.*

This is similar to the saying, "No rose without a thorn."

[Alternatively, "… there is no raisin without a (hard) stem." *See* Proverb 1239. *RWS*]

په دوهٔ وُ بېړو پښې کښېنودے نۀ شي.

391.   *One cannot put his feet in two sailing boats at the same time.*

[It is hard to do two different jobs at one time. *RWS*]

په دې لاس ئي ورکړه په دې لاس ئي واخله.

392.   *Give with one hand, take away with the other.*

Applied to such gifts that are given with one hand and taken away with the other.

په ډک نس (خېټه) مرگ هم ښۀ دے.

393.   *It is better to die with a full stomach than to live in hunger.*

["It is better to die after having dined." Everything is better done with pleasure, with a full stomach. *RWS*]

په ډکه ګېډه مرګ هم ښۀ دے.

394. *Even death is pleasant with a full stomach.*

This expresses the longing of a poor man for food and other wherewithals.

[Everything, even death, is better done with pleasure, that is, with a full stomach. *RWS*]

[In this dialectical variant of Proverb 393, Tair and Edwards interpret "stomach" literally, in contrast with the metaphorical interpretation offered by RWS for both texts. *LNB*]

په ډمانو هم چا جالۍ راکښنلي دي؟

395. *Can boats that float be towed by barbers?*

A difficult job cannot be done by menials. Different people do different jobs.

[For a comment on the role of the barber and other menials, *see* Proverb 615. *LNB*.]

په ډيرو قصابانو کښې غوا مرداريږي.

396. *With too many butchers the cow dies without being lawfully slaughtered.*

This is similar to the English proverb, "Too many cooks spoil the broth."

[The cow that "dies without being lawfully slaughtered" is one word in Pashto, "to become *murdār*", which refers to polluted meat (for example, a cow or sheep that dies of sickness or injury) or impure animals of any kind, (for example, a dog). So "too many butchers" make the normally lawful or *halāl* meat polluted. *LNB*]

په ډيرو لبوني خوشحالېږي.

397.   *Fools alone desire too much of everything.*

Quality is more important than quantity.

[Too much of everything is bad. Only foolish people become happy with excess. *RWS*]

په رِندو کبنې د يوې سترګې خاوند باچا وي.

398.   *Among the blind the one-eyed man is the leader[king].*

A man with some qualities is better than those who have none.

[This internationally known adage appears in a work by the Dutch humanist, Desiderius Erasmus (1466-1536) in the form, "In the kingdom of the blind, the one-eyed man is king";[18] in John Palsgrave's (d. 1554) translation in 1540 of William Fullonius' Latin play, *The Comedy of Acolastus*; and in a scathing poem by the English poet laureate and political satirist, John Skelton (ca. 1460-1529), "But have ye not heard this, How an one-eyed man is Well sighted when He is among blind men?"[19] In the modern period this proverb serves as the theme and title of a well-known English short story by H. G. Wells (1866-1946), "The Country of the Blind."[20] *LNB*]

په زړۀ به دې يوه وي، در پيښنه به کړم بله.

399.   *God says: There will be one idea in your mind, but I will change it into another.*

This is similar to the adage, "Man proposes; God disposes." [*See* Proverbs 303 and 495.]

په زړۀ کبنې ئې ګيدړ ناست دے.

400.   *A jackal sits in his heart.*

This is said of one who is experiencing a deadly fear (that is, a coward).

په زړهٔ کوږ په خُلهٔ خوږ.

401. *Inwardly crooked, outwardly sweet.*

This refers to the hypocrite whose honeyed tongue belies his evil intentions.

[Literally, "Crooked in heart, sweet with mouth." *See* e.g. Proverbs 173, 384 and 444. *RWS*]

په زړهٔ ئې ځنګل ولاړ دے.

402. *A jungle has grown in his heart.*

These words refer to a tyrant.

په زور کلي نهٔ کېږي.

403. *People cannot be forced to live in a community.*

Community life stems from voluntary cooperation.

[One cannot be forced to agree with the community. Unity and brotherhood in a country or community cannot be achieved through any type of force. *RWS, LNB*]

په ساه څهٔ ویسا.

404. *No dependence on life.*

[Life is unreliable, one cannot rely even on breath itself. *RWS*]

په سترګي مشي د چا ښۀ شي خو زړۀ ئې بنۀ شي.

405. *When someone tells him "May you never get tired" of what benefit is it to him except as encouragement.*

If you welcome anyone, what does he get except that he is pleased with the words.

[*stəray məshe!* or "May you not be tired!" is the traditional Pashtun welcome. *LNB*]

په سر دپاسه سر وي.

406. *There is always a head above a head.*

There is always someone superior to any person.

[For example, one can appeal to someone who is stronger or to a higher power or authority. In Pashto, another common rendering of this text is *də sar* ... (not *pə sar*). *LNB*]

په سر (پټکي) کښې دي مسواک دے. په بغل کښې دي خنجر.

407. *A toothbrush in the turban, a dagger in the armpit.*

This text refers to the hypocrite who pretends to be a friend.

[The proverb refers to the duplicity of a so-called Muslim or a mullah, who should be a man of peace. *RWS*]

په سر (پټکي) کښې ئې مسواک او په ترخ کښې ئې چاړۀ.

408. *In his turban a toothbrush, under his armpit a dagger.*

Another reference to the male hypocrite. [A variant of Proverb 407.]

په سر ئې واههٔ خاې ئې چاؤدې.

409. *Though the blow may fall upon his head, it was his testicles that were crushed.*

It is an unusual phenomenon that when damage is done to one individual, it may cause injury to another.

[The word *hāye* (eggs) should replace *khāye* (testicles). It refers to the person who sells eggs, which are traditionally carried in a basket balanced on the head. Or alternatively, it may refer to someone who has stolen eggs and put them in his cap. *RWS*]

[A common feature of proverbs is the use of circumlocution or word substitution (as RWS suggests) to avoid potentially offensive or "impolite" terms; even the substituted word may still carry a double meaning, and both forms of the proverb may circulate. In this case, despite the reference to "testicles", the proverb carries the meaning that a weak person (servant, employee) may unjustly suffer the consequences for a decision made by the more powerful (*khan*, employer). *LNB*]

په سړو کښې توپير دے، څوک لعل دے څوک کاڼي.

410. *Men differ, some are rubies and some stones.*

په سل باندې جوړېږي. په يو باندې ماتېږي.

411. *A hundred will make it, one will break it.*

[It takes one to complete a hundred; by taking only one out, it will "break" the hundred and make it incomplete. See variant Proverb 412. *RWS, LNB*]

په سل باندې جوړېږي. په يو ورانېږي.

412. *The product of a hundred can be destroyed by one.*

This expression was applied, for example, to the sinking of H.M.S.
King George V by the Japanese. That is, it takes a long time to build
but just a little time to destroy. [*See* variant Proverb 411.]

په سپر کبنۍ ئې پوني نهٔ ده ربشلۍ.

413.   *He has not even tested a single fraction (of cotton) in a* seer.

An expression applied to one who has scarcely begun to work. The
seer is a unit of weight [approximately 2 lbs (1 kg) in Pakistan, but
approximately 15 lbs (7 kg.) in Afghanistan *LNB*].

په شاهۍ کبنۍ مولۍ خرڅوي.

414.   *Although a king, he sells radishes.*

This proverb is said of a wealthy man who demeans himself by
earning money through means beneath his dignity.

په شرع کبنۍ څهٔ شرم دے؟

415.   *No shame in doing lawful things.*

[Literally, "What shame is there in the *sharah* or Islamic Law." The
word used here (*sharah*) refers to "religious law" or the "right way" to
live and obey God without fear of "shame". *RWS, LNB*]

په شملکۍ دې شوم غلطه ، په کور کبنۍ دې نهٔ غوندے وو نهٔ کته.

416.   *I was deceived by your turban, for when I came to your home there
was neither a pannier nor a pack-saddle [saddle bag].*

This proverb is said of a man who shows off without having
anything to boast of.

[A pannier (*ghunday*, also called a *kata*, or *zal* in Afghan Pashto) is
the carrying basket or sack which hangs down either side of a donkey,
camel or other beast of burden, in which it carries its load. *LNB*]

په بنهٔ خُله پردي خپلېږي.

417.   *Strangers can be made friends by sweet words.*

[Non-relatives can be made like relatives by sweet words. *RWS*]

په بنهٔ خُله ښار خورے شي.

418.   *A city can be won over by a sweet tongue.*

[Literally, "… by a good mouth (tongue)", a variant of Proverb 385,
"A sweet tongue (mouth) can rule …". Cf. Proverb 1166. *LNB*]

په بنهٔ کار کښې څهٔ تپوس؟

419.   *Why should one ask permission to do a good deed?*

په بنبره په دعا نشي. کوونِ خداے دے.

420.   *Curses and prayer can do nothing. God alone is the doer.*

[Neither curses uttered against you, nor prayers uttered by or for you
(for example, by holy men), will make any difference. For other
proverbial expressions of fatalism, *see* e.g. Proverbs 603 and 653.
LNB.]

په ظاهر لباس غلط د سړي مهٔ شه ، مېنځ ئې ګوره چي چغزي دے که مټاک.

421.   *Don't judge a man by his outward appearance. Look inside to see
whether he is soft or hard.*

The proverb advises that one look inside to see whether he is worthy
or unworthy.

[The text refers to two different types of walnut: one whose meat is
soft, the other hard. This "proverb" is actually a couplet from the
Diwan (collected poems) of the 17th century Pashtun poet Abdur

Rahman Baba (c. 1650-1715), many of whose verses have acquired proverbial authority and usage. *See* Index for "Abdur Rahman Baba". *LNB, RWS*]

په غل غل پیښپژي.

422.   *A thief finds a thief.*

This proverb is more commonly used in the sense of "ill gotten, ill spent," rather than to mean, "it takes a thief to catch a thief."

په غُلو کښې چې څومره چخچي وهي هومره بوئي کوي.

423.   *The more filth is stirred up with a stick, the greater the stench.*

[The application is that an undesirable matter must be hushed-up instead of holding a debate about it. *RWS*]

[The words used in this proverb, and Proverb 424, are impolite, but the proverbs themselves have meanings. *See* note to Proverb 104 and Index entries for "impolite proverbs". *LNB*]

په غوجل کښې چې یوه غوا وچرپژي ټولي پرې ګنده شي.

424.   *When a cow urinates all the cows in the stable are splashed.*

Akin to various common expressions, such as "the fly in the ointment" and "to be tarred with the same brush." Similar proverbs are, "A bad sheep infects the whole flock" and "One rotten apple spoils the [whole] barrel."

په کاني ژوره نۀ لګي.

425.   *A leech doesn't stick to a stone.*

That is, "You cannot get [squeeze] blood from a stone", or, "You can't draw [get] blood from a turnip." A stone-hearted man is not affected by entreaties.

[Though it is common (herein and elsewhere) to translate or explain proverbs with proverbs, notice the difference in nuance: the English proverbs quoted convey a sense of hopelessness and resignation, as well as the futility of trying to get something (for example, money) from someone who doesn't have any. The comment on the Pashto proverb focuses on the stone-like qualities, the "hard-heartedness", of the other person, qualities antithetical to the ideal of Pashtun generosity. *LNB*]

په کک یاد په لک یاد.

426. *In time of need, a little kindness is worth a* lāk.

The Hindi *lāk* means one hundred thousand or a great number.

[Literally, "Remember a bit, remember a *lāk*", or "Remembered a bit, to be remembered a *lāk*." To be thought of at an unimportant event is like being remembered on a great occasion. *RWS*]

په کور کښې دانې نۀ لري او په ژرنده لاس لګوي.

427. *Though there is no grain in his home, he still fights for a turn at the flour mill.*

په کور کښې نۀ کاک نۀ پياز او اربمے د وازګو کوی.

428. *In his house he has neither maize bread nor an onion, yet he belches as if he has eaten fat.*

A man of no means boasts of his power and self.

په کور کښې نيمه ډوډۍ بنۀ ده، نۀ په پردېس کښې تالي ډک د پلاؤ نه.

429. *It is better to have half a loaf of bread in one's own home than a plateful of "palau" in a foreign land.*

palau is a rich food of rice with chicken or beef in it.

[This text has the meter of a Pashto *ṭappa*. *RWS*]

پہ کور کښې ئې سپې د اوبو غلا کوي.

430. *Even a dog has to steal drinking water from his home.*

This proverb is said of a man who is so miserly that he wouldn't give a dog a drink.

پہ کور کښې یو ډز دارو نۀ لري او پلار تہ وائي چې ما تہ توپہ واخلہ.

431. *Though in his house he has not enough powder for one shot, he says to his father, "Buy me a cannon."*

The notion is of doing something beyond one's means.

پہ ګواره کښې بہ ئې برګے سخے نۀ وي او وائی بہ زمونږ د کلي ګواره هغہ دہ.

432. *Although he does not have a single calf in the herd, he still says, "That is the herd of our village."*

Some men boast of things that do not belong to them.

[Proverbs 427, 428, 431 and 432 all provide graphic images of the proud man who boasts of what he does not have. *LNB*]

پہ لاس ورپے ښۀ دے، نۀ پہ کال غوندے.

433. *One ear of corn now [in hand] is better than half a pannier full a year later.*

That is, "A bird in the hand is worth two in the bush."

[The meaning of both the Pashto and English proverbs quoted above (*See* Proverbs 162 and 434) is that it is better to be satisfied with the little that one has, rather than risk losing it to gain something bigger and better. *LNB*]

په لاس چتے بنهٔ دے د هوا د باز نه.

434. *A wren in the hand is better than a hawk in the sky.*

"A bird in the hand is worth two in the bush." [*See* Proverbs 162 and note on Proverb 433.]

په لاس کښې شرشم نهٔ زرغنیږي.

435. *Mustard seed does not sprout in the hand.*

This proverb is spoken when a person wants something done at once.

په لاس ئې ورکړه په لاس ئې واخله.

436. *Give by hand and take by hand.*

A saying that means, what you give, take the same thing back.

په لنګو ګډو کښې بانګ نهٔ وئیلے کبږي.

437. *Among sheep that have given birth to lambs, the call to prayer (azān) cannot be heard.*

The *bāng* ["call to prayer"] is the voice of a sheep too.

[The term *bāng* used in the Pashto text is a play on words, as the same word refers to the "call to prayer" (also called, *azān*) as well as the voice of sheep or the crowing of a rooster. *LNB*]

په مرک ئې ونیسه په تبه ئې راضي کړه.

438. *Force him to face death and he will happily accept a fever.*

Threaten a man with greater trouble and he will willingly accept a lesser inconvenience.

په مړو کښې بد نيشته په ژوندو کښې ښۀ نيشته.

439.　*Among the dead no one is bad, among the living no one is good.*

په مېنه غز نۀ لرم په چا غرض نۀ لرم.

440.　*I have no tamarisk tree at home, so I have nothing to do with others.*

Without obligations, property or family ties, a man is independent.

په نره ئې ګټم په نره ئې خورم.

441.　*I earn with dignity and spend with dignity.*

په نقار خانه کښې د طوطی آواز څوک آورې.

442.　*In the home of the drummers who can hear the twittering of a parrot?*

A weak voice is not heard in the assembly of those who talk loudly.

[The opposition of one man is not listened to ("heard") by the majority. *RWS*]

په ویر کښې هر څوک خپل مړي ژاړي.

443.　*At the time of mourning everyone weeps for his own dead..*

At a time of mourning, he is reminded of the death of his own kinsmen.

په وينځلو به ئي سپين نۀ کړي بابو جانه ،

کوم لمځي چي د وړي اصل ئي تور وي.

444. *Oh Baboo Jan! Washing the black wool carpet won't make it white.*

What is inherently bad cannot become good by effort.

[This is a couplet by the poet Baboo Jan (also spelled Babu Jan). *RWS*]

[This is similar to the Pashto proverb, "Black cannot be made white with soap," that is, for example, scrubbing a black water buffalo will not turn it white. Cf. also "A dog's tail doesn't become straight, even if it is kept in a pipe for a hundred years" and "You cannot beat a horse out of a donkey." Proverbs such as these express notions about the unchanging nature of persons with bad characters (or from an unscrupulous family or troublesome tribe) and, more generally, the difficulty of changing the human heart. *See* Proverbs 173, 401 and 384. *LNB*]

په هر چا خپل وطن کشمير دے.

445. *To each person his own country is Kashmir.*

Similar truths are expressed by the [Dutch, German and English] proverb, "East or West, home is best", [and the saying] "Be it ever so humble, there's no place like home." Kashmir is known throughout the world for its scenic beauty.

[This is one of the most well-known Pashto proverbs. As such, it is a component of cultural literacy and a part of the verbal repertoire of Pashto speakers of all ages. *See* variant Proverb 876; *see* Index for "Kashmir." Kashmir's proverbial beauty is like an earthly paradise.]

Tair and Edwards quote a now proverbial line (which also appears in a popular 19th century song) from a poem by the dramatist John Howard Payne (1791-1852), which expresses a similar sentiment: "Mid pleasures and palaces though we may roam, Be it ever so humble there's no place like home!"[21] *LNB*]

په هغه سپرلي مي څۀ چي سخي کټي مي پکبني نۀ څري.

446. *Of what use is spring to me, when my calves and the young of the buffalo are not here (to graze).*

This proverb is said of a man who cannot enjoy the happiness of others.

[The text expresses indifference to another person's happiness. *RWS*]

په يارانه کبني تل بنګړي ماتيږي.

447. *Bracelets are always broken in friendship.*

There is no bargaining in friendship. For the sake of friendship one should not mind the loss of a precious thing.

[The image suggests beautiful but fragile glass bracelets (*bangṛa*) being broken by an embrace. *LNB*]

په يو باندي چي دوۀ شي، رڼا ورځ پري توره شپه شي.

448. *The bright day turns into dark night for him when two people fall upon him.*

This is a picture of the fate of the weak under the strong, or of the minority under the majority.

[The proverb describes one person facing a fight with two persons, or one person becoming responsible for two dependents. *RWS*]

په يو تيکي کبني دوۀ تُوري نۀ ځائيږي.

449. *Two swords will not go into one sheath.*

One country cannot have two kings. Two strong rivals cannot be accommodated at one place. [*See* Proverb 1071, the same text with a different word order.]

په يو حال يو الله دے.

450. *God alone is constant in his state.*

Everyone in this world changes except God.

په يو غر بل غر مه وله.

451. *Don't dash one mountain against another.*

This proverb is said to one who talks nonsense or boasts of doing the impossible.

[It is also said when one's arguments are consistent. *RWS*]

په يو غوږ ئي ننا باسي، په بل ئي وباسي.

452. *He takes it in with one ear and expels it with the other.*

This proverb is said of one who hears but does not act. "In one ear and out the other."

[Alternatively, it is said of one who does not remember another's advice. *RWS*]

[This saying, in two forms (*See* Proverb 453), has the ring of a translation of the common English proverb, "(Went) in one ear and out the other," cited in "The Proverbs of John Heywood" (1546),[22] describing someone who doesn't listen to advice or correction. *LNB*]

په يو غوږ ئي واوريدۀ، په بل ئي وويستۀ.

453. *He heard it with one ear and ejected it through the other.*

په يو لاس كښي دوه هندوانۍ نۀ اخستلے كېږي.

454.   *You can't hold two melons in one hand.*

It is difficult to do many jobs with small means.

[A number of Pashto proverbs, like this one and Proverb 457, are also common in Persian. No judgment is made about the origin of the proverbs in this collection, whether from Persian, Arabic, Latin, English or other languages; we take the view herein that their commonality and usage among Pashtuns makes them "Pashto proverbs". *LNB*]

په يوه څپېړه شل مخه خوږېږي.

455.   *Twenty faces are hurt by one slap.*

To insult one person means to insult his whole family.

په يوه كودالۍ كوهۍ نۀ شي كنستلے كېدے.

456.   *A well cannot be dug with one pick-axe.*

This text illustrates the common English saying, "Many hands make light work." [*See* Proverb 313.]

پياز دې وي خو په نياز دې وي.

457.   *Let it be an onion, but it should be given with love and pleasure.*

Even a small gift given with pleasure will be highly appreciated.

[This proverb may be said, for example, by a host to his or her guest as the food is served, as a polite apology for the inadequacy of the meal, however generous it is in reality. The saying communicates that what is being served, is served with love and friendship. In Pashtun culture, as in other Middle Eastern and Asian cultures, great value is placed on sharing a meal together. *LNB*]

پير بابا لوئ دے، كۀ د ايلم غرۀ؟ وئيل ئي خداے دي داسي حٮران كړه

لكه زۀ چي دي حٮران كړم.

458. *Which is greater, the Pir Baba or the Ilam peak? May God confuse you as much as you have confused me.*

This is spoken when one is not expected to decide on the superiority of one person over another and hence is confused. The Pir Baba [shrine] and the Ilam, a mountain peak, are the pride of Bunir.

It is said that a Buniri, when asked which of the two was greater, gave the above reply.

[The shrine of Pir Baba and the Ilam Peak are both "great", and one does not expect to choose between them, hence the confusion. The tomb and shrine of Pir Baba is considered the most hallowed shrine in the Frontier. *See* note to Proverb 460 and 653. *LNB*]

پير نۀ الوزي خو مريدان ئي الوزوي.

459. *The* pir *is not flying, but his disciples make him fly.*

It is the disciples and not the *pir*, (a religious leader or "saint"), who interpret his acts as miracles.

[A *pir* is a "saint" or holy man, or one descended from or a "companion" of a holy man, endowed with spiritual power (*barakat*) to perform miracles, heal, and interecede with God on behalf of petitioners. Some *pirs* and their shrines are associated with particular powers of blessing, and are frequented by those with special needs, for example, infertility, headaches, toothaches, and problems with demons. The needs relate to every facet of personal life, including marriage relationships, money and business. *LNB*]

پيره بابا پۀ ډاک ئي وله ؛ پۀ تاتٮرٮرى ديوانه بابا له ځينه.

460. *Oh, Pir Baba, dash him to the ground. Bypassing you, they are going to pay homage to Diwana Baba.*

This proverb is said when a man ignores a person of great dignity to admire one of lesser rank.

"Pir Baba" is the popular name among the Pakhtun for Sayyed Ali Tirmezi, an orthodox 16th century religious leader whose shrine lies in Bunir.

[The shrines of both Pir Baba and Diwana Baba are in Bunir. This is a Pashto *tappa* . *See* notes to Proverb 106 and Proverbs 653 and 656. *RWS*]

پيره پيره، نۀ پيره، نۀ پيره!

461.   *Oh* pir, *if you wish to be my spiritual leader, find out good, if not, to hell with you.*

Discipleship demands reciprocal love and respect. [*See* variant Proverb 462 and note.]

[When in need, someone calls for the *pir,* when he no longer has a need, then he refuses to listen to the *pir.* The proverb is literally, "Oh *pir,* Oh *pir,* no *pir,* no *pir*", but the free translation above carries the meaning. It could also be rendered, "Oh *pir,* if you are a *pir* do good for me ..."; or alternatively, Oh *pir,* if you are a *pir* that will be revealed, and if you are not a *pir,* that will be revealed too." *pirs* are associated with the "folk" and mystic dimensions of Islam (Sufism), which emphasize a relationship with God as Friend and Lover, as illustrated by the poetry of Abdur Rahman Baba. *See* Index for "saint (*pir*)"; cf. "religious leader" and "Abdur Rahman Baba". *LNB, RWS.*]

پيره نۀ پيره.

462.   Pir, *no* pir.

I called you *pir* when you displayed the qualities of *pir*ship, but now that you have changed, you are no longer worthy of being my *pir.* [*See* Proverb 461.]

پېريان خو زمونږ ماماگان دي.

463.   *The* jinns *are our maternal uncles.*

This might be the flattering comment of a superstitious man as he passes through a dark, lonely place.

[The term translated *jinn* is the more common *periyan*, that is demons or ghosts. *LNB*]

پېريانو ته غزنۍ څۀ دے؟

464. *What is Ghaznai to the* jinns?

For a fast and determined man distances are no problem. [*See* Proverb 463.]

[Ghazni is a city in Eastern Afghanistan. *LNB*]

پېړه په لاس په تود تنور پسې ګرځم.

465. *With dough in my hand I search for an oven.*

The reference is to one who attempts to do a job without first preparing for it.

پېژنم پوُړه بنځه ډېره خمبيره ساتي؛ لاس پرې نۀ راکاږي د قلپى غاړه ګنده ساتي.

466. *I know a slut who keeps more leaven than necessary, but does not clean the pot with residue on the edges.*

[The word translated "slut" does not refer to a lady of bad character, but to one who is untidy and dirty; she does not wipe the edges of the pot used to mix her flour. *LNB*]

پيسه په غرۀ کښې سورے کوي.

467. *Money makes a hole in the mountain.*

This is similar to the English proverbs, "Money talks", or "Money makes the mare go." [*See* Proverbs 524, 687 and 689.]

پیسه د لاس خیرے دے.

468.   *Money is the dirt on your hand.*

Money comes and goes and has little true value.

پیسه مبسه   ، او جسي اوتله.

469.   *Although without money, he asks that the bowl be weighed.*

Although without money, the individual expects to make a purchase.

پیشو به شبخه شي ، کۀ په منږکوري پیبنه شي.

470.   *A cat is pious only when he can look at a mouse and resist the urge to kill it.*

[Though the cat appears pious, you will see her true "piety" when she sees a mouse! *RWS*]

[The word used for pious is literally "become a *sheikh*". To "become a *sheikh*" can mean colloquially "a man who grows / has a beard" or one who "becomes pious", the one implying the other. *LNB*]

پیشو په خوب کښې وازدې ویني.

471.   *The cat dreams of fat.*

This refers to a man whose wish to gratify some desire leads him to think constantly about it.

[The reference is to the fat on a piece of meat. The saying may be used to comment on the nature of a person who is obsessed by some unfulfilled desire. *LNB, RWS*]

پیشو د خدائے د پاره منږک نۀ نیسي.

472.   *The cat does not catch the mice for the sake of God.*

    The greedy and selfish person works for his own interest.

[The saying can serve as a comment on a low standard of justice, or alternatively, as a comment on a person's self-seeking nature. *RWS*]

پیشو د منزري ترور ده.

473.   *The cat is aunt to the lion.*

    A reference to the family likeness among felines. Applied to the woman of a noble family who bears the characteristics of her pedigree.

[This is not an original Pashto proverb, but is translated from Urdu. *RWS*]

پیشو زبرګه شوه منږک نۀ نیسي.

474.   *The cat has become pious and no longer catches mice.*

    The hypocrite, when he can find no evil to commit, feigns piety although still essentially corrupt.

پیشو د غوښو څوکیداره کړه.

475.   *They asked the cat to watch the meat.*

    This is as sensible as asking the cat to guard the fish.

It is not appropriate to trust something to the most untrustworthy.

پېغله کۀ توره وي هم کور مې تربۀ ځار شه.

476. *Even though a damsel be black, I shall sacrifice every thing for her.*

Everyone is fond of a virgin even if she be ugly.

[For the idiom "I sacrifice myself (my house, or my head, etc.)" *see* Proverb 524 and 1009. *LNB*]

پينځه واړه ګوتې برابرې نۀ دي.

477. *All five fingers are not equal.*

No two men are alike.

[This common Pashto proverb (circulating in various forms) is used to comment on the differences in character between people. It is based on a realistic and sometimes cynical appraisal of human weakness and diversity. Some Pashto proverbs are known in identical or nearly identical forms or expressions in other Asian and / or European languages. In this case, proverbs akin to "The fingers of the hand are not all alike" are found in 43 languages in Southern and Eastern Europe and Asia, including Turkish, Kurdish, Tajik, Hindustani, Sindhi and Uzbek. *LNB*]

پينځه واړه ګوتې څوک په خُله نۀ منډي.

478. *One does not thrust all his five fingers into his mouth.*

This is said to a person to urge him not to be selfish or greedy.

[It is also used to urge him not to use poor etiquette. *RWS*]

تا او ما سره راضي څهٔ به وکړي خوار قاضی.

479.   *When you and I agree, what can the poor* qazi *do?*

Spoken by a young couple who have married without parental consent and who fear legal objections. The expression contends that when two people have entered into an agreement there can be no outside interference. The *qazi* (*qāzi*) is a judge of a legal court.

تا دې خدا ے جوړ کړي ، نو مونږ ټګان سهي.

480.   *We pray that God may restore your health, even though in your opinion we may have betrayed you.*

The story is told of three companions who set out to commit a theft. On the way they were surrounded by *chowkidārs* [guards]. Two of the thieves escaped, but the third was caught and soundly thrashed. When he was brought home all black and blue, his two companions visited him. At first the victim was angry and silent, but eventually complained that in forsaking him the two had betrayed him. Put to shame, one of them answered, "We pray that God will restore your health, even though in your opinion we may have betrayed you."

[Alternate translation and story: "May God restore your health, no matter if we are called thugs." The story is told of three thugs who, in the main street, caught hold of an elderly person intending to kidnap him. They gave the impression that the old man was their father and they were taking him to hospital. The old man shouted in the bazaar that they were thugs and not his sons. In order that the people around them would believe they were indeed sons of the old man, the thugs replied, "May God restore your health, no matter if we are called thugs." *RWS*]

تر خوړل ئي لا اُمید بنهٔ دے.

481. *Anticipation is better than eating.*

تر دې تر باجوړه لنډے نه څي بي لوړه.

482. *Up to this place and onward to Bajaur the donkey will not move without being clubbed.*

This refers to a lazy person who will not work without prodding.

[The animal is not specified, but an "ox" or "donkey" is understood. *RWS, LNB*]

تر کوره نه تر ګوره.

483. *Not just to the home but unto the grave.*

Friendship should extend not only to the home, but as far as the grave.

[Friendship is forever, but see contradictory Proverb 484. *RWS*]

تر کوره وم درسره، تر ګوره نهٔ یم درسره.

484. *I was your companion during the walk to your home, but will not go with you to the grave.*

Some friendships are superficial and short lived.

تربور خوار لره خو ئي په کار لره.

485. *Keep your cousins poor, but use them to your own advantage.*

The Pakhtuns usually do not like their cousins to be superior to them.

[The cousin or *tarbur* (father's brother's son) is a Pakhtun's traditional rival as well as his natural ally in disputes with outsiders. *tarburs* are also rivals for the inheritance of scarce family land. *See* Proverbs 486, 716 and 1264. *LNB*]

تربور کۀ دې خر وي لته پرې مۀ اړوه.

486.   *Even if your cousin be a donkey, don't ride him.*

According to Pakhtun tradition, *tarburwali* (that is, inter-family or inter-clanal enmity), is considered to be the most dangerous form of enmity. [*See* Proverbs 485, 716 and 1264.]

تروریٔ په ډېر اهرس، رنگ ئي بد کي د اولس.

487.   *The aunt's greed puts the people to shame.*

The misbehavior of even one member of the family disgraces the whole family or tribe.

[This proverb appears to be in the Bannu dialect. *RWS*]

تروریٔ وئیل چي سل قحطي به په ځان تېرې کړم، ولې د سپي مخ به ونۀ وینم.

488.   *The fox said, "I will go on a hunger strike indefinitely, but I won't look at the face of a dog."*

Some men will starve rather than face an enemy.

[The expression is about cowardice. *RWS*]

تریاکي دوه په ایکي.

489.   *Oh opium eater! Two with one.*

This is equivalent to, "Killing two birds with one stone."

[The English proverb quoted by Tair and Edwards refers to accomplishing two objectives with one action (*see* Proverb 945). *LNB*]

تره کۀ مضبوطه ده، د زور په مخکښنې هيڅ نۀ ده.

490. *Though the boulder is heavy, it will yield to strength.*

Nothing can withstand the use of force.

تش په توره ماته ګوره.

491. *Look at me, but don't expect anything.*

This proverb is spoken by a person who is being exploited.

[Alternatively, "Look at me, (here I am) without any reward or payment." *RWS*]

تش منګے په باد غړېږي.

492. *An empty water pitcher makes a noise in the wind.*

Wind blowing across the neck of an empty vessel causes a whistle. Cf. the English proverb, "Empty vessels make much noise."

[A very little force is required to coerce the weak. *RWS*]

[The apparently parallel proverb in English appears in a wide variety of forms, for example, an "empty barrel", "empty bowl", "empty can", "empty kettle", and an "empty wagon"—each of which is said to "make the most noise". The reference in the English, however, is to foolish persons who are the most talkative or noisy, for example as quoted in Shakespeare's (1564-1616) *Henry V*, "I did never know so full a voice issue from so empty a heart: but the saying is true, 'the empty vessel makes the greatest sound.'"[23] *LNB*]

تشه تلې تشه راتلې، د پاچو دورې دي تلې.

493. *You were coming and going empty handed, raising the dust with the edges of your trousers.*

This is said to a person who uses his time uselessly.

تشه لاسه تۀ می دشمن ئې.

494. *Oh empty hand, you are my enemy.*

Thus laments the man who is either without the means to defend himself from his enemy, or without the money to meet his financial obligations.

[Lack of strength and resources—physical, familial, economic, relational—affect a Pashtun's ability to successfully meet the challenges to honor posed by daily life. Without means, for example, a man cannot even show proper hospitality to guests. Having an "empty hand" is thus an "enemy" of a man of honor. *LNB*]

تقدير په تدبير پورې خاندي.

495. *Fate laughs at prudence.*

This is similar to the adage, "Man proposes; God disposes." [*See* Proverbs 303 and 399.]

تلوار ګرندي ته پمیچو واچوه.

496. *Put the share of the hasty fellow on the chaff.*

تماشګیر د نخښې مینځ وولي.

497. *The spectator hits the bull's-eye.*

Criticism is far easier than performance.

تندر په تالاش پریوت، خرهٔ ئي د راموړي یوړل.

498. *A thunderstorm struck Talash, and carried away the donkeys of Ramora.*

This is used to illustrate the fact that sometimes a man suffers for the crime of another.

A calamity striking one place may have adverse effects elsewhere.

تنحْرِیه! په خپلِي خُلِي نیولیه.

499. *Oh partridge, you are the victim of your own tongue.*

One's good qualities sometimes get him into trouble. The lovely flower is plucked because of its beauty.

تنگ دي خداے قبر هم د چا نهٔ کړی.

500. *Even one's grave may not be narrow.*

When a home is criticized for being small, the occupant replies in these words.

[This may be understood as a rebuff (in the structure of a blessing / curse), "May God not make anyone's grave narrow!" Alternatively, it may also be used in reply, for example when a visitor comments jealously on the large size of a house, viz. "Even a grave can be large ("not narrow"), so don't be jealous that my house is so big." *LNB*]

توتان په وار پخیږي. وړوکي ورته بیړه کوي.

501. *Mulberries ripen at the proper time, but children are in a hurry for them.*

Although everything comes at its appointed time, it is human nature to be impatient.

توتو ما وخوره!

502. *Come, Oh dog, bite me!*

An ironic reference to a person who is trying to goad his enemy into attacking him, thus inviting trouble upon himself.

تور تور څۀ دي. دا واړه غوشایۀ دي.

503. *What are these black objects? They are all dunghills.*

The Pakhtun says this when a useful commodity is reduced in value by someone unwilling to share it.

تور دلے که تور دے ما په گل منلے دے.

504. *Even though Tor Dalai is black, I have taken him for a flower.*

The beloved says this about her lover, despite his defects. Tor Dalai was the hero of a famous Pakhtun romance, "Dalai and Shahai".

تور دے بچے تور دے کۀ لرې لرې گرځي بچے بیا د خپلې مور دے.

505. *My child is black; yes, black. Even if he wanders away, he is still his mother's child.*

These are words of affection used by a mother when her child begins to walk.

تور مار په شا گذار کوي.

506. *The cobra turns on its back, then strikes.*

This proverb is said of an enemy, who will strike while pretending to be incapacitated.

تور مُلا ئي په سرو شنو نۀ دے، خو چي بېرې وي.

507. *Tor Mullah does not mind whether they are ripe or unripe, just so long as they are berries.*

A greedy man will eat his favorite food irrespective of its quality. [*See* Proverb 85 note.]

تُوره په اصل غوڅول کوي.

508. *A sword cuts according to the quality.*

When a man is challenged, his success depends upon his mettle [courage or strength of character.]

تُوره په څنګ کښې کوتک غواړي.

509. *You have a sword under your arms, yet you ask for a club!*

This proverb is used when a man, though well provided for his own defense, calls for an inferior weapon.

[The saying exposes one pretense for avoiding a conflict. *RWS*]

تُوره په کټو ده غشي په ویشتو دي.

510. *The proof of the sword is in the testing, that of the arrow is in its striking power.*

This meaning is similar to the English proverb, "The proof of the pudding is in the eating," [or "Seeing is believing" *RWS*].

توره ویرول کوي. سپينه ورول کوي.

511. *Black brings fear, white brings rain.*

This refers to clouds. Analogous to the proverb, "Barking dogs seldom bite."

[The notion is that "black" (clouds), perhaps like "barking dogs", may look aggressive and threatening, but actually may not bring rain. *See* Proverbs 43, 685 and 1226. *LNB*]

تُوري پور غُوښتو، خُاځي نور غوښتو.

512. *Torai was asking for the payment of debt while Zazi was requesting further credit.*

A man cannot pay back his debt when still in need.

[This is said ironically when a person has nothing and so nothing can be expected from him. *RWS*]

تُوري چي وهلے شي، وينه توئيږي.

513. *When the sword strikes, blood flows.*

War leads to bloodshed.

تُورِ ميروګے وهي، نوم د آدم خان کېږي.

514. *It is Merogai who fights, but the credit goes to Adam Khan.*

The chivalrous acts are Mero's, but they are attributed to Adam Khan.

This is said of one who takes credit for another's work. Adam Khan was the hero of a popular romance, and Mero his comrade-at-arms, who made sacrifices for his hero.

تۀ چي پشت پا ګروۍ، په کور کېنې څومره زر لرې.

515. *When you scratch the upper part of your feet, how much money do you have in reserve?*

Never get into a situation that may cause you physical disability and hence material loss. This is similar to the warning, "A stitch in time saves nine."

It is generally believed that a wound caused by scratching the upper part of the foot takes a long time to heal.

[An alternative translation might be, "When you scratch the underneath (soles) of your feet, how much ...?" According to superstition, an itch in the soles of the feet is a sign of money. *RWS*]

تهٔ دلته او شل دې په قنبر کښې.

516. *You are here, your spear is in Qambar.*

This is said of one whose belongings are in one place while he is in another.

تبر په هبر باقی روزګار.

517. *Live together and bury the axe.*

The advice is to "Forgive and forget."

[In the First Edition, the Pashto text was written *ter pa ter*, "gone and past"; the proverb is also found with the common *ter pa her*, "forget the past" (cf. the familiar proverb *ter pa her rātlunki shmāra*, "Forget the ones that have gone and count the ones that are coming". *LNB*, *RWS*]

[Tair and Edwards' gloss (translation) hints at the American idiom usually rendered "Bury the hatchet", based on the Native American practice of burying hatchets, scalping-knives and war clubs after smoking a "peace pipe" with one's enemies, signifying the forgetting of past differences and hostilities. The Latin proverb, "Forgive and forget" brings to mind the Chinese proverb, "Forget injuries, never forget kindnesses." *LNB*]

تیر د ارهنډي ساتي او غنم کونډه غواړي.

518. *He uses the wood of castor for the plow and still expects the best wheat.*

Inferior materials will not produce excellent articles.

تېر ساعت په بېرته نۀ راځي.

519. *Time gone by will never return.*

تبل د کونځلو وځي.

520. *Oil is extracted from the sesame seed.*

All men of quality go through the mill.

[As oil is squeezed from sesame seeds, so quality men go through times of testing which lead to perseverance and good character. *LNB*]

تپ د دوارو لاسو خبرّي.

521.   *A clap requires the use of two hands.*

It takes two to make a quarrel.

[It also takes two for friendship. *RWS*]

[Interestingly, this proverb, first cited in Pashto by Thorburn,[24] is also found in German and twenty-four Asian languages including Persian, Tajik, Hindustani and Sindhi. Without textual evidence, it can be difficult to trace international proverbs to a single source or language. Sharing between languages is quite common (for example, many English proverbs are of Latin or Greek origin). *LNB*]

تکه هر چرته چې وي، د خوار په کور پريوځي.

522.   *A thunderbolt always falls on the home of the poor.*

Calamities always seem to befall the destitute.

ټول عمر دې تير شو په اوبو کښې، اُوبهٔ نهٔ پيژنې کبه.

523.   *Oh fish, though you spent your entire life in the water, you don't know what water is?*

Applied to the person who spends his life in an occupation without ever understanding it thoroughly.

جار دي شم روپۍ، چي هم خپر ئي هم گدئ.

524. *Oh wealth, I die for you, because you are both a shelter and resting-place for me.*

  "Money talks", or "Money makes the mare go." [*See* Proverbs 467, 687 and 689.]

  ["I die for you", literally "I sacrifice (myself) for you" is an idiomatic expression of love. Here, money is loved because it provides protection and comfort. *See* Proverbs 476 and 1009. *LNB, RWS*]

جار بابا وكړۀ او دستونه په ادي ولگيدل.

525. *The purgative was taken by father, but the stools were passed by mother.*

  Spoken when punishment falls on the wrong shoulders.

جرگه د كارغانو هم ښه ده.

526. *Even the council of the crows is good.*

  A joint effort is wise.

  [The *jirga* or council of elders is an integral part of Pashtun culture, enabling the leaders of a community to resolve problems without recourse to civil law. A *jirga* can range from just five people to a large gathering, depending on the scale of the issue under discussion. *RWS, LNB*]

جنت بنهٔ ځاے دے. خو تلل ورته د زړهٔ په چاودهٔ دي.

527. *Although Paradise is a wonderful place, to reach it requires a prodigious effort.*

جنگ د غوايانو وو، او ماتبدل جوار.

528. *The battle was between the bullocks, but it was the maize crop that was crushed.*

   The fight was between powerful men, but the weak and poor were ruined. [*See* Proverb 1194.]

جنگ سوړ شو، موذی تود شو.

529. *When the war subsided, the coward became aggressive.*

جنگ ئې کور وکړو، او کرکنپې په صحرا نهٔ خوري.

530. *He quarreled at home, yet he does not eat berries in the jungle.*

   This proverb is said of the person who, after a quarrel with his family, sulks and complains in the company of his friends. Righteous anger against an enemy, though justified, should not become a burden to others.

   [It is about a person who protests in an inappropriate place. *RWS*]

جنگه جنگه تود شو، کربوړے مي پخکړے دے.

531. *Oh fight, fight! Warm up, warm up! I have cooked a lizard for you.*

   With this sort of expression small children will urge-on two quarreling companions.

جو وربشې يو دي.

532. jaw *and barley are the same thing.*

It makes no difference if one thing is called by different names. *jaw* (the Urdu word for "barley") and *urbəshay* (the Pashto word for "barley") are the same thing. Cf. the English proverb, "Six of one, half-a-dozen (or, "a half-dozen") of the other."

جيټ هاړ دننه ، ساوڼ بادرو په وُنه ، اسو کتک په غنه ، اؤ نورو له لمبه

خمبه پُنبه.

533. *May and June spent in a room:*
      July and August 'neath the trees:
      Under the thorn-bush two months more:
      Then six full months designed to please with barn chock-full and
      blazing fire,
      And cotton bag for sleeping ease.

[Literally, "… for the remaining months (using three rhyming words) *lumbə, khumbə, pumbə*", that is, flame (in the wood fire), baskets-full (of food) and cotton (sleeping-bags)." *RWS, LNB*]

چا پوښتلې که لا تربدلې.

534. *Have you been asked? Or are you just interfering.*

چا ته مخ او چا ته شا.

535. *To some you show your face, to others your back.*

A reference to discrimination in showing favors.

چا ته نارینه په ګټ [ګوټ] کښې نارینه.

536. *To whom do you show courage, only when in the corner of your home?*

The coward is brave only where he finds himself safe.

[The proverb can be understood as a mocking question and charge, "To whom are you courageous (a brave man)—only in the corner of your house?!" That is, he is a "real man" only at home, or when secure or hiding in his house. *LNB*]

چا چې ورځې شي کږې، ورته بلا شي خپلې وزي.

537. *When misfortune comes on one, even his own goats become a calamity.*

Misfortune can turn comfort into trouble.

چا عقل د مور په نس کښې نۀ دے زده کړے.

538. *No one ever learned wisdom in his mother's womb.*

Wisdom comes only after experience. Experience is a wise teacher.

چا کول چې ما کول.

539. *Who was going to do this except me?*

"Fools rush in where angels fear to tread."

[This saying is an expression of repentance over something one has done. *RWS*]

[The proverb says literally, "Who was doing it that I was doing it" and expresses regret for reckless actions, "rushing in" to do something unwise; thus Tair and Edwards' citation of "Fools rush in ..." (Alexander Pope, 1688-1744).[25] *LNB*]

چا وکړي په خپله! ګله ځله د بله!

540. *Who has done it to you? "Myself." Then why do you blame it on someone else?*

This proverb refers to a story about a giantess [lady giant] and a man named "Pakhpulla" (that is, "myself"). He set fire to the huge woman's hair and then escaped while she was crying for help. "Who has done this to you?" asked her companions. She replied, "Pakhpulla." Assuming that she was declaring herself to be the culprit, they said, "Then why do you blame someone else?".

چا وئیلي لافي هغه تل په لاري پاتې.

541. *Braggarts have always been left behind.*

[He who brags or boasts is always left behind. *RWS*]

چار کوټې پنج ملکانان.

542.   *Four homes and five lords.*

Each one claims sovereignty over a common property, small though his share may be.

[The items are four in number, and the claimants (*malaks*) are five. *RWS*]

چار محکمه زړهٔ محکمه.

543.   *A perfect job leads to a confident heart.*

[A stable job makes the heart stable. If you have a perfect job, don't worry. *RWS*]

چاړهٔ کهٔ د سرو زرو شي، خو په خپته د منډلو نهٔ ده.

544.   *Though the dagger be of gold, it is not wise to thrust it into one's belly.*

A dangerous thing, though apparently precious, should be avoided. [*See* variant Proverb 1224.]

چت تهٔ جوړ کړه نقش له ما پرې غواړه.

545.   *First build the roof yourself, then ask me to decorate it.*

Do not ask me to do everything for you, let us share the work. Equivalent to the common English expression, "Put first things first."

چټے هم آسمان ته پښې ونیسې، وائی زهٔ آسمان ټینگوم.

546.   *Even the wren braces his legs and says, "I am holding up the sky."*

This is said of an insignificant boaster.

چچ په لاس تور مصلي وے، ارمان ارمان دے چي خواني وے.

547. *Alas, alas! Oh that I were young even if I had to be a gypsy with winnowing basket in hand.*

[Literally, the phrase translated as "gypsy" is *tor musali*, a term for black or dark skinned Indians. *RWS*]

چچ وائي به دِ کوله، توره بلا وله.

548. *Oh gypsy! Better stick to your own profession of winnowing and get rid of serious trouble.*

This is said of a person who, having left his own profession for another, suffers both losses and regrets.

چرته چي ډب وي، هلته ادب وي.

549. *Where there is a slap there is obedience.*

"Spare the rod and spoil the child." [*See* notes to Proverb 310.]

[The proverb articulates the view that respect and proper behavior or manners (*adab*) are learned through discipline or force (*dab*). It is applied not merely to children, as the English parallel proverb might suggest, but to any situation where obedience, propriety or proper work are expected. For example, an employer might say this as part of a verbal censure of a subordinate; a politician might use it to defend harsh laws and policies. *LNB*]

چرته چي زړۀ څي هلته پښې څي.

550. *Where the heart leads, the feet will follow.*

Your feet will take you wherever your inclination lies.

چرته سنگروبه چرته د بنو پلاؤنه.

551. *Where is* sangṛoba *and where is the* palau *of Bannu?*

It is quite impossible to find the *palau* of Bannu in little *sangṛobə*. That is, a man should entertain according to his status.

[Another way to phrase this is: How can *sangṛoba* (the poor man's rice dish) match the *palau* (the rich rice dish with beef or chicken) of Bannu? *RWS*]

چرته کلے هلته ډیران.

552. *Where there is a village there is always a dunghill.*

[It is man himself who causes pollution or problems. *RWS*]

چرته هندوان چرته تُوتان؟

553. *Where is the Hindu, and where is the mulberry tree?*

A tale is told of a Hindu who wished to eat the fruit of the mulberry. He climbed the tree. When he had gorged himself, he found that he could not get down. After a long and annoying wait he was happy to see a Pakhtun arrive. The man having helped him exclaimed, "What business has a Hindu in a mulberry tree?"

The implication was that no one should strive beyond his capacity. Related to an American expression "Water over your head", [or "Biting off more than you can chew."]

[An alternative interpretation given by others is that wherever there are Hindus there are mulberries, because the stereotypical Hindu is too weak or incapable of climbing the trees—or is perhaps too embarrassed or unable to do so because he wears a wrap-around *lungi*. *LNB*]

چرته ئي وهي اؤ چرته دنګهري.

554. *Where has it been struck [hit, beat] and whence comes the sound.*

This is said of an article that refuses to perform its normal function.

چرسي زوئ نۀ زوئ.

555. *A charsi is no son.*

A *charsi* (or user of the narcotic *chars* [hashish]) is damned and not accepted as a son.

چرګ په ډيران مۀ کسه په تول ئي کسه.

556. *Don't look at the hen [rooster] on the rubbish heap, but consider its weight.*

Think of how weighty a man is irrespective of the place where he lives.

[That is, think of his influence and how he can be of advantage to you. *See* Proverb 557. *LNB*]

چرګ په ډيران مۀ ګوره په تبخي ئي ګوره.

557. *Look at the chicken in the frying pan, not at the dunghill.*

Don't judge by outward appearance, but consider an object's usefulness.

[Proverb 557 is a variant of 556, and shows how minor lexical changes can be made to texts as they circulate orally. They both begin, "Don't look at"—(556 uses *kasa*, from the verb *kasəl*, and 557 uses *gora*, from the more common *katəl*)—"the chicken on the dunghill or rubbish heap (*ḍerān*)", but instead "look to its weight (*tol*, 556), or "look at it in the frying pan (*tabakhey*, 557)." The chicken or rooster is pictured as foraging for food on the rubbish heap—but the observer needs to look beyond appearances. *LNB*]

چرګ ته خپله چاره په اوبو کښي ښکاري.

558. *The chicken sees the knife in the water.*

Death comes to the chicken by means of a knife. This is said about
a calamity that can be foreseen.

چرګ چي په زور نيسي هم شور کوي، اؤ چي په قلاره ئي نيسي هم شور
کوي.

559. *Whether you capture a chicken by force or slowly, it will still make a
noise.*

This refers to the person who complains regardless of
circumstances, no matter whether something is beneficial or
detrimental to his wellbeing.

چرګ خو يو مارغۀ دے، چي چا ونيو د هغۀ دے.

560. *The common chicken belongs to whoever has caught it.*

"Might makes right", or as in the expression, "Possession is nine-
tenths [or "nine points", or "eleven points"] of the law." [*See* Proverb
196, 665 and 695.]

چرګ دي بولي که نۀ صبا کېږي.

561. *Let the cock [rooster] crow whether it be dawn or not.*

Whatever the outcome, one should perform his duty.

چرګ دي يم خو حلالوه مي مۀ.

562. *I am your chicken but do not kill me.*

I am your slave, but do not take undue advantage of me. Used generally to mean that one should not take unfair advantage of his friends.

[The term used for "kill" in this proverb refers to the lawful slaughter (*halāl*) of animals for meat, (cf. Proverbs 52 and 832). *halāl* means "permitted" in the sense of something being religiously "clean", "pure" and therefore "lawful" as opposed to *harām* "forbidden" (*see* Proverb 381). *LNB, RWS*]

چرګ که بنې له نیسې هم تغیږي، او که بدې له ئ نیسې هم تغیږي.

563.　*Whether you catch a hen [chicken, rooster] for its benefit or to harm it; it will chuckle [cackle] in either case.*

The reference is to a foolish man who cannot distinguish right from wrong.

چرګ له د دوک داغ بس دے.

564.　*For a chicken the pain of the hot skewer is sufficient.*

To a poor man minor losses are a serious burden.

چرګه چې چرچک وهي، چرګوړی پسې چک وهي.

565.　*When the hen clucks, all the chickens run after her.*

The voice of a leader draws followers.

چرګه د جولا لاړه نوم پرې د ملک وشو.

566.　*It was the weaver who lost the hen, but the* malək *who took the credit.*

The poor weaver's chicken was slaughtered, but the guests thought that it was the *malək's* own chicken. Thus, credit went to the *malək.*

چرګه د چرګوړو سره لاړه قندهار ته.

567. *The hen took her chicks and migrated to Kandahar.*

This is said of someone who leaves his home with his family to seek greener pastures elsewhere. [Cf. the modern American proverb,] "The grass looks greener on the other side", ["The grass is always greener on the other side of the fence." *See* Proverb 871.] Kandahar is a city in southern Afghanistan.

چرګه د مالګي په څټلو څۀ پوهېږي.

568. *What does the hen know about licking salt?*

This is said of someone who is unable to appreciate a good thing.

چرګه زما ده اؤ اګۍ د شاه زمان کره اچوي.

569. *Although the hen is mine, she lays her eggs at the home of Shah Zaman.*

This proverb is used when the product of one's property is enjoyed by others.

چرګه مې چا اوړي ده. خو دا قيصه د مړي ده.

570. *It is true that someone has stolen my hen, but this story is about a murdered man.*

This proverb is used when a serious affair overshadows something relatively insignificant.

چرمبنکی د پښو په شامت د مارانو ووتۀ.

571. *Because of its feet the lizard was removed from the snake family.*

This proverb refers to someone who, because of some physical or other oddity, becomes a social misfit.

چرې بختيار چرې د خدا ے لار.

572. *What comparison can there be between God's way and that of Bakhtyar.*

God's conduct is infinitely superior to that of man.

Bakhtyar is a common name among the Pakhtun, meaning "lucky man."

[How do you expect just and Godly behavior from Bakhtyar, who is an ordinary, simple man. Only in God do we find true justice. *LNB*]

چرې چې ډنګ شي. د ابی کوډے تر څنګ شي.

573. *Whenever there is the tap of beating drums, the mother packs up her kit and follows the sound.*

This is said of someone who always seeks out revelers.

چرې دې وهم چرې د باسي.

574. *Look where I beat and find where wind is passed.*

Used when an action produces an unexpected reaction. [*See* Proverb 209.]

[This is an example of a proverb that, although suggestive, avoids the use of offensive terms, viz. "I beat you on one place, the sound (of passing gas) comes from another place." *See* variant Proverb 554. *LNB*]

چنبتن ووئيل سپي ته اؤ سپي ووئيل لکۍ ته.

575. *The master gave orders to the dog, the dog gave orders to his tail.*

This is equivalent to the American expression, "Passing the buck."

چغال الو ته نۀ شو رسیدے. وئیل ئي دا تاروۀ دي.

576. *The jackal, when he could not reach the plums, said, they are sour anyway.*

Grapes are sour. When a person cannot obtain what he wants, he may resort to abusing it or he may make lame excuses as in the "sour grapes" [literally, "plums"] reply above.

[This may be an allusion to Aesop's (c. 620-560 BC) well-known fable of the fox who tried in vain to get some grapes beyond his reach and went away saying, "I see they are sour."[26] *LNB*]

چغال په نعمت شکر کولو، چرګه ئي د خولۍ نۀ پریوته.

577. *When the jackal tried to thank God for his blessing the chicken flew out of his mouth.*

According to the popular fable, a jackal had caught a hen and was carrying her into the jungle when he met a cockerel. From his safe perch in a tree, the cockerel, in order to help the hen escape, crowed to the jackal, "Brave sir, you must thank God for providing you with such a juicy morsel." When the grateful animal opened his jaws to pray, the chicken flew away to safety.

Similar animal tales are common in oriental and western literature from ancient times through the middle ages. For example, *The Canterbury Tales*, [written between 1387 and 1400 A.D.] by the English poet Chaucer, includes fables that illustrate trickery or the evils of flattery.

چمیار له هغۀ خي. چي پښې ئي سوزي.

578. *Only the man whose feet are burning goes to a shoemaker.*

The proverb means, a man in danger will struggle. It also means that only a barefooted man and not one who has shoes will go to the shoemaker. A man will only approach one who can satisfy his needs.

چونچی له جارو، جارو له ډاق.

579. *A small peg is removed by the brush and the brush is removed by the truncheon.*

The mighty rules the weaker; or, every disease has a cure.

چونګ کوې که پونګ کوې، خو دا پټے به للون کوې.

580. *Whether you pass wind or weep, you will have to weed this plot.*

Whatever the circumstances, you must complete this work.

It refers to an order that must be obeyed under all circumstances.

چې څوک بد کوي کارونه، هغه بد ویني خوبونه.

581. *He who commits evil deeds has nightmares.*

The evil man has a guilty conscience.

چې (څوک) په طمع د سورو شي. هغه پاتي په مبرو شي.

582. *He who waits for horse riders to accompany him will be stranded in the desert.*

He who waits for others will be left behind, so the meaning is "Trust in thyself." Alternatively, "Those who wait to accompany important people will be left behind", as the latter would not accompany them.

[Do not expect help from others. *RWS*]

[This proverb reinforces the importance of autonomy and self-determination that are so central to the ethos of being Pashtun and "doing *pakhto*". The oft quoted proverbial notion "Trust in thyself" is balanced by other proverbs that urge "Trust in God" (or fate). Hans Christian Andersen advises "To trust in thyself and God is best, In His Holy will forever rest."[27] *LNB*]

چې اباسين په کاسو شي، هم به وچ شي.

583. *Even Abasin will run dry if it were distributed in bowls.*

   A large property, when divided into small plots, will vanish in no time. The Abasin is the mighty River Indus. [*See* Proverb 55.]

چې اسمان غرېږي، زانۍ کمر ته ننوځي.

584. *When the sky roars with thunder, even the cranes take shelter in protective ledges.*

   When a despot is angry, even his close friends avoid him.

چې اوبۀ تر خُلي شي، زوئ لاندې ترپنبو شي.

585. *When the water reaches his mouth, a man will place his own child under his feet to save himself.*

   Some will sacrifice those dearest to them for self-preservation.

   [The reference is to a person—father or mother—no gender is indicated. *LNB*]

چې اوبۀ وي، تيمم ته څۀ حاجت.

586. *When water is available, ablution with dust or earth is not needed.*

   When a leader is available, those of lesser importance need not be consulted.

   tayyammum (an alternative form of ablution) is performed before obligatory prayers.

   [Literally, "When there is water, there is no need for *tayyammum*." According to Islamic law, ablution with clean sand, soil or dust (*tayyammum*) before prayers is permitted when water is not available for the normal ablution (*awdas*; (Ar.) *wuzu*). *LNB*]

چې اوخوري د نر لغته، داسې به کښېني لکه عورته.

587. *A brave man's kick will force him to sit like a woman.*

This is a reference used to show contempt for the boaster.

چې اور ولګي، اوچ اؤ لامدهٔ ګډوډ سره سوزي.

588. *When fire breaks out, it burns both wet and dry.*

Calamity is no respecter of persons, it strikes down both good and bad. [*See* Proverb 202.]

چې اور ولګي، هغه وخت اوبهٔ نهٔ وي.

589. *When the fire blazes, water is never available.*

Some objects, or persons, are never present when needed.

چې اورې هغه وایه، چې وینې هغه مهٔ وایه.

590. *What you hear you may talk about; what you see should be kept secret.*

The things one hears don't carry as much weight as those he sees with his own eyes.

چې اوږه نهٔ خوري. بوئی به در نه نهٔ څي.

591. *If you do not eat garlic, your breath will not smell.*

The innocent man has nothing to fear.

چې اوويشت نۀ شي، خبر به نۀ شي.

592. *He who has never been shot cannot know anything about it.*

Suffering is known only to sufferers.

چې باد نۀ وي، بوټي نۀ خوځي.

593. *If there is no wind, the plants do not sway.*

A negative counterpart of the proverb, "Where there is smoke, there is fire" [or, "There's no smoke without fire."]

[These adages observe that every effect has a cause. *RWS*]

چې بتې خوري، مولې به زغمي.

594. *He who eats barley must stroke the pestle.*

He must prepare the barley before eating it.

He who wants anything must work hard to get it [or must pay something for it. *RWS*]

چې بد غورځي، بد به پرځي.

595. *He who is a mischief-monger is dashed to the ground.*

چې بد مې غواړي، په بدو دې واوړي.

596. *May he face evil who wishes me harm.*

چې بل ته کوهے کنې، هم پخپله به پکښې پریوځي.

597.   *He who digs a well to trap others, will fall into it himself.*

That is, evil begets evil.

[A similar sentiment is expressed in a poetic form in Proverb 1218.
LNB]

چې بوډئ مړه وي، نو ټول ښار به موړ وي.

598.   *When the old woman is satisfied, the whole city is satisfied.*

When the matriarch of a home is happy, the whole house is happy.

چې بې ذاته اشنائي کا، اور به بل په خپل تندي کا.

599.   *Those who befriend the ill-bred will burn their own foreheads.*

This means that they will come to trouble.

چې پرون دې خوله رانه کړه، نن پرون دے.

600.   *Since you did not give me a kiss yesterday, consider today as
yesterday.*

This is similar to the saying, "It is never too late to mend," [that is,
to mend or change our ways; cf. the proverbs, "It is never too late to
learn" or "Better late than never." *See* Proverb 247. *LNB*]

چې پلار ئې برگے وي، زوئ ئې ټکے وي.

601.   *If the father is a hybrid, the son will be a mischief-maker.*

This is analogous to the English saying, "Like father, like son."
[*See* Proverb 799.]

چې پور ګڼې نور وګټه.

602. *If you expect to collect the debt, you should earn more.*

Don't depend only on the collection of debt.

چې پوره ئي نۀ وي، نو سر ئي د کاڼي د لاندې کا هيڅ پرې نۀ کېږي.

603. *Unless fate has decreed his end, you can crush a man's head under a rock and he will suffer no more.*

This is similar to the popular idea that a person cannot be killed unless his "number is up."

[This is a clear expression of the notion of fate; that one's life and destiny are determined. Even if struck on the head with a rock, he will suffer no loss if it is not his appointed time. *See* Proverbs 72, 73 and 276, and Index entries for "fate" and "time". *LNB*]

چې پوزه ئي څاڅي بلا ترې پاڅي.

604. *He whose nose is dripping becomes the source of trouble.*

A person who appears to be harmless may bring harm to others, both friends and enemies.

[Alternatively, it can mean "the source of trouble looks miserable", that is, his misery is as obvious as a dripping nose. *RWS*]

چې په اخور دې لوے شي نو غاښ ئي مۀ ګوره.

605. *Do not examine the teeth of the animal that has grown up in your manger.*

He who has long been your friend should not be put on trial. One whom you intimately observe need not be probed further.

چې په چیکړه کښې خپژي، ځاڅکي به در پورې وي.

606.   *He who walks in the mud will be splashed with it.*

Man cannot escape the consequences of his deeds. [Also, as in the
proverbial statement,] "You can tell a man by the company he keeps,"
[a man is affected by those with whom he "walks" or associates.
LNB]

چې په ځان کښې ويني په جهان کښې ويني.

607.   *What one sees in himself, he also sees in the whole world.*

What we see in ourselves governs what we see in others.

چې په خوست کښې دي، هغه په کتاب کښې نشته.

608.   *That which is found in Khost does not exist in the book.*

The people tell a story about a certain party from the Khost area
who brought a case before a mullah for his decision. The latter gave a
decision according to the law, but it was unacceptable to the
plaintiffs. They insisted that he find in his books a law that coincided
with the customs of their homeland. Try as he might, the mullah
could find nothing in the law that met their need. Angrily he said,
"What is found in Khost does not exist in the books."

To this day people in many remote areas govern themselves by
tribal law rather than the official law of the land. Khost is a [city and]
province in Afghanistan.

["Khost" represents both the Pashtun tribal heartlands and the practice
of *pakhtunwali*, the tribal code of honor, here contrasted with the
"Book", that is, the Holy Qur'an. Both Islam and *pakhtunwali* are
important criteria of Pashtun ethnic identity, and are primary, and
sometimes competing, sources of moral authority in Pashtun society.
This is one of a number of proverbs by which Pashtuns mark
themselves (and certain customs) as distinct and autonomous, even in
relation to Islam. *See* Proverb 341. *LNB*]

چې په دومره وېش کښې مې هم برخه نۀ وي، نو بيا خو مې خوله چينگه وينگه ده.

609. *If in a large scale [redistribution] I am left out, then I am worthless.*

[Literally "If in a large scale *weysh* I do not have my share, my mouth drops open." The term *weysh* refers to the Pashtun custom of periodically redistributing or exchanging lands within or between villages to ensure fairness in the allotment of houses and fertile plots. It was previously practiced, for example, by the Swati Yousafzai Pakhtun. The idiomatic Pashto expression, *khulə chinga winga da*, "my mouth drops open," is somewhat similar to the British term "gob smacked", conveying here not only astonishment, but also the fear of becoming landless—"then I am worthless." *See* Proverb 1285. *LNB*]

چې په زړۀ سره مئين وي يو ځاے کيږي.

610. *Those who love sincerely are certainly united.*

چې په زړۀ ئې د يار غم وي ځۀ به خوب کا.

611. *How can one sleep when the sorrows of his beloved hang heavily over his heart.*

[This is one line of a verse from Rahman Baba.[28] *RWS*]

چې په زور ورسره نه ئې برابر، د هغۀ تر څنگه مه کښېنه زړۀ ور.

612. *If you cannot equal him in strength, do not sit jauntily beside him.*

One should not pretend to be equal to his superiors.

[This is a line of verse from Rahman Baba.[29] *RWS*]

چې په سر دې درد نۀ وي، داغ پري مۀ ږده.

613. *When you have no headache, do not beat it.*

It is foolish to worry without cause.

[This could mean, "If your head doesn't hurt" (if there's no reason to
be worried), "don't scar or brand it" (poke it with a hot stick), or more
likely, "don't show it" (for example, don't show you are upset by
wrinkling or pressing your forehead). *See* variant Proverb 702. *RWS,
LNB*]

چې په سر ئي چاړۀ شي، خدا ے ئي په زرۀ شي.

614. *Only when the dagger hangs over his head, does he remember God.*

چې په کلي غلبله شي، د ډم د نائي بنه شي.

615. *When something exciting happens in the village, the menials reap
the most pleasure.*

[The word translated "menials" (cf. Proverbs 1074 and 1075) literally
refers to the itinerant barber (*nāyi*) and musician (*ḍəm*), both of whom
are landless, menial servants at the bottom of the social ladder; no
Pakhtun would marry into these groups. The barber also performs
circumcisions and functions as a messenger to announce, with the
beating of a drum, engagements and weddings. The musician, though
beloved for his music, is associated with sensuality. The above
proverb states that it doesn't matter if something sad or happy occurs
(that is, a death or a wedding), both mean profitable work—and thus
happiness—for the itinerant barber and musician (and other menial
workers, like cooks). *LNB*]

چې په کومه کټوی کښې دې برخه نۀ وي، اور ورپسې مۀ بلوه.

616. *When you have made no share in the cooking pot do not put the fire
under it.*

One should not concern himself with that which offers him no advantage.

چې په ګوړه مري، په زهرو ئې مۀ وژنه.

617.   *One who can be killed with sugar need not be killed with poison.*

[See also the variant form of this text, Proverb 1066, where this proverbial strategy is aimed specifically at the "enemy" (*dukhman*). *LNB*]

چې په ګیدړ پسې ووځي، نو تابیا د زمري کوه.

618.   *When you go out to hunt the jackal, be prepared to meet a lion.*

That is, always go after your enemy well prepared.

چې پخپله برائي کا. له بناغلیو سره ځۀ لره سیالي کا.

619.   *He who boasts of his own prowess is actually unable to compete with the brave.*

چې پخپله ځان ته خان وائي خان نۀ دے.

620.   *He who calls himself a Khan is never a Khan.*

It is for others to call him a Khan and recognize him as such.

[It is not the tradition in Pashtun society for a man to call himself a Khan, even though he may be a Khan. *RWS*]

[The ethnic title "Khan" can refer to a tribal leader (cf. *malək*), or chief, or senior male of a Pashtun clan; a wealthy landowner or village landlord who has dependents; or a man of status and reputation. It is often incorporated into Pashtun names (for example, Adam Khan; *see* Index entries under "Persons") or used as an honorific, although the title is now used by non-Pashtuns (for example, in India) as a mark of status. Pashtuns are rarely self-effacing, and every man sees himself as a "great man" or "Khan"—as equal to or better than another. The proverb serves to restrain such boasting. *LNB*]

چې پخپله ورشې بيا څۀ له مرور شې.

621. *When you go somewhere uninvited, why should you complain if not received properly.*

چې پيسې وي، نو ښځه د کلابته راځي.

622. *When there is money, the woman will come even from Kalabat.*

A story is told of a young man from Swabi [Swabi District East of Peshawar] who was engaged to marry a girl living across the Indus in Kalabat, a town in the Hazara District north of Rawalpindi. Because the prospective bridegroom was poor, her father refused to give her in marriage. The young man went to India and was soon rich. He sent news of his wealth back to his family. The prospective father-in-law, getting wind of the situation, decided generously to convey his daughter to India by *dholi.* When the procession reached its destination, the father called upon the young man, who now pretended not to recognize him. "Friend", said the father, "I am your father-in-law, I have brought your wife." The boy replied ironically, "It is true that when there is money, the woman will come even from Kalabat."

[The *dholi* mentioned in the above story is a covered chair mounted on wooden poles or beams and carried on the shoulders of two men. It is the traditional form of transporting a bride in South Asia. *LNB*]

چې تر يوې وياله ټوپ کا، بله ورته آسانه شي.

623. *When you cross [jump across] one stream, the next becomes easier.*

Each successive hurdle is easier to cross.

چې تنگ شي، نو په جنگ شي.

624. *When one is pushed into a tight corner, he will fight.*

This is similar to the idiomatic expression, "fighting with one's back to the wall."

[When one is hard pressed, desperate, with nowhere else to turn, he will take his "last stand" and fight. *LNB*]

چې توره کټوی باندې کړي، غمونه تر پښو لاندې کړي.

625. *When Tora puts the cooking pot on the hearth, she puts all her worries under her feet.*

The reference is to one who is absorbed in menial duties and has no time for other responsibilities [or to think about other things.] She puts all her worries [*ghəm, see* Proverb 333] "under her feet", that is, behind her.

[Or alternatively, "When the black (*tor*) cooking pot is placed on the fire she puts ..." That is, if food is available, there is nothing to worry about. *RWS*]

چې تیغ چلیږي، وینې بهیږي.

626. *When the sword strikes, blood is shed.*

چې جاسوس ئي د کوره وي، مینه ئي توره وي.

627. *When there is a spy in the house, the family cannot keep its love private.*

A secret can be kept only when there is no spy among the conspirators. When a spy belongs to the household itself, the house will be ruined [literally, "become black"].

[The term *tor*, meaning "black", refers to being accused, especially of sexual offenses. *LNB*]

چې جنگ سوړ شو. مرئ تود شو.

628. *When the battle ended, the slave became bold.*

Cowards are bold only after the battle has ended.

چې چا پښتو وکړه، ښځۍ به ئې وربي ټولوي.

629. *He who would follow* pakhtunwali, *his wife will eventually gather the chaff.*

This proverb is said of a man who, with meager resources, follows the traditions of *pakhtunwali* and puts himself in serious financial straits. *Pakhtunwali*, the Pashtun code of honor, includes competition with a rival, often at great expense.

[The image is of one's impoverished women gleaning grain or ears of corn—a picture of the possible cost and dire consequences of doing *pakhto. See* Proverb 341. *LNB*]

چې چا سر په زمکه ایښے وي خپل یار ته،

په آسمان باندې ختلے لکه نمر وي.

630. *He who has prostrated himself before his beloved, has risen like the sun to the heavens.*

[A line of verse from the *Diwan* of Rahman Baba, which also appears in the form, *che ye sər pa zməka ekhay wi wo yār ta ...*[30] *See* notes to Proverbs 106, 421 and 1266, and Index for "Abdur Rahman Baba". *RWS*]

چې چا سره اوسې، په مذهب به د هغو شې.

631. *Whomsoever you live with, it is likely that you would adopt their ways.*

This is similar to the proverb, "When in Rome, do as the Romans do."

[The Pashto proverb is descriptive, not prescriptive; that is, it is axiomatic that one tends to adopt the lifestyles and behaviors of those one lives with. *See* Proverbs 89, 885 and 1255. *LNB*]

چې خان نهٔ وي، جهان به څهٔ کړي.

632.   *Without me, what need would there have been for the universe?*

چې ځوان وم، د هرې هپې خان وم، چې زوړ شوم د خوارې خواري پرور
شوم.

633.   *When I was young, I was a leader of every raid, but now that I am old I am only a chewed stall of hay.*

چې خې خې ابازو له به راخې.

634.   *Wherever you journey, you will eventually return to Abazai.*

This is similar to the proverb, "East or West, home is best." [*See* Proverb 445.]

[Abazai is a small town on the outskirts of Peshawar. *See* Proverb 1223. *LNB*]

چې حقاني مينه ئې نهٔ وي، ميئن ئې مهٔ کړي د ملا په تعويزونو.

635.   *If there is no true love, he cannot be made into a lover by the mullah's amulet.*

An amulet or phylactery may contain sacred writings.

This proverb is usually spoken by women who have been rejected by their husbands. Women often seek after mullahs, asking them for amulets so that their husbands may love them.

[Amulets (*taweez*) may contain verses from the Holy Qur'an considered to possess special blessing power. This text is in the meter of a *ṭappa*; see Index for "*ṭappa*". *LNB, RWS*]

چي څنګه دېس، هغسي بېس.

636. *As the country, so the appearance and the clothing of the people.*

Every country or nation has its own way of life. They are not similar.

چي څوک اودهٔ وي، د هغو نر کتی زېږي.

637. *He who sleeps, will find that his buffalo gave birth to a male [calf].*

A tale is told of two Gujars, each of whom had a pregnant buffalo. (A Gujar is a herdsman of cattle, especially buffalo.) Both animals gave birth during the same night. One owner slept, but the other, who had remained awake, exchanged his male calf for his friend's female. When the sleeper asked his fellow Gujar the following morning, what his buffalo had produced, the answer was, "He who sleeps will find that his buffalo gave birth to a male."

[The female buffalo is valuable for the milk she produces. *LNB*]

چي څوک دې په محفل کښې نهٔ پېښتي ورګډه، څهٔ له ور ګډوې خپله ډېده.

638. *When no one in an assembly bothers about you, why should you enter there at all.*

An uninvited guest is unwelcome.

چي څوک مئين توب کوي، هغه خوبونه نهٔ کوي.

639. *He who loves does not sleep.*

This proverb applies more to ambition than to love. The ambitious man is never careless and is untiring in his pursuits.

چې څومره بهر د‌ے، هومره دننه د‌ے.

640. *As much as it may appear outwardly, it is much more so inside.*

A man's surface qualities are outnumbered by his hidden virtues.

[The contrast between "outside" and "inside" (outer / inner) qualities, outward appearances versus heart realities, is a common theme in proverbs. *See* Proverbs 173 and 421. *LNB*]

چې څومره خُلِي هومره خبرِي.

641. *The more tongues, the more versions.*

چې څۀ تیار وي هغه د یار وي.

642. *Whatever is ready is offered to the friend.*

One who is a friend need not expect formalities.

چې څۀ درپورې وینم. خدائیګو ګورِې غوندې دې وینم. چې څۀ درپورى نۀ
وینم هرګز دې نۀ وینم.

643. *When I hope to get something from you, I consider you as sweet as sugar [guṛ]. When you have nothing that interests me, I have nothing to do with you.*

The friendship of greedy people is only for selfish gain. *guṛ* is un-refined sugar, also called *shakari.*

[While a Pashtun longs for a true friend, he often encounteres the sad reality of human selfishness, insincerity and hidden agendas, as expressed in the now proverbial observation commonly attributed to Abdur Rahman, "Every man has a purpose (*matlab*) in friendship; I have not seen a man who was a friend for the sake of God alone." See Proverbs 164 and 1331. *LNB*]

چې څۀ رنگ شاړه هسې کربوړے.

644.   *As the boulder, so the lizard.*

Man is a slave of his environment. [*See* Proverbs 820 and 944.]

چې څۀ کرې هغه به ریبې.

645.   *As you sow, so shall you reap.*

[This well-known proverb appears in the collections of many nations. The English version circulates in slightly different forms, for example, "As they sow, so let them reap", "What a man sows he must reap", or the simple warning, "You reap what you sow," etc. One of the earliest occurences of this truth occurs in the Greek manuscript of the *Injil Sharif* translated into 17th century English, "God is not mocked: Whatsoever a man soweth, that shall he also reap."[31] If you sow kindness, good habits or positive words, you will reap accordingly; the opposite is also the case. Abdur Rahman Baba wrote, "Sow flowers that your surroundings become a garden. Don't sow thorns; for they will prick your own feet."[32] The ancient axiom of sowing and reaping expresses one of the most logical of life's lessons and a fundamental law of nature, as well as a basic principle of God's justice. *LNB*]

چې خاوند ئې نيني چيچي، نو سپے ئې خاورې خوري.

646.   *If the master is eating roasted maize, his dog will naturally eat earth.*

[If the master has nothing substantial to eat, what will be given to his dependents. Roasted maize is very similar to popcorn. *RWS*]

چې خبر شي بې اثر، تري نه پټه خُلۀ بهتر.

647.   *When words become useless [ineffective], it is better to keep silent.*

چې خپل زړهٔ بد نهٔ کړې، پردے زړهٔ به ښهٔ نهٔ کړي.

648. *Until you strain your nerve, you cannot please others.*

It is with making painful efforts [literally, straining "your heart"] that one can please others.

چې خدائے سړے ساتي، نو د زمري په خُلهٔ کښې ئې هم ساتلے شي.

649. *If God wishes to save a man, He can keep him safe even in the lion's mouth.*

چې خدائے کوی هغه به اوشي، خو د اوښ ګوډه تينګه وُتړه.

650. *Whatever God wills will happen, but it is better to bind tightly the foreleg of the camel.*

God's will is irrevocable, but we must take precautions.

[The first half of the text is an unattributed reference to a *Hadith*, *see* Proverb 651. The proverb above has hints of the well-known Arabic saying, "Trust in God, and (but) tie your camel." In other languages the same truth is expressed using a variety of different images, for example, "Call on God, but row (your boat) away from the rocks" (Indian), and "God gives nuts, but He doesn't crack them" (German). The proverb encourages personal responsibility and counters the temptation to presume upon God, to assume that He will grant food and clothing, protection and shelter, without any effort on our part. *See* Proverbs 157 and 905. *LNB*]

چې خدائے کوي هغه به وشي، د نبي د خُلې حديث دے بل به نشی.

651. *What God wills will happen; this saying [Hadith] of the Holy Prophet will never change.*

[This could be a reference to the important *Hadith* of Gabriel which outlines the creedal principles of Islam known as the "Six Pillars of Faith" (*arkan al-imān*), which includes belief in God's foreknowledge and determination of all affairs, good and bad. This doctrine of the Divine will or "fate" (Ar. *qadar*) is balanced by the individual's need to make right and ethical choices; the tension between resignation and human agency is reflected in a number of Pashto proverbs and the folk wisdom of many nations. *See* Proverb 650.]

چې خدائے مهربان شي، هندو ورته مسلمان شي.

652. *When God bestows His blessings on someone, even a Hindu will be a Muslim to him.*

That is, even his greatest enemy will become kind to him.

[Or, "... a Hindu will become like a Muslim to Him." This is used when someone shows kindness to a person who otherwise is deemed to be undeserving. God treats him as if he were a believer. *LNB*]

چې خدائے نۀ کوي، پير بابا به څۀ کړي.

653. *When God is unwilling to act, what can Pir Baba do about it?*

Fate rules our lives. "Pir Baba" now has an indefinite connotation and [used in this metaphorical way] simply designates a respected man. [*See* Proverbs 458 and 460, and similar Proverb 656.]

چې خدائے ورسره بد شي، دستي له شرعي رد شي.

654. *When God becomes angry with an individual, he immediately turns away from the religious code.*

When a man incurs God's wrath, he will violate the Islamic Law [literally, *Shariah*] and hence will be punished.

چې خدائے ئي نۀ کا، بنده به څۀ کا.

655. *If God does not do it, what can man do.*

چه خدائے ئي نه کا، دیوانه بابا به څۀ کا.

656. *When God chooses to do nothing, what can Diwana Baba do about it?*

Diwana Baba is a saint whose shrine stands in Bunir in the Swat district of Pakistan. Every year thousands of pilgrims visit the shrine to pray, especially for their worldly desires. [*See* Proverb 460 and 653.]

چه خوارانو روژۍ ونیوۍ، نو ورځي هم سترۍ شوۍ.

657. *When the poor kept the fast, the days were lengthened.*

Those who are fated to be unlucky have their share of trouble.

چه خوري خوري، چه وائي وائي، چه مري مري، چه پائي پائي.

658. *When he eats he is eating, when he talks he goes on talking, when he is alive he goes on living, and when he dies he submits to death.*

Such is the way of life.

چه خوشے ګرځېدۍ، آخر به پرځېدۍ.

659. *When you wander about alone, it is only natural that eventually you will fall.*

[One is reminded of the proverbial wisdom of King Solomon (*Bacha Suliman*), "Two are better than one, because they have good reward for their toil. For if they fall, one will lift up the other; but woe to one who is alone and falls and does not have another to help."[33] *LNB*]

چه خُله سپینه لرم یاران مي ډېر!

660. *When I have a charming face, my friends are many!*

When I have wealth and power, my friends are also many!

[This is a cynical expression about the material tendency of society. *RWS*]

چې د بونېر ئې، ګل د ثمېر ئې.

661.   *If you are from Bunir, you are a rhododendron blossom.*

With this proverb the Buniris praise their own tribe. [*See* note to Proverb 305.]

چې د پوزې نه ئې نېسې، نو ساه ئې خېژي.

662.   *Even if you catch him by the nose, he will die.*

This proverb is said of a man in a very bad condition or state of affairs.

چې د تورې وزې سور وي، د هغۀ په تنډه نور وي.

663.   *The forehead of a man who wears a scarlet edged sword shines.*

The brave will rule.

[Alternatively, "He whose sword handle is red (with blood), his forehead will shine." *RWS*]

چې د چا دوستي ډېره وي، هغه به دولت بائېلي. چې د چا دشمني ډېره

وی هغه به سر.

664.   *He whose friends are many will lose his wealth. He whose enemies are many will lose his head.*

[In Pashto proverbs, wise sayings that highlight the dichotomy between "friend(s)" and "enemy(ies)" are common. *See* Index entries for both key words. *LNB*]

چې د چا زور وي، د هغو کور وي.

665. *To him who is strong goes the home.*

The meaning is similar to the English proverb, "Might makes right." [*See* Proverbs 196, 560 and 695.]

[The strong person has complete authority in his (or her) home. *RWS*]

چې د ځوانانو نيستي شوه، نو منو هم منه زار شو.

666. *Since youths are now in short supply, even Manu has become Manuẓar.*

When there is a scarcity of capable people, even ordinary individuals are considered [or pose as being] superior.

چې د خدائے وو نعمتونه هغه تاسو ونيوه، نو زۀ به خاوري خورم.

667. *Whatever bounties God offers us, you have devoured them, while I must eat dust.*

Some enjoy all the blessings of God while others are left in poverty.

[The bounties of God are common for all and should be equally distributed. *RWS*]

چې د خدائے ويره ئي نۀ وي، څۀ د ورۀ پناه څۀ د غرۀ پناه.

668. *When he has no fear of God, whether a man be behind a mountain or behind a door is one and the same thing.*

No obstacle will prevent the confirmed sinner from committing sins.

[Literally, "What refuge is a mountain, what refuge is a door (that is, a house)." Providing "refuge" (*panā*) is a part of the Pashtun code of honor, and someone pursued by an enemy may seek refuge in a tribal fortress or village. This text may also be interpreted as a threat against an enemy: "If there were no fear of God your mountain refuge would be like the refuge of a door!", that is "If I didn't fear God I would have no problem catching you." In another version of this proverb, the second phrase stands alone as a boast: "What difference does it make if there is a a door or a mountain between us?", that is "You can run but you can't hide from me anywhere." *LNB*]

چې د دوه ؤ سرو سره جګړه شي، د دريم پکښې ښه شي.

669.   *When two persons quarrel, the third party gains.*

"Divide and rule".

[As Tair and Edwards note, this proverb is similar to the well-known Latin political axiom, *Divide et impera*, also translated and known in the form "Divide and conquer", that is, factions that fight each other, and nations divided within, are more easily defeated or ruled. *See* Proverb 715. *LNB*]

چې د زړونو پريوځي، د غرونو پريوځي.

670.   *He who falls from the hearts of his fellows falls from the mountains.*

He who becomes unpopular falls from his pedestal.

چې د کلي په سبلمه ورشي، نو وارۀ ويوښنته.

671.   *When you approach a village, make inquiries from the children.*

It is the unsophisticated children who will speak the truth about everything in the village.

چې د مچ کوچو ته زړۀ کېږي، نو ځان ته دې مېښنه واخلي.

672.   *If a fly has a craving for butter, he should purchase a buffalo for himself.*

If a man of low degree complains that he lacks the good things of life, he should strive to attain them.

چې د ملنګ د کلي لار ده، هغه زمونږ لار ده.

673.   *The way of the* malangs' *village is our way.*

The *malang* is a beggar. Since there are no villages made up of beggars, they have no body ["way"] of custom and traditions. The expression is ironic.

چې د وادهٔ مېرمن متیزه لاړه، نو سرود چاته غږېږي؟

674.   *Since the bride has eloped, for whom is the music being played?*

When careful preparations have been made to greet a person who ultimately fails to show-up, this proverb is spoken.

چې د یو سُود کېږي، د بل کور نړېږي.

675.   *While one benefits, another's home crumbles.*

چې دوه پړخي، یو خو غورځي.

676.   *Whenever two wrestle, one is thrown.*

چې دوه غرکي خُلۍ نیسي، یوه به درنه خلاصیږي.

677.   *When you hold two churning skins, one will certainly fall from your hand.*

This is said of the greedy man who plants his feet astride two boats and falls between them.

[The greedy man tries to grasp more than he can handle, and ends up suffering loss. *LNB*]

چې دې وکښنه ، ما وى مصرى، ده.

678. *Before you drew the sword, I said it was Egyptian.*

The saying is used in the sense of, "Before you spoke, I had known the truth."

چې دې نۀ پوښتي مۀ گډېږه.

679. *When you are not asked, don't interfere.*

چې دې نۀ خاربنتبږي، مۀ ئ گروه.

680. *If any part of your body is not irritated, don't scratch it.*

This is similar to the proverb, "Let sleeping dogs lie." [*See* Proverbs 206, 208 and 702.]

[Avoid unnecessary involvement. *RWS*]

چې دوډئ وي نو مېلمه کے څۀ دے، او چې ايمان وي نو مرگ څۀ دے؟

681. *When there is food in the house, what matter if a guest arrives. When there is faith, what is death?*

That is, a guest is no problem and death need not be feared.

چې ډول دِ وى په څنگ، د وهلو ئ څه ننگ.

682. *When one has a drum at his side, why should he not beat it?*

When a person lowers his moral standards, he is not ashamed of indulging freely in immorality.

[Or alternatively, "… why should he be ashamed of beating it?" The drum is associated with musicians and a class of menials called *ḍəm. See* note on Proverb 615. *RWS, LNB*]

چې ډېر خاندي ډېر به ژاړي.

683. *The more you laugh the more shall you weep.*

"He who laughs first, laughs last", assuming that this popular expression is taken to mean that comedy is never far from tragedy.

[The English proverb about laughter occurs in various forms, most commonly, "He who laughs last, laughs best", as well as "He who laughs first, laughs loudest" and "He who laughs last, laughs longest." The Pashto text affirms the reality that life's joys are often followed by tears. *LNB*]

چې ډېر غواړي جنگونه، هغه دوه کوي ودونه.

684. *If one enjoys quarreling, let him be a polygamist.*

[Literally, "If one likes a lot of fighting, he should get married twice!" While relations among Pashtun women in a given household are generally harmonious, there may be rivalry between co-wives, for example, over the scarce "resource" of male attention (expressed in terms of gifts, favoritism, special treatment of one wife's children over a co-wife's, etc.). Quarreling between two wives is proverbial, as in the above proverb and others like it, for example,"One hundred men can live in peace, but not two women." *See* Proverbs 3, 797, 1229, 1334. *LNB*]

چې ډېر غوربزي، نو نۀ وربزي.

685. *When there is excessive thunder, there is no rain.*

This is analogous to the expression, "Barking dogs seldom bite", or "He is all bark and no bite." [*See* Proverbs 43, 511 and 1226.]

چې رنگ دې په قيصه زېر شو، تورُو ته مۀ ځه.

686. *If you turn pale upon hearing the story, avoid the battle front.*

چې روپۍ وي ، بزرګې چبلي دبري.

687. *When there is money, the spotted goats are plentiful.*

Another in the group of proverbs related to "Money makes the
mare go." [*See* Proverbs 467, 524 and 689.]

چې رښتیا را رسي ، نو دروغو به کلي وران کړي وي.

688. *By the time truth is known, lies will have destroyed the village.*

[*See* Proverb 1087. *LNB*]

چې زر لري بازار د غرۀ په سر لري.

689. *If you have cash, then you have a market even on the top of the
mountain.*

"Money makes the mare go", as so often in Pakhtun proverbial
literature. [*See* Proverbs 467, 524 and 687.]

چې زر لرې زاري د څۀ ده.

690. *If you have money, there is no need to make requests.*

The wealthy man can demand rather than ask.

چې زر وي نو زیار د څۀ دے؟

691. *When there is money, there need not be striving.*

چې زړه شوې پاکیزه شوې.

692. *When you reach old age you become pious.*

چې زما او ستا بایدهٔ دي، لري او نزدې څهٔ دي.

693. *When you and I agree, there is no question of distance.*

چې زما تر سر شي تېره، خدا ے دې نهٔ کړي دنیا ډېره.

694. *When I leave my worldly wealth behind, may God not increase it.*

This proverb suggests that the individual does not want others to profit by his good fortune. Hence, by implication, "Eat, drink and be merry, for tomorrow you shall die". [*See* comments on Proverb 389, and Proverb 999.]

چې زور د زورور شي، کندو کښې ئې غنم خپل شي.

695. *When the strength of the powerful is exerted, the wheat in the barn becomes one's own.*

This observation is similar to the English proverb, "Might makes right." [*See* Proverbs 196, 560, 665.]

چې زوئ ورور ئې وي وژلي، د هغهٔ لاس وي چا نیولے؟

696. *When your son or brother has been murdered, who then has tied your hands?*

When a Pakhtun's relative has been murdered, no law on earth can keep him from taking revenge.

[Alternatively, "When he is the murderer of his son and / or brother, who can tie his hands?", that is, who else can prevent him from murdering others if he doesn't care about killing his own relatives? RWS]

چې ژوندے یم بنهٔ مې وایه، چې مړ شم مهٔ راپسې ژاړه.

697. *While I am alive speak well of me, and when I die do not weep for me.*

چې سپینه غوا توره څټي، توره دې سر وُخوري چې سپینه نهٔ څټي.

698. *When the white cow licks the black, may the black lose its head if it fails to lick the white.*

When a man of superior status pays homage to one of low degree, the latter is obliged to respect him in return.

چې ستاسو کره درشم نو څهٔ به راکړې، چې زمونږ کره راشې نو څهٔ به راوړې.

699. *When I call on you at your home, what will you give me? And when you call on me at my home, what will you bring for me?*

This is spoken of a selfish person.

چې ستاسو غوا لنګیږي نو زمونږ غوے به لنګ شوے وي.

700. *When your cow is bearing a calf, our ox will also have given birth!*

This proverb is said of a person from whom an ordinary performance cannot be expected, much less anything great.

چې سر حیات وي خولۍ ډېرې.

701. *When the head is alive, caps are many.*

When one is alive and striving, he will eventually be able to meet his wants.

چې سر دې نۀ خوږيږي نو داغ پرې مۀ ږده.

702. *If your head does not ache, do not treat it.*

Avoid creating unnecessary troubles for yourself. "Let sleeping
dogs lie", or "Don't upset the apple cart." [*See* Proverbs 206, 208 and
680; cf. variant Proverb 613.]

چې سر ئې د مار وي که چرمنبکی وي هم ئې مۀ پريږده.

703. *If its head resembles that of a snake, kill it even though it be a lizard.*

Do not spare anyone who may be a threat in the future.

چې ښۀ کوې ښۀ به مومې.

704. *If you do well you will be rewarded.*

چې طلب ئې کوې پرې پېښ بۀ شې.

705. *That which you search for, you will find.*

"Seek and ye shall find."

[Diligent effort and seeking will be rewarded. As Tair and Edwards
note, this Pashto proverb echoes a well-known saying of Jesus Christ
which encourages people to "seek" God and Truth with the certainty
that "those who seek will find."[34] Earlier, a 10th century BC proverb
of King Solomon (*Bacha Suliman*) in the Old Testament advised men
to "seek Wisdom" (personified), who promises "I love those who love
me, and those who seek me find me."[35] *See* Proverbs 248 and 906.
LNB]

چې غاښونه وو نو چنې نۀ وي.

706. *When there were teeth, there was no grain.*

The complaint of a person who, when he could have made good use of an opportunity, found none. Now that he has the opportunity, he is in no position to profit by it. [That is, he now has no teeth to chew the grain.] The "grain" here refers to a variety of chickpea [or garbanzo bean].

چې غټ وي نو لټ وي.

707. *The bulkier, the lazier.*

چې غرڅېرب (څورب) وي نو نېر (نور) غرځهٔ ئي هم څېرب وي.

708. *If the mountain is fertile, its wild goats will be fat.*

The wealth of a country is the wealth of its people.

[The variant words in parentheses in the Pashto script are in the Bannu dialect. *RWS*]

چې غلا ئي وشوه نو څوکيدار ئي وُساتلو.

709. *After his house was burgled he kept a* chowkidār.

Hiring a *chowkidār* (or watchman) would prevent further losses. The proverb warns that "A stitch in time saves nine" [that is, take appropriate action while you can]. However, the meaning is closer to "Closing the barn door after the horse has gone" [or "… after the horse has bolted" or "is stolen", meaning: one is taking action too late to do any good. *LNB*]

چې غل نهٔ تښتي نو مل دې وُتښتي.

710. *If the thief does not take to his heels, at least allow his companions to flee.*

چې غنم لاړ شي نو په دروزه ئې اور وُلګه.

711. *When the wheat is gone, let the stalks be burned.*

When you have lost a precious thing, you might as well let everything else go with it.

چې کتوی خُتي نو په وادهٔ به دې باران کبږي.

712. *If you keep licking the cooking pots, rain will certainly fall on your wedding day.*

The proverb is spoken to young children as a warning to those who are greedy.

[This "proverb" is a Pashtun superstition. *RWS*]

چې کلي سره وهلې ئې نو نهٔ ئې وهلې.

713. *When you are beaten along with the others of the village, you are not really beaten.*

If everyone is beaten with the same stick, there is no disgrace.

چې کلي په نامه لري. یو خوئ تر نورو ښهٔ لري.

714. *Naming a village after a man signifies that he had qualities superior to those of his contemporaries.*

[Or, that he had at least one quality that was superior to those of his contemporaries. *RWS*]

چې کلي دوه شي د چغلو ښنه شي.

715. *When the village is divided the backbiters rejoice.*

This is similar to the proverb, "Divide and rule". [*See* Proverb 669.]

چی کم وی لوبوه ئي. چی لوئي شي نو تربور دے جنگوه ئي.

716. When he is small let him play [or, play with him], but when he grows
up and becomes your tarbur, make him fight with others.

The *tarbur* is a rival [or cousin—the two are often synonymous.
See Proverbs 485, 486 and 1264 *LNB*].

چی کوز ګوري. هغه وُربوز ګوري.

717. The man who looks down sees only his downcast face.

Life holds no joy for those with pouting expressions.

چی کوي مي نۀ نو ګنجي مي مۀ بوله.

718. If you don't want to marry me, do not call me a "bald-head".

Do not find fault with me when you have already made up your
mind not to befriend me.

چی کُول شي نافرمانه. تول ئي واړه شي کریانه.

719. When a generation revolts and becomes disobedient, all their
weighings are false measures.

چی ګوته خوږ شي نو سترګي ژاړي.

720. When the finger is injured, the eyes weep.

When calamity comes to a man, his whole family suffers with him.

چي لاړ شي تر بلخه، درسره به وي خپله برخه.

721. *Even if you travel as far as Balkh (Bactria), your fate will follow you.*

    Distance cannot alter destiny.

چي لاس مات شي نو غاړي له ځي.

722. *When the arm is broken it is bound to the neck by a sling.*

    When in trouble, one seeks the help of his own kith and kin [friends and relatives or kinsman], just as the arm and neck are parts of the same body [and support each other].

چي لري خُلهٔ چالاکه، خپله بده به کړي پاکه.

723. *He who is cunning will clear himself.*

    He will turn his sins into virtue.

چي لرې مي، لرم به دې. چي لرې مي لرم به دې.

724. *If you respect my honor, I will respect yours, but if you defame me I will defame you.*

چي لرې هغه به پېرې.

725. *Whatever "you have" you will vend it.*

    A man's character is reflected in his actions.

[This rhyming proverb (*lare … pere*) uses the Pashto verb *perəl*, literally, "to purchase" or "to buy", which has been rendered "vend" above, connoting the idea of "trading" or "selling"—that is, "One trades what one has." Based on what "you have" in stock (within you), you will buy from or sell to others—your actions reveal who you really are. *LNB*]

چې لوړ‌ہ‌ړي کور ئي نړ‌ہ‌ړي.

726.   *He who rises high shall find that his house falls.*

"The wealthier the more miserly"; or, one who thinks highly of himself will come to trouble.

[The above reference ("The wealthier the more miserly") is not an English proverb we know of, but if "miserly" is corrected to "misery", this may be an allusion to a quote from Chaucer's definition of tragedy, "A certeyn storie … / Of him that stood in greet prosperitee,/ And is y-fallen out of heigh degree/ Into miserie, and endeth wrecchedly."[36] One is reminded of King Solomon's (*Bacha Suliman*) warning in the Old Testament ("Pride goes before destruction and a haughty spirit before a fall"), often quoted proverbially as "Pride goes before a fall,"[37] and King David's now proverbial lament (over the death of King Saul and his house), "How the mighty have fallen!"[38]. The Pashto proverb expresses a similar truth. *LNB*]

چې لنگیدے نۀ شوې نو بلاربیدې څۀ له؟

727.   *If you were unable to bear a child why did you become pregnant?*

This proverb is spoken to one who attempts to do a job that ultimately proves to be beyond his capacity, or to one who could not foresee the magnitude or consequences of the job.

چې له خپله عقله پلے وي، هغه تل په غم نتلے وي.

728.   *He who lacks intelligence will always be in trouble.*

چې یار سره یاری لري عیب ئي مه گوره.

729.   *When he is faithful to his friends do not find fault with him.*

[Or alternatively, "When you are faithful to your friend, do not find fault with him," that is, don't focus on his faults." *RWS*]

چي له ياره وائي له خانه وائي.

730. *What he says about his friends he says about himself.*

چي ماما سر وگروي د خوريي طمع پيدا شي.

731. *When the maternal uncle scratches his head his nephew's expectations are aroused.*

Nephews always expect something from their uncles.

چي مار لنډے شي لا ګرندے شي.

732. *When the snake grows shorter it becomes faster.*

The more trouble you cause for an enemy the more active he becomes.

چي مرګ شته ښادي نشته.

733. *When there is death there is no joy.*

As long as one fears death he can have no joy.

چي مړ شو هغه پر شو.

734. *He who dies is defeated.*

What can a dead (powerless) man do.

[Or alternatively, "He who dies becomes guilty," that is, he cannot justify or defend himself. RWS]

چې مزري پرنجے وکړو نو پیشو ترې اړتاوه شوه چې لیوهٔ پرنجے وکړو نو منرک.

735.   *When the lion sneezed, the cat was tossed about, and when the swine sneezed, the rat was tossed about.*

This proverb derives from a popular myth that, in the beginning, when God Almighty created the animals, He first made the higher animal species. From these the smaller animals evolved.

The epigram is used to compare the brave man with the coward. The swine and the rat are symbols of cowardice; the lion and cat are symbols of bravery.

چې مور مبره شي پلار پلندر شي زوئ د لوئي لارې قلندر شي.

736.   *When the mother becomes a step-mother, the father then becomes a step-father, and the son is left to wander on the highways.*

چې نامردو اسونه وکړل نو اول ئې په خپل کلی وترپول.

737.   *When the cowards got horses they galloped first over their own village.*

When cowards gain power they destroy their own kith and kin [relatives].

چې نن سپک شي صبا ورک شي.

738.   *He is disgraced today, he is destroyed tomorrow.*

Disgrace ultimately leads to destruction.

[This proverb underlines the dreadful consequences of dishonorable behavior. Pashtun society is shame based, and what people say (or "what people might say") can destroy one's reputation and inevitably that of one's family. This serves as a powerful mechanism for social control. One may become disgraced through (perceptions or accusations of) sexual impropriety, cowardice, disloyalty to family and religion, etc. *See* Proverbs 738 and 487. *LNB*]

چي نۀ ځي نو وا بۀ دې خلم، چي نۀ خورې نو څه به دې کړم.

739. *If you refuse to go, I will pick you up (and carry you), but when you do not eat, what can I do about it.*

This is said to a child or anyone who is reluctant to eat. This is similar in meaning to "You can lead a horse to water but you cannot make him drink." [*See* Proverb 11.]

چي نۀ دې وه د پلار او د نيکۀ اوس دې نوې ونيوه.

740. *Instead of following the way of your ancestors, you have adopted a new way.*

[In contrast with the western fascination with innovation and all things "new", Pashtuns often attach importance to that which is associated with the traditions of their ancestors, and resist practices which they perceive as undermining their identity, autonomy, customs and values. In Islam a high value is placed on following the *sunna* (custom) of the Prophet and resisting *bid'a* (innovation), which some view as a danger to the community. *LNB*]

چي نۀ دې وي په خوا هغه تا ته شي بلا.

741. *What you never think worthy of consideration becomes a calamity*

[What you didn't think of becomes a disaster or a problem for you. *RWS*]

چي نۀ دې وي د موره داسي مۀ وايه چي ورره.

742. *If he is not the son of your mother, do not call him a brother.*

Do not trust a man who is not a close relative.

چې نه کار نو په هغې کېنې څۀ کار؟

743. *When no meddling is requested why should one interfere?*

When you have nothing to do with it, why meddle in it?

[If something does not concern you, do not interfere with it. *RWS*]

چې نۀ کبړي بیا د نهه کروئ نه اګره نۀ کبړی.

744. *When it is not being cooked, even nine ladles will not make it.*

The proverb refers to cooking porridge. Without the will to work, no job can be completed.

چې نۀ مرم هر څه بۀ واورم.

745. *As long as I live I will listen to many things.*

Live long and have many varied experiences.

In one's life one comes across many unexpected things.

چې نۀ مني د یار پندونه په سر به تل وړي د غم بارونه.

746. *He who does not heed the advice of friends will always bear the burden of grief.*

[This rhyming proverb contrasts "the advice of friends" (*da yār panduna*) with the "burden of grief" (*da ghəm bāruna*) one will bear, literally "forever carry on his head", if he rejects the wise counsel and admonition. Another version of this text substitutes *panduna* for *bāruna* making for a delightful alliteration, a play on the words: *panduna* = advice, *panduna* = "load" (carried on one's head). One who listens to advice is considered wise; a friend's advice is especially sweet, and one who rebuffs such counsel will suffer grief. *LNB*]

چې نۀ ورکوي مولا څۀ به ورکوي دولا.

747.   *When God does not give what can Shah Dawla give?*

Shah Dawla was a saint in the Punjab province of Pakistan.

[The Sufi saint Hazrat Shah Dawla (d. 1676) of Gujrat is most famed for his attraction to wild animals and the miracle of the *Chudās* or "Rat Children" (children born brainless, small-headed, long-eared and rat-faced, who were nonetheless blessed by the saint). Like other saints, Shah Dawla's intercession could procure a child for a childless couple, but the supplicant had to make a vow either to present the child at the shrine or to make an offering—failure of which would lead to the next child being born a *chudā*. This fear has brought about both reverence and prosperity for the shrine.[39] The proverb advises that however blessed the intercession, if the Sovereign God does not give and answer, the saint can give nothing. *LNB*]

چې نۀ ئي کړي حبيب څۀ به وکړي خوار طبيب.

748.   *When God chooses not to heal someone what can the poor doctor do.*

[Like Proverb 653, this proverb counsels submission to God's sovereign will. In this text, the contrast is between *habib* ("Beloved") and the poor *tabib* ("doctor"); other proverbs contrast the power and will of God over that of the holy man (*pir*). *LNB*]

چې نيم سپرے په دڼی ولی نو نيم سپرے ماتېږي.

749.   *If you strike a half-seer stone against a four seers one, the half-seer will be smashed.*

The weak always remain weak. A *seer* is approximately 2lbs.

چې وچولے مې خپل وي، سپرلے به پۀ ما تل وي.

750.   *When fate is on my side, it will always be spring for me.*

A fortunate man will always enjoy life.

چې وخت د سنت شي د يتيم پوزه ويني شي.

751. *When the time of circumcision approaches the orphan's nose bleeds.*

The unfortunate ones, even at the propitious moment, are still losers.

چې وخت د ښکار راشي نو لاچۍ له غُل ورشي.

752. *When the time for the hunt approaches, Lachai the bitch begins to ease [relieve] herself.*

This proverb is spoken when those who wish to profit from an opportunity lose it.

چې وخت د ګينتو شي، خوراک د چټاکو شي او غُل د ټټو شي نو قيامت
به رانزدې شي.

753. *When time is measured in hours and food in* chiṭaks *and when men ease [relieve] themselves in latrines, then the day of doom will be nearer.*

Spoken ironically by those who are compelled to observe conventions [that is, modern practices and formalities *RWS*].

[A *chiṭākəy* is a 50-gram weight, the smallest measure used in the buying and selling of food and produce. *LNB*]

چې ورېږي باران مزې کوي خواران.

754. *When it rains the poor make merry.*

This proverb is an ironic reference to those living in mud houses during the rainy season.

چي ورکے وي په پښنو ځي چي لوئي شي په اوږو ځي.

755. *When he is young he walks firmly on his feet, but when he grows up he swaggers.*

چي ویر وي خو په سر توري دپ وي.

756. *When there is lamentation let it be thorough.*

That is, the grieving shall be complete [literally, "with a bare head" RWS].

چپ وئي خورپ غل به شي چپ ور ئي کرپ گل به شي.

757. *When you eat it, it will become excreta. When you give it, it will turn into flowers.*

The proverb refers to the evil consequences of miserliness [stinginess, selfishness, greed] as against the blessings of generosity.

چپ هاتهيان ساتپ نو دروازپ دنگپ جوړوه.

758. *If you plan to keep elephants make your doors wide and high.*

If one wishes to live as a chieftain or leader, he must bear the responsibilities and prepare for the difficulties of his position. Tough jobs need much planning.

[Difficult jobs require bigger and more costly investments. RWS]

چپ هلک (جینپ) وُنه ژاړپ نو مور هم پئ نۀ ورکوي.

759. *As long as the infant does not weep the mother does not give it milk.*

When in need, ask.

[If one does not complain, he does not get it. RWS]

چې هوس دے. دغه هومره بس دے.

760. *If there is desire that is enough.*

چې هوسۍ وهي د هغو تازيانو خُلِي توري وي.

761. *The hounds that chase the deer have black noses.*

Those who are born to do great things have the needed strength and skill.

[That is, they are known or obvious. *RWS*]

چې يو خوا گورم ډانگ دے، چې بل خوا گورم پړانگ دے.

762. *[When I look to one side there is a club to beat me, when I look to the other side there is a leopard to eat me.]*

[This is similar to the English saying,] "Between the devil and the deep blue sea," [that is, to be between two equally dangerous options. *See* Proverb 323. *LNB*]

[Cf. an alternative version of this text, "On one side a cliff to fall from, on the other side a leopard." *RWS*]

چې يو لور ئي تر ملا وي مۀ ئي ځنې رغوه.

763. *If he carries only one sickle, do not desert him.*

If a man has only an ordinary weapon for self-protection, one should accompany him.

[Alternatively, "… do not befriend him," that is, do not make any agreements with him. *RWS*]

چې يو مړ نشي بل به موړ نشي.

764. *If one does not die the other does not become rich.*

[This is similar to the English proverb based on the Latin,] "One man's loss is another man's gain."

چې يو وهم بل پرې ژنګېږي.

765. *When one is being beaten the other sobs.*

[The idea is that if one person is being beaten, someone else feels the pain, that is, suffers the destructive consequences of another's behavior: "If I strike one, the other weeps." *See* Proverbs 266 and 409. *LNB, RWS*]

چې يوه سترګه دې ړنده شي په بله لاس کښېږده.

766. *When one of your eyes becomes blind, put your hand over the other.*

This expression implies that, when you lose one of your precious belongings, you will protect the others more carefully.

چې يوه ګوته بل ته ونيسې نو څلور ځان ته کېږي.

767. *When you point only one finger at someone else, the remaining four point toward you.*

While one is pointing out [judging] a weakness in another person, he should remember that he himself has many more. [*See* Proverb 782.]

چې ئې ياد کړې په وړوکتوب هېر به ئې نۀ کړې په زوړتوب.

768. *That which is learned in childhood will never be forgotten even in old age.*

چې ياري کوي هغه خواري کوي.

769.   *He who makes friends must expect to share their burdens.*

It may also mean that it is difficult to find a friend.

[Friendship involves struggle, hard work and painful "burden bearing" of the hardships of others. *RWS, LNB*]

چې يار ئې کنې په بده ئې پياز وي.

770.   *Though you may consider a man your close friend, he will surely have an onion under the belt of his trousers.*

That is, he will certainly be a faithless friend.

[Sometimes you may consider a person to be a loyal friend, but he may not be. *RWS*]

[The "onion in the trouser belt" refers to a folk practice whereby someone who swears an oath later can disavow it on the grounds of "uncleanness"; thus, the proverb is a comment on insincerity or duplicity. *LNB*]

چې يم خو زۀ يم.

771.   *If there is anyone, it is I.*

The statement amounts to a big boast.

چې ئې وغواړې په خُله خورې به ئې په څۀ؟

772.   *If you beg for it with this mouth, then with which mouth will you eat it?*

When a man degrades himself through speech, how can he eat? The mouth itself has been degraded.

[This proverb could also be said of a person who does not like to make requests. *RWS*]

چې ئې زده شي د مور په پۍ هېر به ئې نۀ شي په زړبوډگۍ.

773. *Things learned at the mother's breast will not be forgotten even in old age.*

چې ئې غواړي نو پرې واوړي.

774. *He who longs for it will eventually come face-to-face with it.*

[Alternatively, "He who longs for it will stand by his demand." He will not give up seeking that which he longs for or demands, until is it his. *RWS*]

چې ئې نۀ زده د کمیسۀ غاړه هغه ئې خوري په لکه غاړه.

775. *Although she does not know how to make the collar, she enjoys her food and holds her head high.*

Although the woman does not know how to keep a house, she nevertheless lives well and is unduly proud. The reference is to the person who holds a position for which he is unqualified.

[Literally, "Although she does not know how to make a collar of a *kemis* (shirt), she eats with high head (proudly)." *RWS, LNB*]

چې یوه کډه وځي د بلې زړۀ وځي.

776. *When one family leaves, another is grieved as it thinks it might follow suit.*

[The "leaving" here is a reference to emigration or migration, such as the departure or moving on of a caravan. *LNB*]

چیتر چې په ترتر شي زاړۀ سخي ورته سخوندر شي.

777. When the March rains come, the weak calves fatten into young
      bullocks.

چیتر چې ورنده شي په خنبو کبنې نۀ ځائېږي، پگن چې ورنده شي په پتو
کبنې نۀ ځائېږي.

778. When there is excessive rain in March, there will be no place in the
      storehouse; when there are heavy rains in April, there is no room in
      the fields.

      The proverb refers to grain.

چیتر دے په تر تر د ے.

779. The rain of spring is very light.

      [In spring it rains rapidly with short breaks. RWS]

چېرې هدو، چېرې گیدړ.

780. Look at Hado (the foolish dog). How can he catch a jackal?

      Small or foolish people cannot achieve greatness [or perform great
      jobs].

چیندخ په پوله (لوته) وُخوت کشمیر ئې ولید!

781. The frog sat on a dike and saw Kashmir.

      An ironic comment addressed to the person who boasts of his
      achievements.

      [A variant proverb says,, "The frog climbed on a dirt-clod and saw
      Kashmir." LNB]

خُان ته ګوره بل پرې نيسه.

782. *Look first at yourself, then look at others in the same way.*

Judge others as you judge yourself.

[Often we judge others but may be guilty of the same thing. The theme of "judging" is common in proverbial literature. The annotation above refers to the Biblical axiom well-known in English, "Do not judge, or you too will be judged. For the same way you judge others, you will be judged and with the measure you use, it will be measured to you." A Japanese proverb says to, "Search seven times before you judge" and Buddhist wisdom cautions, "Easily seen are others' faults, hard indeed to see are one's own. Like chaff one winnows others' faults, but one's own one hides, as a crafty fowler conceals himself by camouflage." The great humanitarian, Mother Teresa of Calcutta (1910-1997) gently reminds us, "If you judge people, you have no time to love them." *See* e.g. Proverbs 6, 421, 767. *LNB*]

خُان ستړے بنهٔ دے که زړهٔ ستړے بنهٔ دے؟

783. *Which is better to be tired physically or to have a tired heart?*

خُان بنهٔ دے کهٔ مل.

784. *Which is better, being alone or with a comrade?*

[Or, "Which one is better, the self or one's friend or comrade?" *RWS*]

خانه خپله خانه تر هر چا را باندې کرانه.

785. *Oh self! You are most precious to me.*

Used seriously to indicate human dignity.

[Literally, "Oh self, my self! You are more precious to me than anyone else." *RWS*]

خائے هغه تود وي چې اور پرې بلبږي.

786. *The place where fire burns is hot.*

Only the person in trouble can appreciate his dilemma [can sense or perceive properly the degree of trouble. *RWS*]

خنې ولولي ملا شي خنې ولولي بلا شي.

787. *Some read and become learned (a mullah). For others, reading is a calamity.*

Knowledge can either benefit or destroy man. It is the use he makes of knowledge that determines his worth. The mullah is a Muslim trained in traditional doctrines; he may be the head of a mosque.

[Literally, "… and some become learned and become a calamity." *RWS*]

څپلۍ پيزار نۀ دے او پګرۍ دستار نۀ دے.

788.   Chappals *are not shoes, a cap is not a turban.*

The proverb signifies that no one of low degree is worthy of leadership.

In earlier times the turban and the shoes (*paṇi* [a special type of shoe with a curled-up toe]) were signs of dignity. Neither cheap footwear such as *chappals*, nor inferior headgear, was fashionable.

[The proverb can be rendered, "A sandal (whether the cheap *chappal* usually made of plastic or rubber, or the better quality leather *tsapləy*) is not a shoe, and a turban (*pagrey*) is not (that is, it is more than) a turban cloth." *See* Proverb 328. *LNB*]

ختۀ ئې غتۀ ده او غواړي خبر.

789.   *Though he is of noble birth, still he begs.*

[The healthy person must work for his livelihood. *RWS*]

څښتن حيات مال ئې ميرات.

790.   *The master is alive, but the property is gone with the wind.*

[Literally, "... but the property is without an owner." *RWS*]

څښتن سپي تهٔ وُوئيل او سپی لکۍ تۀ.

791.   *The master spoke to his dog and the dog spoke to its tail.*

A saying often used for amusement, as when the boss gives orders to his officers who in turn order a subordinate to "mind the baby".

څلور لوښي چې سره پراتۀ وي نو هم کله کله ګړببړی.

792. *When four pots lie together they sometimes make noise.*

Even the best of friends quarrel or differ among themselves.

[Disagreement among friends is natural. When people dwell together, disagreements may sometimes arise. *RWS*]

څملې يو ځائۍ او خوب بل ځائۍ وينې.

793. *You sleep in one place and dream in another.*

This is said of one who keeps company with one group of friends and speaks well of another.

څنګه تره هسې کربوړے.

794. *As the rock is, so is the lizard.*

څنګه چړ داسې بوچړ.

795. *As he begs, so he gets.*

Even a beggar receives according to his skill.

[*char* is a technical word used for collecting bread for the pilgrims of any distant holy shrine. *RWS*]

څنګه ژرنده هسې ئې دوړه.

796. *As the flour mill, so will be its flour.*

Actions bespeak the man.

["Like father, like son." *See* Proverbs 601 and 799. *RWS*]

څنګه حال دے؟ ویل ئې د دوؤ ښځو د خاوند نه مي بنۀ حال دے.

797.   *"How are you?" "I am still happier than the husband of two wives."*

This exchange refers to the individual who, though in trouble, is happier than the man with two quarreling wives.

[This is a two-part dialogue proverb. For examples of other "dialogue proverbs" and proverbs refering to multiple wives ("wives, multiple"), see the Index. *LNB*]

څنګه مخ هسې څپیړه.

798.   *As the face, so the slap.*

A man's appearance governs the treatment he receives.

څنګه میاندې هسې لُونه.

799.   *As the mother, so the daughters.*

This is analogous to [the old axioms, "Like mother, like daughter" and] "Like father, like son", [referring to the apparent continuity of family characteristics. *See* Proverbs 601 and 796. *LNB*]

څنګه نیت هسې مراد.

800.   *As your intentions, so your reward.*

"As you sow, so shall you reap." [*See* Proverbs 284 and 645.]

[The notion of "intention" (*niyat, niyyah*, vow, intention, purpose; cf. *irāda*, purpose or will) is important in Islamic spirituality. Every religious act, for example, prayers, fasting, the *Hajj* pilgrimage, must begin with the formulation of the proper intention, and works are judged according to the intentions. For mystics, the utterance of the *niyat* expresses an intention to turn away from everything created to enter into the awsome presence of the Divine.[40] *See* Proverbs 280, 1005 and 1148. *LNB*]

څوک چې تاته وُوائی چې غوږ دې سپي یوړو نو تهٔ به اول په سپي پسې
مندې وهي کهٔ په خپل غوږ به لاس ږدې؟

801. *If someone tells you a dog has carried away your ear, will you chase the animal or will you put your hand to your head [ear]?*

First verify, then believe.

څوک چې خدا ے شرموی د اوبښ د پاسه ئي سپي وُخوري.

802. *When God puts a man to shame, the dogs bite him even though he is on a camel's back.*

No man can escape defamation if it is God's will.

څوک چې ستا په مینه کښې ماته کړي پندونه. نهٔ د ے چا لیدلے اباسین په
لوئ بندونه.

803. *To him who advises me not to love you: Large dams cannot stop the Indus [Abasin].*

When strong emotions flow, nothing can stop them.

څوک چې کښنیوځي په خپله خُله کښنیوځي.

804. *It is one's own tongue which is risky.*

This is analogous to the popular saying, "Whenever you open your mouth, you put your foot into it."

[The meaning of the Pashto text is: whoever is caught, is caught by his own tongue (mouth). The image is of a bird being caught in or falling into a net. *RWS, LNB*]

[There are a number of variations of the "foot in mouth" idiom (meaning, to make a blunder or *faux pas*, to get into trouble), including the advice, "If you keep your mouth shut you will never put your foot in it." *See* Proverbs 499 and 1080; *see also* Proverbs 216 and 882, and Index entries for "tongue". *LNB*]

څوک حیران دي د خدا ے په کنجو، څوک حیران دي د رخت په کنډو.

805.   *Some worry about how to spend the bounties of God, others are concerned with patching their tattered clothes.*

Used as a complaint against the unequal distribution of wealth.

[Alternatively, "Some are puzzled or confused about …" *See* Proverb 808. *RWS*]

څوک دي په پینډه کښې کېوي که هسي لاس وینځي؟

806.   *Do they allow you to eat with them or are you washing your hands for nothing?*

People wash their hands before eating. The remark is addressed to one who wants to enter into a society that rejects him.

[For the sake of hygiene as well as courtesy, it is the Pashtun custom to wash hands before eating, inasmuch as Pashtuns often use their hands to eat out of a common plate as a token of friendship and intimacy. *LNB*]

څوک مۀ وهه په ګوته تا به نۀ وهي په لته.

807.   *Avoid beating a man with your finger and he will not kick you.*

If you don't threaten a man with harm, he will not take excessive revenge.

څوک وائي چې څۀ ئي کړم؟ څوک وائي چې څۀ وکړم؟

808. *Some say, "What shall I do with it?" Others say, "Where shall I find it?"*

The text points out the gulf between the "haves" and the "have-nots."

څوک ئې په کلي کښې نۀ پرېږدي او دے وائي زما اسباب د ملک کره کښېږده.

809. *They will not allow him to enter the village although he says, "Take my luggage to the home of the malək."*

This proverb is said of a man who claims an importance not acknowledged by the people.

[The man is not even allowed in the village, but wishes his luggage to be taken to the *malək's* house. A *malək* is the head of a village. *RWS, LNB*]

څومره چې خرګے وي. دومره ئې بارګے وي.

810. *As the donkey, so the load.*

Man is rewarded according to his ability; or, man shoulders responsibilities according to his abilty.

څومره چې خر وي نصیب ئې غر وي.

811. *Sometimes fools reach high positions.*

[Fate isn't bound by a person's cleverness or ability. *RWS*]

[Literally, the proverb refers to the donkey whose "fate" (*nasib*) enables it to climb mountains. *LNB*]

ٹومره چې دي پرونۍ وي هومره پښې غزوه.

812.   *Stretch your feet according to the length of the sheet.*

[*See* Proverb 814.]

ٹومره چې کوره اچوپ هومره شربت خوږېږي.

813.   *The more [raw] sugar you add to the syrup, the sweeter it becomes.*

shərbat is a cold drink, not a cola, made from fruit juices.

[*shərbat* is the name given to any sweet drink. Raw sugar (*guṛa*) is made from sugar cane grown in many parts of the North West Frontier Province. *RWS, LNB*]

ٹومره چې دي ٹادر دے دومره پښې غزوه.

814.   *Stretch your feet according to the length of your (chadar) sheet.*

The *chadar* is a sheet worn as a mantle by men. This text is similar to the proverb, "Cut your coat according to your cloth" (that is, the amount of cloth you have), [a proverb common in English, Dutch, Spanish and other languages; cf. the Assyrian proverb, "Stretch your legs according to your quilt." *LNB*]

[The *chadar* (or *tsādər*) is made of cotton or wool; it is worn in a different style by women. The meaning of the proverb is that one should do the best he or she can with the means or resources he / she has, and not overstretch one's bounds. *See* Proverb 812. *LNB*]

ٹومره خُلِې دومره خبرې.

815.   *Many tongues, many words.*

[Alternatively, "Too many mouths, so much talk." *See* variant proverb 1079. *RWS*]

خۀ به چتے وي او خۀ به د چتي بنوروا.

816. *How small a wren and how little its soup!*

This proverb is used sarcastically when a man of inferior quality attempts great deeds. That is, small people cannot achieve great objectives.

[The proverb refers to the low quality or standard of what is done by inconsequential people. *RWS*]

خۀ په کاسي کښې ئي راکوې په غلبيل کښې ئي راواچوه چې توئي شي.

817. *Why give it to me in a bowl; put it into a sieve so it will spill on the ground.*

[This sarcastic proverb refers] to the granting of a favor. The friend grants the favor only after persistent prodding.

خۀ چې خداے ته وي منظوره هغه کېږي.

818. *Whatever is God's will, will take place.*

God's will shall prevail.

خۀ خټکے خوږ وو او خۀ پرې باندې ترې ګد شول.

819. *On the one hand the melon itself was sweet, yet more sugar was sprinkled on it.*

This is said of a man of noble birth who, given the proper education, proves himself a worthy member of society.

څه دې کمے دے چې په ژرنده کښې دې کور دے؟

820. *What scarcity can you suffer when you live at the water mill?*

One should not complain of want if he has an abundance. Man is a slave of his environment. [*See* Proverbs 644 and 944.]

[This proverb is said about a person who has the benefit of natural advantages. *RWS*]

خۀ ژرنده پخۀ (ورانه) خۀ غنم لامدۀ.

821. *On the one hand the mill was defective, on the other the wheat was wet.*

Sometimes more than one defect causes failure, that is, troubles don't come alone.

[The notion is that troubles never come singly. It is not the fault of one thing alone; the other thing too, has something wrong with it. *See* Proverb 824. *RWS*]

خۀ شل او خۀ شل نيمي.

822. *Whether it be twenty or twenty-and-a-half (it is one and the same).*

A little difference is immaterial.

خۀ مې په هغه سپرلي چې نۀ مې غوا څري نۀ سخي.

823. *Why bother about the spring season in which neither my cows nor my calves will graze.*

We should be concerned with our own interests, not those of others. Of what use is a thing which does not benefit me.

[The proverb expresses indifference about another's concerns. *RWS*]

خه مئ راندۀ خه اوبۀ خړي.

824. *On the one hand the fish were blind and on the other the water was muddy.*

This proverb describes a man "on the horns of a dilemma." [*See* Proverb 821.]

خپۀ ورور راوړے خپۀ خور.

825.   *No difference between the child of a brother and that of a sister.*

حاجت بلا ده که ترې خبر شي. خۡای د تلو نۀ وي تۀ ورلۀ ورشي.

826. *Being in dire need is a great tragedy. A man of status, to whom others should come, may be forced by necessity to go to them.*

[This rhyming proverb may also be rendered: Need is a curse you may know, because it takes you to the place which is not worth approaching. *RWS*]

حاجیان دې خداے دروغژن نۀ کړي.

827. *May God not make* Hajjis *as liars.*

Hajjis are those who have completed the holy pilgrimage to Makkah. The proverb is used ironically to chide people who, while pretending piety, will still not refrain from lying.

حرام مال د هیچا نۀ هضمېږي.

828. *No one can devour [that which is] ill-gained .*

[The stolen or "ill-gained" goods (*māl*) are literally "*harām*", a religious term meaning "forbidden" or "illegal", the opposite of "*halāl*", "permitted" or "lawful". The term is also used, for example, with reference to unclean or forbidden foods in contrast with that which is permitted. *LNB*]

حصار ګیدړ د زمري سره هم جنګ کوي.

829. *A cornered jackal will fight even a lion when surrounded.*

[This is similar to the English proverb,] "Even a worm will turn" [and its variants, "Step on a worm and it is sure to turn," "The trampled worm will turn." *LNB*]

[Alternatively, "A surrounded jackal will fight even a lion." Even the scrawny jackal if cornered or surrounded by powerful lions will "turn" (that is, change its normal character) and stand and fight rather than run away. *RWS*]

حکم چند چي ليبي نۀ کوي تيارۀ ده!

830. *When Hukam Chand (a Hindu) does not want to play, he says, "It is dark."*

This proverb is said of a person who always makes lame excuses.

حکومت سره حکمت پکار دے.

831. *To rule requires wisdom.*

Rulers need wisdom.

حلال کړے چرګ دے که د سپي په خوله کښې ئې ورکړې نو يو به ئې سي.

832. *He is like a slaughtered chicken which even a timid dog will carry away.*

This proverb is said of a good-hearted person of whom even the timid man will take advantage.

حيله کوه زما برخه خوړه کوه.

833. *Be economical with others but make my share large.*

خاموشي نيمه رضا ده.

834. *Silence is half consent.*

[*See* Proverb 835; cf. Index entries for "tongue", "mouth"]

خاموشي لوئے كمال دے.

835. *Silence is a very good quality.*

"Silence is golden."

[There are a number of international proverbs and witty quotations about the the virtues and consequences of silence and the dangers of the tongue. King Solomon (*Bacha Suliman*) wryly observed, "Even a fool is thought wise if he keeps silent, and discerning if he holds his tongue."[41] The English economist and journalist Walter Bagehot (1826-1877) remarked, "An inability to stay quiet is one of the most conspicuous failings of mankind." It is sometimes wiser to be silent than to speak, as in the proverb, well-known in many languages, "Speech is silver, silence is golden." *See* Proverb 1165; cf. Proverbs 647 and 1088. *LNB*]

خان خفه بي بي خوشحاله.

836. *The Khan is angry, his wife is happy.*

This proverb refers to an extravagant woman who, in defiance of her husband, spends lavishly.

خان ستا د خبره می توبه شه خو دا سپي دي را نه کوري کړه.

837. *Oh Khan, to hell with your charity, please call off your dogs.*

I don't want help, but please do not give me trouble.

خان ورک شو چونگ ملک شو.

838. *The Khan has passed away, and the "Chung" has become chief.*

When there is a shortage of leaders, the menials replace them.

[Although *chung* is used here as a person's name, it literally means a "handful," that is, a "handful" of lesser people. *LNB*]

خانان به بیا سره خانان وي په مېنځ کښی توئی شول نوکران ئی زېر ګلونه.

839. *The Khans will always remain together as Khans, but along the way the servants are scattered like yellow flowers.*

The chiefs reunite while the menials suffer.

[This saying in the form of a *tappa* (folk poem) says that Khans will become friends with each other, but the poor servants, whose youth is likened to yellow flowers, perish in the feud. *RWS*]

خانده خانده، بنهٔ کور دي وړے دے.

840. *Go on laughing, you have won the game.*

خاوره د سخر د نغري نه اخیستے کیږي.

841. *Ashes are brought from the home of the father-in-law.*

This refers to the re-moulding of the bride's way of life when she has joined a new family.

[*khāwra*, "ashes", is also used to refer to earth in various forms, including the clay used to build houses. *See* Proverb 842. *LNB*]

خاوره د لوئي خاور گاړي نه اخله.

842. *Take your clay from a large clay-pit.*

If you make a request, it should be made to a generous, large hearted person.

[Clay is used for making pots, bricks, etc. In Proverbs 841 to 846, the term *khāwra* can be translated earth, dirt, dust, clay or ashes. *LNB*]

خاوری په سر ابرې په توپل.

843. *When you jump into the ashes, the dust will fall upon your head.*

[The proverb connotes] disappointment on all sides, or being in a very miserable condition.

[The term *topal* can refer to a cap or the top of the head or turban. Thus the saying can be translated literally, "Dust (or clay) on the head and ashes on the turban." *RWS, LNB*]

خاورې د لوئې ډېران اخله.

844. *If you wish to take manure, take it from a large dunghill.*

If you make a request, always ask of those with generous hearts. [*See* Proverb 842.]

خاورې راغلې ابرو له ايرې باد يوړې.

845. *The dust came to take refuge with the ashes and the ashes were carried away by the wind.*

This proverb is said of a weak man who takes refuge with an even weaker person weighed down by his own troubles.

خاورې يو خاورې به شو.

846.   *We are made of earth and we will become earth.*

Reminiscent of the Christian saying, "Dust thou art, and unto dust thou shalt return."[42]

[Death is the common lot of all mankind, as this Pashto proverb about the finality of life affirms. Cf. the now proverbial phrase from the English burial (funeral) service, "We therefore commit his body to the ground; earth to earth; ashes to ashes; dust to dust ..."[43] *LNB*]

خاوند نوم د خدا ے د ے.

847.   *"Khāwand" (Lord) is a name for God.*

This proverb shows the veneration the husband receives from his wife.

[*khāwand* can mean "master", "Lord", "owner" or "husband". *RWS*]

خبره تر خبرې پورې يادېږي.

848.   *One word brings another to mind.*

One action recalls another.

خبره چې "افغانۍ" کوي نۀ ئې پلار کوي نۀ ئې ادۍ کوي.

849.   *That which "Afghani" says was never said by his mother or father.*

This is said concerning someone whose statements are not in accord with family traditions. Or alternatively, he who talks in Persian differs from his Pashtun parents.

[The saying may also be about the Afghan who doesn't care about his relations, whose actions are not just or proper. *RWS*]

خبره د خدای د پاره د پاره کوټک د ورور عزیز د پاره.

850.   *A word for the sake of God, a stick for the sake of your relatives.*

   When asked about justice one should speak the truth, but when
one's relatives are embroiled in dispute, he should take up arms in
their cause, whether the action be right or wrong.

خبره زده کړه بیا ئي وکړه.

851.   *First learn then talk.*

خبره لږه، عمل ډېر.

852.   *Fewer words, more action.*
   "More matter, with less art."[44]

خبره ئي د اوبو تیږه ده.

853.   *His word is like a rock in water.*

   That is, "His word is his bond".

[That is, a man's word is as clear as a clean rock in water. There is no
ambiguity with it. The well-known English proverb cited by Tair and
Edwards appears in many forms and in a number of languages, for
example "My word is my bond"; "An Englishman's (or "an honest
man's", or "a gentleman's") word is his bond". In the field of law, a
"bond" is a legal document obliging one person to pay money to
another; in this proverb it refers to a solemn promise—based on one's
word alone—that a pledge will honored no matter what the cost. *See*
Proverbs 1 and 387. *LNB, RWS*]

خبرې ښې کوي لکی ئې کږې کوي.

854. *His words are fine but their tails are bent.*

His words are just, but his conclusions are bad, [that is, their intent or ends are twisted. *RWS*]

خبرې ډېرې سر ئې يو.

855. *Many discussions, one conclusion.*

[When a debate is long and words are many, a person wants to get to the conclusion quickly. *RWS*]

خپل به آزار شي بېزار کېږي نه.

856. *One's own kith and kin [relatives] may suffer persecution but will not get fed up with one another.*

[Relatives or kinsmen (*khpəl*) stick together in times of trouble. *LNB*]

خپل به دې وژروي پردے به دې وُخندوي.

857. *Your relatives will make you weep (for your faults) while a stranger will made you laugh.*

[In a variant form, this is also said of a true friend (*dost*) compared to an enemy (*dukhman, dushman*): "A friend makes you weep, an enemy makes you laugh," that is, a relative or friend will tell you the truth. Here the comparison is between a relative (*khpəl*) and a stranger (*praday*). See Proverbs 215, 862 and 1298. *LNB*]

خپل به سره خپل شي د چغلخور په خُله به غل شي.

858. *Those who are relatives will remain united, and the backbiter's mouth will be filled with excreta.*

The scandalmonger cannot disgrace a member of a close family. Cf. the proverb, "Blood is thicker than water." [*See* Proverbs 182 and 875.]

خپل په برغولي کښې هم ښۀ وي.

859.   *One's own food, even when served on the lid of the cooking pot [is better].*

A family always prefers its own meals to those cooked by others.

[This is not merely a matter of taste, but of economic and familial autonomy so important to Pashtun pride and honor. *LNB*]

خپل په خُلې خوري او د بل په سترګو خوري.

860.   *His own he eats with his mouth, that of another he devours with his eyes.*

This proverb is applied to the miser who enjoys his own possessions without sharing them, while gazing covetously at the possessions of others.

خپل ځان ساتلے ښۀ دے بل ته مۀ وايه چي غل ئي.

861.   *Protect your own belongings and do not call another a thief.*

[Self-protection is better than blaming others, justly or unjustly, for one's own lack of vigilance. *RWS*]

خپل خپل پردے پردے.

862.   *A relative is a relative, and a stranger is a stranger.*

[There is no comparison between a relative and a non-relative. There is a clear distinction between them. *RWS*]

خپل خپل دي پردي مغل دي.

863. *Relatives are relatives and strangers Mughals.*

"Mughal" here refers to the descendants of the Turkish invaders who ruled India from A.D. 1526 to 1857. Some Pakhtun tribes remained at war with them throughout their rule.

[The term "Mughal" in Pashto is also used as a metaphor for an enemy. *RWS*]

خپل خر ترلے بنهٔ دے که غل اشنا وي هم.

864. *Even if a thief is one's friend, one should tie his own donkey.*

Make friends with everyone, but trust no one.

خپل دا په نس د بل دا په وس.

865. *Things done for yourself are close to your heart; things for others you do only if you can.*

[The word translated "heart" (*nas*) is the Pashto word for "stomach". *RWS*]

خپل دا مي خپله کړي د بل دا مي هم خپله کړي.

866. *That which is mine must come to me; that which is another's should also come to me.*

This proverb is said of a selfish and greedy person.

[A way of saying, "What is mine is mine, what is yours is also mine." *LNB*]

خپل دې که مړ کړي سويري ته به دې واچوي.

867. *If your own kin kills you, at least he will put you in the shade.*

If your relatives kill you, at least they will not disgrace you.

خپل دې هغه دے چي صبا بېگا ئي مخ ويني.

868. *That person is your comrade whose face you see every morning and evening.*

The one who is very fond of you is just like a relative.

خپل سر په خپله نهٔ خرئيل کېږي.

869. *One cannot shave his own head.*

This expression is ironic. No one can live to himself. It is also a way of saying, sometimes you need others' help for a job.

[Alternatively, it can also mean "one cannot see his own faults." *RWS*]

خپل عزت په خپل لاس کښې دے.

870. *One's honor is in his own hand.*

By his attitude a man earns honor or disgrace.

خپل عقل او پردے دولت هر چاته ډېر ښکاري.

871. *One's own wisdom and another man's wealth appear very good to everyone.*

"The grass looks greener in the next field". [*See* note to Proverb 567.]

[While one considers his own wisdom to be sufficient (a man is always wise in his own eyes), the other man's wealth always seems to be a lot compared with one's own. *LNB*]

خپل عمل د لارې مل دے.

872. *A man's actions are his companions.*

A man cannot escape the consequences of his actions, [and they accompany him like a friend (*mal*) on the road of life. *LNB*]

خپل کور یا خپل گور.

873. *For a woman either the home or the grave.*

Home is the best place for a woman.

[There is no explicit mention of "woman" in the Pashto text; the choice is between "one's own house or one's own grave." A commmon variant proverb applies this explicitly to women, which is the understanding of the translation above. *RWS, LNB*]

[The proverbs of most nations tend toward a misogynous (negative or hateful) view of women. Many Pashto proverbs express a male ideology and understanding of appropriate female behavior. Proverb content and use may serve to construct and maintain the gender culture of a society. In the case of the Pashtun, such proverbs (along with *Hadith* and explicitly religious texts and understandings), reinforce the traditional role of women in relation to men. The seclusion and protection of women (*pərdah*) is an aspect of the honorable organization of domestic life and an integral element of *pakhtunwali*. Applied more generally, this proverb suggests that if a man cannot possess his own home, it is better to be in his own grave. *See* Proverb 1168 and Index entries for "woman, women". *LNB*]

خپل گور هر چاته تنگ لیدۀ شي.

874. *Everyone considers his grave to be narrow.*

Each one fears the troubles and agonies of death.

خپل نۀ پردي کیږي.

875. *One's kin can never become a stranger.*

However unpleasant the attitude of one's kinsmen, they can never turn into strangers. "Blood is thicker than water." [*See* Proverbs 182 and 858.]

خپل وطن هر چا ته کشمير دے.

876. *To each one his own country is Kashmir.*

Everyone admires his homeland.

[One's native land or country is likened to the Shangri La paradise of Kashmir, with its beautiful snow-capped peaks east of Pashtun homelands. *See* Proverb 445. *LNB*]

"خپل" هغه دے چي په تنګسيا کښې دي پکار راشي.

877. *A true comrade is one who comes to your aid in time of trouble.*

"A friend in need [that is, a friend who helps when one is in need] is a friend indeed."

[As Tair and Edwards note, the Pashto saying is similar to the English proverb about the character of true friendship. Both texts are close to the ancient Latin saying, "A sure friend is made known when (one is) in difficulty" or "... is known in unsure times."[45] *See* Proverbs 911 and 1173. *LNB*]

خپلو شوملو ته څوک تروې نۀ وائي.

878. *No one calls his [own] whey sour.*

We are all loath to acknowledge our own weaknesses. Everyone admires his own objects, no matter how defective.

خپله برخه آسمان نۀ ويني.

879.   *He cannot see his own portion of the sky.*

This proverb refers to one who, though without property or status, is still very proud.

خپله برخه آسمان نۀ لري.

880.   *A portion of the sky does not even exist for him.*

This differs from the previous proverb in that it is said of a very poor man.

خپله پيره لاس راکړه.

881.   *"Oh my* pir, *give me your hand."*

This is spoken by someone in distress. A *pir* is a holy man or mystic. [*See* Proverbs 142, 459 and 461, and Index entries for "Saint (*pir*)", "holy man".]

خپله خُله هم قلا ده هم بلا ده.

882.   *One's own tongue is a fort as well as a calamity.*

You can use your tongue both for good and bad purposes.

Your tongue may save you from danger, but it may also endanger you.

خپله ډنگوي د بل نۀ آوري.

883.   *He beats his own drum so hard that he fails to hear that of another.*

This proverb is said of the extreme egotist who refuses [or doesn't care to hear] advice from others.

خپله دوډۍ په پردي شکارۀ کېنې ده.

884. *One man's bread in another man's basket.*

This is a complaint offered by the true owner of a possession or property claimed by another.

خپله غوايۀ په لوړه خبـژه چي څوک څۀ رنگ کړي هغسې تۀ کړه.

885. *"Oh my bullock, climb a hillock! Of what the others do, take stock."*

This proverb is addressed to an inexperienced and undisciplined person about to perform a particular task. He is advised to observe from a vantage point and follow in the steps of the experienced.

[Alternatively, "Oh my bullock, climb to a height and see what others do—then you do that too." The proverb also suggests something like, "When in Rome, do as the Romans do." *See* Proverbs 89, 631 and 1255. *RWS*]

خپله غوبنه وڅکونده د بل دا هم دغه شان خوربـژي.

886. *Pinch your own flesh, that is how it will hurt others.*

An echo of "The Golden Rule" principle. [*See* Proverb 302 and Index for proverbs on "Friendship". *LNB*]

خپله کوره ګله کوره!

887. *"Oh my home! How like a flower you are!"*

[One's own home is better than all others. *RWS*]

خپله لاسه ګله لاسه.

888. *"Oh my hand, you are flower-like."*

The hand is a man's most trusted companion. Whatever is done with one's own hand is preferable.

[Whatever you do yourself, with your own hands, is preferred over and is more satisfying than something done by others. The proverb has a similar structure to Proverb 887. *RWS, LNB*]

خپلې خُلّي وهلي شپاړس.

889.   *Their mouths have destroyed sixteen people.*

Careless talk can destroy many people.

[This reminds one of the saying, "Careless talk costs lives," first used on posters in World War I as an admonition against talking too freely in a time of war, lest a spy was listening who could gain information that would cost lives. A similar American saying was popular during World War II, "Loose lips sink ships." In Pashtun culture, where men live and die for honor, lies, gossip and malicious rumors can destroy reputations, and lead to unending and costly blood feuds. *LNB*]

خټک به زړېدو نۀ کۀ د بل غمونه ئي نۀ کولٍ.

890.   *The Khattak would never have become old had he not been worrying about the problems of others.*

The Khattak, brooding over the problems of others, destoys his own health.

[The Khattak tribe is famous among the Pashtun for their kindheartedness. *RWS*]

خداے او مړو سره و پېژاندهٔ.

891.   *God and the dead have recognized one another.*

The proverb refers to man's meeting with his Maker after death, when he must face God's righteous judgment.

[This saying points to matters that two individuals or groups understand between themselves. *RWS*]

خدائے باچا ئي راكوي شيخ مير ئي نهٔ را كوي.

892.   *It is Almighty God who is giving it to me and not Sheikh Mir.*

    An ironic proverb stressing man's misuse of power. The use of "Sheikh Mir" is an indefinite but powerful referent, as several leaders named Mir appear in Pakhtun history. The meaning is that the real bestower [of power, etc.] is God and not some pious man.

[The sense is, why should one fear men, when he knows that the true Giver is God, not men. *RWS*]

خدائے به وي ياران به نهٔ وي.

893.   *God will always remain while friends will perish.*

خدائے په رښتيا خوښيږي.

894.   *Truth pleases God.*

خدائے چا ليدلی نهٔ دے ولې په قدرتونو ئي پيژني.

895.   *Who has ever seen God? He is known only by His performance (skill).*

[Alternatively, "No one has ever seen God. He can be known by His might, providence or power." *RWS*]

خدائے چې مهربان شي نو بنده نهٔ دے چې پښيمان شي.

896.   *When God bestows His gifts He, unlike man, has no reason to repent.*

خداے چې مهرِي ته په قهر شي نو وزرې ورکړي.

897. *When God becomes angry with the ant, He gives it wings.*

This is a jibe at those who attempt things beyond their reach.

خداے خبر دے چې ترۀ کافر دے.

898. *God knows that the uncle is an infidel.*

Uncles are in certain cases said to be unfriendly.

خداے د حق ملگري دے.

899. *God is on the side of truth.*

[Literally, "God is the friend of truth" (*See* Proverb 894). This is one of a number of proverbs in the form, "God is (is not) a friend of ..." *See* Proverbs 900, 901. *LNB*]

خداے د صبرناکو مل دے.

900. *God is the companion of tranquility.*

[Literally, "God is the companion (or friend) of patience." *RWS*]

خداے د ناروا مل نۀ دے.

901. *God does not defend the unlawful.*

[Literally, "God is not the companion (or friend) of the unlawful." *RWS*]

خدائ دي هيخوک داسي نهٔ کا چي خپله درنه کا د بل سپکه.

902.   *May God create no one of the type who makes his weight heavy and that of another's light.*

That is, May God not make a person who boasts about himself and disparages another.

[A person who is important or significant is referred to as "heavy" or "weighty" (*drund*). A self-important person exalts himself at the expense of another, whom he disdains and dishonors as "light" or insignificant (*spək*). LNB]

خدائ شړلے نهٔ سمبږي.

903.   *Those whom God has made outcasts will never mend their ways.*

[The reference is not to caste but to the incorrigible, whom God casts out. To be cast out (*sharəl*) of a village for example, is a form of punishment imposed by a council (*jirga*) on habitual offenders. LNB]

خدائ مړي ژوندي کوﻟے شي خو عادت ئي نهٔ دے.

904.   *God can bring to life a dead body but this is not His habit.*

خدائ مل کړه کار په چل کړه.

905.   *Make God your companion and use your head.*

The sense is as in the English proverb, "God helps those who help themselves."

[Literally, "Make God your companion and start your work." The advice is to learn or adopt the skill to do a job properly. Though in a class of common Western sayings attributed to the Bible but not actually contained in it, the English proverb, "God helps those who help themselves" is in fact a piece of folk theology that appears in many cultures, sometimes used to justify one's efforts to aquire or attain some personal end. *See* Proverbs 650 and 905. LNB, RWS]

خدائے وائی تۀ حرکت کوه زۀ به پکښنۍ برکت واچوم.

906. *God says, "Strive and I will bless."*

[Those who act, who make an effort (*harakat*), are blessed (*barakat*) by God in their doing. In this variant of Proverb 301, this proverbial wisdom is ascribed to God Himself, who pledges to release His blessing on our efforts. *LNB*]

خدایه پاکه دومره دۍ خوار کړو چې د غواؤ غوړو ته دۍ کښینوؤلو.

907. *Oh God! You brought me [him] to such poverty that I am [he is] forced to use cow's butter.*

This is an ironic comment on the stupidity of anyone who speaks disparagingly of a good thing.

[Cow butter is a luxury. The use of the third person ("him ... he is") in the gloss is an alternate translation. *LNB, RWS*]

خدایه! تل به تۀ ئې.

908. *Oh God! You are eternal.*

خدایه! تۀ داسې مۀ شې لکه بنده.

909. *Oh God! Be not like a man.*

خدایه! دوستی مې د سیاله سره کړې.

910. *Oh God! Let me be a friend of my equals.*

[Literally, "Let my friendship be with my equal." *RWS*]

[A Pashtun prefers friendship, marriage and even enmity, with one (or with a family) who is his equal in status, resources and power. *LNB*]

خدایه! دومره تنګسیا راولې چي دوست او دښمن و پیژنم.

911. *Oh God! Visit upon me such tribulation that I may distinguish friend from foe.*

It is in times of need and trouble that a man knows who is his friend or foe. [*See* Proverb 877.]

خدایه هر چا ته روزي ورکوې خو د ټوخي نه بغیر نه.

912. *God gives everyone the necessities of life but not without at least a cough.*

This is a reminder to man that he must work for a living.

[The reference is to a person who has performed a service for another and "coughs" to hint at payment or a gratuity. One needs to make some effort and not presume upon God. *LNB*]

خدای ئي در وُښنایه در ئي مهٔ کړه.

913. *May God show it to you, but may He not give it to you.*

This is an ambivalent aphorism used as both a prayer and a curse.

خدای یو دے روزي ئي ډېرې دي.

914. *God is one, but His ways are many.*

[That is, "His blessings or provisions (literally, *rozi*, "daily bread") are many." *RWS*]

[The proverb contains two contrasts: God:one::blessings:many. The unity or oneness of Almighty God is foundational in the Islamic, Christian and Jewish faiths. "God is One" is taught by all the prophets; for example, Moses (*Musa*) says, "The Lord our God is one Lord."[46] Out of His majestic oneness many wondrous blessings flow. *LNB*]

خدایه! زور راکړې کبر را مه کړې.

915. *Oh God! Give me strength but not pride.*

[This is one of a number of proverbs in the structure of an invocation or prayer, "Oh God! ..." *See* Proverbs 916-923. *LNB*]

خدایه! بنادي را کړې د خپل نغري را کړې.

916. *Oh God! Give me joy, the joy of my own hearth.*

خدایه! شکر دے چې د کلال خر دې نۀ یم پیدا کړے.

917. *Thank God that You have not created me the donkey of the potter.*

This is used when a person is shocked by the tyrannical treatment of servants. The potter's donkey is the most degraded of animals.

خدایه! بنۀ مې کړې د بنۀ پلار زوئ مې کړې.

918. *Oh God! Make me good; make me the worthy son of a good father.*

خدایه! صبر د سپي راکړې خوئی د سړي راکړې.

919. *Oh God! Give me the patience of a dog and the character of a man.*

خدایه! ګنجي ته نوکونه ورمۀ کړې.

920. *Oh God! Do not give nails to the scurvy-headed man.*

This proverb is said of a man of low status who, upon attaining power, misuses it.

[The Pashto word translated "scurvy-headed" literally means "bald". The allusion is to a man scratching his bald head with his "fingernails". *See* Proverb 225. *LNB*]

خدايه! لوئ مي کړې لوئي را مهٔ کړې.

921.   *Oh God! Make me great but spare me from arrogance.*

خدايه لويه! ما وساتې له بده زويه.

922.   *Oh Great Almighty God! Protect me from a bad son.*

خدايه! يو خرگے يو تبرگے را کړې نور د دوزئی نه مي خلاص ئي.

923.   *Oh God! Give me only a donkey and an axe and do not concern yourself further about my livelihood.*

This proverb is attributed to the Khattaks, a hardy people who can endure great hardships and earn their living with small means.

خدمت عظمت دے.

924.   *Service is greatness.*

[Those who are greatest are those who serve. The virtue of service affirmed in this proverb has been extolled by philosophers, writers and poets of East and West. "The greatest virtues are those which are most useful to other persons" (Aristotle); "The sole meaning of life is to serve humanity" (Leo Tolstoy); "The most acceptable service to God is doing good to man" (Anonymous). The notion of humble, selfless service was also crucial in the non-violent Khudai Khidmatgar ("servants of God") nationalist movement (1930-1947) founded by Khan Abdul Ghaffar Khan ("Badshah Khan", 1890-1988). That there is "greatness" (*azmat*) in even the smallest acts of service (*khidmat*) is eloquently expressed in the words of the poet Emily Dickenson, "If I can stop one heart from breaking, I shall not

live in vain; If I can ease one life in the aching, Or cool one pain, Or help one fainting robin up to his nest again, I shall not live in vain."
LNB]

خر ابا کړه کار پرې تېر کړه.

925.   *To serve your own purpose you may call even a donkey your father.*

خر ته دي خدائے ښکر نۀ ورکوي.

926.   *May God not give horns to a donkey.*

May God not give power to the unscrupulous or foolish person.

خر چې تر مکې لاړ شي هغه خر دے.

927.   *Although a donkey goes to Makkah, he is still a donkey.*

A fool will always remain a fool no matter if he visits a holy place.

[Alternatively, "If a donkey goes ..." His character remains unchanged. *RWS, LNB*]

خر چې د خرۀ نه کم وي غوږ ئې د پرېکولو دے.

928.   *If a donkey does not behave as a donkey should, his ears should be cut off.*

A man should choose an equal as his rival. If he does not, he should be punished.

[If a donkey's qualities are less than another donkey's, he deserves to have his ears cut off. *RWS*]

[An alternative interpretation suggests that "if one donkey is inferior to another," it is the superior rival who should be cut down to size. *LNB*]

خر چې لټ شي خپله کټه هم نۀ وړي.

929. When a donkey grows stubborn it will not even carry its own pannier.

This is used to upbraid and scold a stubborn person who refuses to budge when pressed.

خر خان ته اريان دے مالک ئي بار ته.

930. *The poor donkey is worried about himself and the master is worried about the load.*

This proverb is said of a servant who, though too ill to work, is ordered by his master to do so.

خر د باره سره خوري.

931. *He wants to gobble-up both the donkey and its load.*

This proverb is said of the greedy person who strives to possess everything.

خر د خويد په خوراک څۀ پوهيږي.

932. *What does the donkey know about the eating of green fodder (grass).*

A fool cannot appreciate the value of a good thing.

[The word for "green fodder" is *khwid*, literally, "green barley"—a luxury a donkey rarely sees. *LNB*]

خر د فقير مړ شو او وران پرې د کلي سپي شول.

933. *It was the* faqir's *donkey that died, but the dispute arose among the dogs of the village.*

This is spoken when someone's losses become a bone of contention among his rivals.

[The *faqir* is a beggar whose meager possession (a dead donkey) is fought over by the village dogs. *LNB*]

خر ښکر غواړي او پيشو وزر غواړي.

934. *The donkey wants horns, the cat wants wings.*

This proverb is said of unscrupulous people who grasp and misuse power.

خر غيرت کړے وو نو لارۍ ووهو.

935. *The donkey stood his ground and was killed by the bus.*

This proverb is said of the foolish person who takes unnecessary risks.

[The proverb says literally that "The donkey acted with *ghayrat* ..." and paid the consequences. *ghayrat*, a core value in Pashtun culture, refers to a combination of zeal, courage, honor, pride, autonomy and self-definition. The proverb, then, is a warning about the price of stubbornly "doing *pakhto*", for example, acting aggressively or taking revenge. *See* Proverb 341 *LNB*]

خر مۀ تړه د سرو ريبنمو په پړي، اصل ئي کم اصل دے په خاورو کښې به رغړي.

936. *Do not tie your donkey with a silken red rope, it is of ill-bred stock and will roll in the dust.*

Do not attribute dignity to a lowborn person, because sooner or later he will disgrace himself [and abuse the privilege].

خر مې شه خر به مې شه شی تر یو ځایه را سره هم شه!

937. *Be my donkey, be my donkey driver, also come along the way with me!*

This proverb is said of the selfish man who wishes to shift his entire burden on to another's shoulders.

[This is spoken about one who takes advantage of a friend or other persons. *RWS*]

خر نۀ دے قچر دے پرې پورې د خرۀ سر دے.

938. *It is a mule rather than a donkey, but on its shoulders lies the head of a donkey.*

This proverb refers to a well-born person who has failed to uphold the family's honor.

خر نۀ منجبړي موړے منجبړي.

939. *The donkey is not prancing, but its peg has begun to jump [prance].*

This is used when two persons of equal rank, about to settle a discussion amicably, are joined by a third person of lower degree. The newcomer takes sides and soon foments a quarrel. It is not the donkey that prances but the peg helps him do so.

[Generally, donkeys do not prance, but the peg (a short wooden stick) helps him to do so. *LNB*]

خر هغه دے خُل ئې بدل دے.

940. *The donkey is the same, but it carries a different pannier.*

This proverb is said of someone who, having changed positions and his way of life, appears to be a different person, although in fact he is unchanged.

[That is, the changes are only outward; the donkey has merely "exchanged" (literally, *badal*) his load. *See* Proverb 247. *RWS, LNB*]

خر ئي په رشي پوري وُترلو نو ورته وائي چې مهٔ خوره.

941. *They tied the donkey beside a heap of corn and told him not to eat it.*

This proverb is used when someone is ordered to do something contrary to his nature. It is similar to the proverb, "Hang your clothes on the tree but don't go near the water" and shows how difficult it is to prevent a man from doing what is in his nature.

[Tair and Edwards here quote a Mother Goose English nursery rhyme for children: "Mother, may I go out to swim?" "Yes, my darling daughter. Hang your clothes on an alder limb, And don't go near the water." (In European folklore, alder trees were considered a charm against evil spirits that inhabited lakes and ponds.) The English saying is a kind of warning, whereas the Pashto proverb is a comment on human nature, that is, a donkey will invariably eat the nearby corn (like the cat in Proverb 475 who will eat the meat or fish he is asked to "guard"). *LNB*]

خرارہ یوہ سوته کني او بلي ته سترګي وهي.

942. *The lark scratches one dung pat but keeps its eye on another one.*

This proverb is said of a greedy and cunning man.

خرارې د واره سره لاړې.

943. *Oh lark, you were done away with one stroke.*

This is said of one who enters into competition but then does not participate.

The meaning is that a weak person quickly succumbs even to a minor trouble.

[This proverb can also be said of one who is quickly eliminated from a competition. *RWS*]

خربوزه د خربوزی نه رنگ اخلي.

944. *The musk melon derives its color from another [musk] melon.*

That is, man is a slave of his environment. [*See* Proverbs 644 and 820.]

خرما او ثواب دواړه.

945. *Dates and spiritual rewards go together.*

This proverb is used to express the idea of "killing two birds with one stone."

[The term *sawāb* refers to the reward or benefit one receives from God for good deeds and following the pattern of the Prophet, for example, breaking the fast by eating dates, thus the two go together (*see* Proverbs 291 and 489). *LNB*]

خرو ته ګوره په ډيران شپو ته ګوره.

946. *Look at the donkeys and see how they pass their nights on the rubbish heap.*

A person who cannot protect himself should not spend his time in a place that is open to all hazards.

خرو سره کښېنه خر به شې ښو سره کښېنه ښۀ به شې.

947. *Sit with donkeys and you become a donkey. Sit with good people and you become good.*

Good company is far better than bad.

[Society molds a man and "Bad company corrupts good morals." *RWS, LNB*]

خرو سره تيرسري خوند نۀ کوي.

948. *A headstall [bridle] does not look nice on a donkey.*

An ugly face cannot be made beautiful with ornaments.

[Ornamental bridles or halters are for horses, not donkeys. *RWS*]

خروار د موټي نه معلومېږي.

949. *A heap is distinguishable [known] by a handful.*

One handful of corn reveals the quality of the entire heap.

The proverb also has a political application: a nation is judged by the few.

خرۀ دې شړه چي خښنۀ ونۀ کړي.

950. *You should drive away your donkeys so that they do not foul the place.*

This is an expression of contempt applied to one whose behavior and speech are unworthy of his station in society.

خرۀ کا په هرې چولۍ ناره کا.

951. *Keep donkeys and go around shouting about them in every home and every desolate place.*

Keep the company of fools and be a nuisance and in constant trouble.

[Donkeys cause trouble by braying in every street. The foolish person exposes himself everywhere by talking. *RWS*]

خرهٔ کله کا بیا کیله کا.

952.   *First round up the donkeys, then complain.*

Duties first, then demands.

خرهٔ لِپژده لعنت پرِپژده!

953.   *Load the ass and don't keep on cursing him.*

Do your own job instead of cursing others.

خره ورسک دِي سپين شو او د خُبنتن کور دِي وُ نهٔ پیژاندهٔ.

954.   *Oh donkey, (the hair on) your forehead has become white and still you are unable to recognize your master's home.*

This proverb is said of an old and experienced fool who does not recognize his destination.

[Alternatively, it is said of the person who does not learn lessons despite a long span of life. *RWS*]

خرهٔ همپشه په بی طمعِي خائے کپنپي ولاړ وي.

955.   *Donkeys are always found standing in unexpected places.*

Fools will be found where others fear to tread. [Cf. Proverb 539.]

[This is said of a person who is not found in the proper place at a time of need. *RWS*]

خرِي ته چا یی مخِي وُوِي په وله ئي خرِي اوبهٔ نهٔ خُپنلِي.

956.   *Someone described a she-ass as beautiful and it stopped drinking muddy water from the stream.*

A fool when flattered only brags about it.

[This is about the misconception of a person who, when praised, forgets his real position or status. RWS]

خرې ته ئې وئيل زوے دې وُشو! وئيل ئې څۀ ئې كوم خپل بار به وړي خپل به وړم.

957. *They said to the donkey, "A child [son] has been born to you!" It replied "Why should I care for him. He will carry his own load, and I will still carry mine."*

A poor man's children will not release him from the burden of life.

[This is a two-part dialogue proverb with a common "statement and reply" structure: "To the donkey they said, …" and "He replied, …" For examples of other "dialogue proverbs" see the Index. LNB]

خرې موږې خوږې موږې!

958. *Oh ass my mother, you are my darling!*

A mother will say this ironically about herself when she knows that her sons love her only when they want something of her.

[Though one's mother may be a simpleton ("Oh mother like an ass"), she is nonetheless dear to him. RWS]

خر سپے د ګيدړ ورور وي.

959. *The gray dog is the brother of the jackal.*

This proverb is said of someone who, despite outward differences, resembles others in his habits.

خره مرغۍ ټوله خراړه ده.

960. *Every gray bird is a lark.*

Those with the same characteristics should be treated alike.

خرے چي غُريږي څه به ئي ليدلي وي.

961. When *Khaṛe (a gray dog) growls, it will certainly have seen something.*

The proverb suggests the need to be alert, because the dog's growl is a sign of some danger.

[*Khaṛe* is the name given to a dog (not mentioned literally) in this proverb and also describes its coloring: *khaṛ* is the gray-brown color of earth. *LNB*]

خس کم مۀ ګڼه په سترګو کښې به دې پريوځي.

962. *Don't belittle a straw; it may fall into your eyes.*

Don't look down on or disregard an insignificant person, as he may some day prove to be a source of trouble to you.

خشاک مي خشاک وُسو او سبو مي خوټ وُ نۀ خوړ.

963. *The fuel has all been burnt and my spinach has not even boiled.*

[The proverb refers to the uselessness of one's struggle. *RWS*]

خلق ژاړي خو پيغله خاندي.

964. *The people weep, the damsel laughs.*

This is indicative of the carefree attitudes of maidens or youths.

خَلق لېوني پورې خندېدل لېونۍ په خلقو پورې.

965. *The people were laughing at the madman, while he was laughing at the people.*

Sanity is relative.

خُله خوري سترګي شرمېږي.

966.   *The mouth eats and the eyes are directed to the ground.*

This proverb is said of the person who, having become obligated to another, cannot hold his head high because of his debt, [and looks down to the ground in embarrassment or shame (*sharmigi*). RWS]

خُلۀ دي نۀ دو وربا خُلۀ دو.

967.   *That's not a mouth—it's more like the opening of a trouser leg.*

This proverb is said of one whose mouth is always emitting nonsense.

خُله ئي په اوګره سوي وه او زبېرګي ئي د خُنکدن کاوۀ.

968.   *While the porridge burned his tongue, he pretended to be in the throes of death.*

This proverb is said of someone who makes "much ado about nothing", or "makes a mountain out of a molehill."

[The proverbial English sayings "much ado about nothing", (also the title of a comedy by William Shakespeare[47]), and "(Don't) make a mountain out of a molehill", are mocking comments on the foolishness of making a great deal of unnecessary fuss about something insignificant. *LNB*]

خليه پليه منځ ته وتليه.

969.   *Oh little straw, you have entered the arena.*

An ironic comment addressed to one who, though of meager talent, enters a competition and makes a ridiculous showing.

[In this rhyming proverb (*khaliya paliya mendz ta watəliya*) a person's impressive or ridiculously good performance puts him or her at the center (*mendz*) of attention. *RWS, LNB*]

خندا پسې ژړا وي.

970. *After laughter there is weeping.*

Sorrows follow in the wake of joy. [*See* Proverbs 102, 250, 378 and 683, and Index entries for "sorrow" and "joy".]

خوار او مراد لري خبره ده.

971. *There is a vast difference between a poor man and luck.*

The poor are seldom lucky.

[The poor seldom get what they long for, or alternatively, they long for what is above their status. The word translated "luck" (*murād*) refers to his wishes or desires. *LNB, RWS*]

خوار به چا له څۀ ورکړي سابۀ په کنډولي کښې.

972. *What can the poor man give to others—only spinach in a bowl.*

The poor man's gift is bound to be insignificant, though given in sincerity.

خوار چې له ژورې تير شي بيا ئې څه دار دے؟

973. *When a poor man has passed through ravines, of what else should he be afraid?*

Among the Pakhtuns, a poor man is thought to be extremely concerned with his personal safety.

خوار خپله خواري نۀ کړي جګجکې وروړي.

974. *The poor man does not live within his means and is constantly making requests.*

The opposite way of life is obviously prescribed here for the poor.

خوار خوشې مې وُلِیدهٔ هوس مې ورته وُشو.

975.	*I saw her helpless and felt a desire (to assault her).*

This is spoken ironically when someone in a helpless condition is imposed upon by another.

[In Pashtun culture, shameful treatment of women is avenged, but when someone is viewed as weak or in a poor condition, there is no fear of revenge to contain the other's behavior. *RWS, LNB*]

خوار دلې هم خوار، په هندوستان هم خوار.

976.	*Poor here, poor in India.*

Wherever he is, a poor man remains poor.

خوار سپائي پخپله ځان ستائي.

977.	*The timid soldier praises himself.*

خوار شړۍ نهٔ موندله چې وُئي موندله نو په ژړا شو چې دا دولس ګزه نهٔ ده.

978.	*The poor man could not find a blanket, but when he found one he began weeping and complaining that it was not twelve yards.*

This proverb is said of a person who strives to gain his essential needs and then demands more after their satisfaction. The satisfaction of one want [demand or desire] leads to yet another one.

خوار شو هغه کلے چې فرض ئي خوار سُنت ئي ښنکلے.

979.	*Spoiled are those villages that have carried out their compulsory duties carelessly while expending their energies on the non-obligatory.*

[Alternatively (in the singular), "Spoiled is that village that has ..." RWS]

[The proverb's meaning rests on a contrast between two Islamic terms: compulsory, obligatory religious duties (*farz*) and optional or non-obligatory religious duties (*sunnat*). For example, a part of a Muslim's daily prayer ritual (Arabic *salāt*, Persian *namāz*) is *farz*, that is, compulsory and commanded by God; while the *sunnat* element of the prayers is not compulsory (for example, when traveling), it brings extra reward. The village whose misplaced priorities cause it to focus on non-essentials will be "spoiled" or reduced to poverty. RWS, LNB]

خوار شې پښتونه چې اول ئي مينځ خورې بيا ئي پوستکه.

980.   *Oh Pakhtun, cursed be thee! First thou eatest the flesh, and then the skin.*

[The image is of one who first eats the inner portion of a fruit, then the skin. RWS]

خوارو له غوښت غله ده.

981.   *For the poor, even millet is food.*

خواره پليه سورو سره دې څۀ دي؟

982.   *Oh poor sluggard afoot, what have you to do with the horsemen?*

Only equals should compete with one another.

[A man on foot ("afoot") cannot compete with the horseman. LNB]

خواره حيله به دې خوار کړي.

983.   *Oh poor man, dependence on others will destroy you.*

[Or alternatively, "... dependence on others will make you (more) poor." RWS]

خواره خُله او څربې خبرې.

984. *A whining mouth and proud words.*

This is said about a person of low status who boasts overmuch.

خواره خواري د خرو د خاوندانو ده.

985. *Owners of donkeys are always in trouble and misery.*

He who associates with fools will always be in trouble.

[Alternatively, "Hardship and misery is the fate of the owners of donkeys." *RWS*]

خواره خواري شوه د منږکانو باچائي شوه.

986. *Poverty has prevailed and the mice have begun to rule.*

When social conditions deteriorate, evils appear.

خوار هغه شو چې لږ ئې تر پامه هیڅ شول.

987. *He who has despised a small thing becomes poor.*

This is similar to the English saying, "Something is better than nothing."

خواري د چا اوبۀ نۀ ورې.

988. *No man's labor is lost.*

Earnest effort does produce results.

خواری چي مړي شي نو دي مړي شي.

989.   *When the poor become rich they should die.*

[The proverb uses word play and alliteration in the feminine forms of
the Pashto words *maṛi* (rich) and *mṛi* (dies). LNB]

خواري ناديدي دروازي دي وُليدي.

990.   *Oh poor woman, you who have never experienced the advantages of
wealth or status, you now have seen the doors.*

     Thus will a mother ridicule her son's wife.

[The term *nādidak* (*nādidi*) is used of someone who shows off to
friends something she has never had before (for example, a new ring,
a new watch). The proverb makes fun of the boaster for being proud
of seeing or having something for the first time. It is customary
among Pashtun for the daughter-in-law to move in with her husband's
family, where the mother-in-law reigns supreme. LNB]

خوارۀ هغه خوري چي خداے پري خوړؤلي وي نۀ چي خُله ئي لويه وي.

991.   *He whom God has ordained to eat, will eat, and not he whose mouth
is large.*

     Worldly blessings depend on God's will, not on one's big talk and
boasts.

خوارۀ خوارۀ به درته وائي وژور ته به دي بيائي.

992.   *He will talk sweetly while leading you to the abyss.*

     This proverb is said of a man who deceives others with flattery and
thus ruins them.

خوب چې کوې خاوري به يوسي، شاه د هغو چې شوګيرې پسې کوينه.

993. *He who sleeps will get nothing. The beloved is for him who keeps vigil night after night.*

The vigilant, not the negligent, achieves his objective.

[This saying is in the form of a *tappa* . For a discussion of this text *see* Proverb 1159. *RWS, LNB*]

خوب چې کوې خوب به ويني.

994. *He who sleeps will have pleasant dreams.*

The proverb means that work of quality will produce results. It can also mean, that the one who sleeps will only dream and do nothing concrete.

خوبيدلے د مړۀ ورور دے.

995. *The sleepy one is brother to the dead ones.*

In sleep, as in death, one is unconscious.

[*See* the second meaning of the previous proverb. *LNB*]

خود غرضه (مطلبی) په خټه اور لګوي.

996. *A selfish man will even set fire to the mud.*

Selfish people use any means to achieve their ends [for example, compelling someone to do a difficult or impossible favor for them like building a fire on top of mud. *LNB*]

خور مې خور خورزه مې د زړۀ تکور.

997. *My sister is my sister; my niece is the darling of my heart.*

In arranging a marriage between cousins, this aphorism is a ritualistic way of praising the brother whose son wishes to wed your sister's daughter.

[Marriage between first cousins are prefered in Pashtun society. *LNB*]

خوراک د خپلې خوښې جامه د بل د خوښې.

998. *The choice of food should be your own, the choice of clothing should be another's.*

People do not see what and how you eat, but they do see how you dress.

خوره څښه حساب کتاب مۀ منه.

999. *Eat, drink and hang the expense.*

"Eat, drink and be merry."

[Eat and drink without fear or worry about payment. *See* Proverbs 389 and 694. *RWS, LNB*]

خوره خوره آس به دې وړي.

1000. *Eat it up! Eat it up! The horse will still carry you.*

Do your villainy and let others bear the responsibility [or burden].

خوري زوزان بار پرې مُهران.

1001. *He eats thorny shrubs and carries a cargo of sovereigns.*

The reference is to a simple camel bearing valuable coins. The proverb is applied to a man who lives modestly while his work entails great responsibilities.

[The Pashto word translated "sovereigns" (*mahrān*) refers to old "money". A "sovereign" was a gold coin worth one pound sterling used in Britain from the 15th to the 20th centuries. *LNB*]

خوريه! څۀ رنګ چي دي (زړۀ) چاؤد دے دغسي مي (زړۀ) چاؤد دے.

1002. *Oh sister! As narrow is thine (heart), so is mine.*

The meaning is, "As you are, so am I!" The proverb is spoken by a woman to a friend, for example, just as you are fed-up with your chores or luck, so am I.

[Alternatively, "Just as you (your heart or situation) are narrow (or split or broken), so am I." The proverb illustrates and turns on the careless use of adjectives that carry double meanings. *RWS, LNB*]

خوريے د ماما دښمن کېږي.

1003. *The nephew becomes the enemy of his maternal uncle.*

A nephew forgets the affection his maternal uncle feels for him.

[In Pashtun culture, a man may not allow his sister and her sons to have their share in the paternal heritage. Where no inheritance is expected, the normal rivalries over land and heritage don't apply, and so there is often a special affection between a man and his *māmā* (maternal uncle, i.e. his mother's brother, or father / mother's sister's husband). *RWS, LNB*]

خوړ کښې کاني ډېر دي خو کار په سېر تمام دے.

1004. *Although there are many stones in the ravine, the one weighing one seer fits the need.*

There are many types of people, but the important one is he who fulfils the need.

[In Afghanistan and Pakistan, many *khwar* (ravines or dry river beds) are filled with rocks and boulders. Getting something done is often based on who you know or are related to, more than on skill, position or merit alone. The proverb advises one to look for the "weighty" (a *seer* is a measure of weight; *see* Proverb 413) or significant person. *LNB*]

خوږ په نیت کوږ.

1005. *Sweet, but with bad intentions.*

[This rhyming proverb with ending alliteration—*khog* (sweet) and *kog* (crooked)—warns that appearances can be deceptive. On the importance of "intensions" (*niyat*) see Proverb 800. *LNB, RWS*]

خوږه وروره د سترګو توره د دوزخ د اوره د دښمن د زوره د قرضه پوره دې
خدای وُساته.

1006. *Oh my dear brother, the pupil of my eye, may God save you from these troubles: the flames of hell, the power of the enemy, debts and credits.*

This is more a prayer than a proverb. It is spoken to honor one's nearest and dearest.

[Some Pashto proverbs (*see* e.g. Proverb 906) are structured as invocations (prayers), blessings and curses. To a Pashtun, these three "troubles"—whether otherwordly ("hell fire") or this-worldly ("powerful enemies" and "debt")—are equally dangerous, dishonoring and deadly.

[In a outstanding display of verbal art, this proverb contains a number of delightful poetic devices including *assonance* (repetition of the same vowel sound), *alliteration* (repetition of the same initial consonant), *colliteration* (the clustering of similar consonant sounds), *rhyme* (similarity in the sound of word endings), *internal rhyme* (rhyming of the last word in a line with one or more words inside the line), and various "sound echoes" throughout: "*khoga wrora, də sturgo tora də dozakh də ora də dukhman də zora də qarza pora de khoday wusāta.*" *LNB*]

خوشحاله ختکه په درنو درونده په سپکو سپکه.

1007. *Oh Khushal Khattak! You are honorable in the company of dignitaries but are considered degraded by those who are themselves degraded.*

Noble people behave nobly, while the mean act meanly towards others.

This is a well-known saying of the famous warrior poet Khushal Khan Khattak [1613-1689].

خوشي اشنايي د نيا او د نمسي.

1008. *The blood relationship between grandmother and grandson produces no material benefits.*

When there is a great difference in age or status, an identity of interest or views is not possible. The proverb can also be used to mean, the old will die soon, leaving the young helpless.

خونه مي در [نه] ځار شه خو لاړي د پاسه.

1009. *Let my home be yours, but only the portion above the hanging pole.*

This proverb is said in irony of a selfish person who makes generous offers, but does not mean what he says.

The "hanging pole" is a long rod suspended from ropes at a height of about six feet from the floor of a room [used to hang or air out quilts, for example, so the offer of a "house" is merely "roof space". *LNB*]

[It may also refer to a "supporting pole" which supports the roof or a wooden pole used to support a frame before the cement is poured. *RWS*]

[Literally, "(May I) sacrifice (*zār* in Yousafzai, *jār* in Afghan Pashto) my house ..." The common idiom "may I sacrifice (my head, my house, my life, etc.)" expresses a Pashtun's willingness to sacrifice himself / herself for the sake of friendship, love or honor.[v] *See* Proverb 524. *LNB*]

---

[v] [In Afghan Pashto, the idiom is *khuna me jār sa* and it appears in this form in Tair's original major proverb collection, *Rohi Mataluna:Pashto zarbul amsal bumgha Urdu tarjuma* (*Rohi Mataluna:Pashto proverbs with Urdu translation*), Mohammad Nawaz Tair, Pakhto Academy, Peshawar University, First edition, 1975, Volume I, p. 431.]

خوئ له اصله دے تاثیر له مجلسه دے.

1010. *One's manners are a product of his heritage but they are tempered by society.*

[That is, one's manners (habits) are inherited or learned from one's family, but this is tempered by society or the company one keeps. *RWS, LNB*]

خیال هم خواري غواړي.

1011. *Proper dress demands care.*

To acquire anything worthwhile demands efforts.

خبرات په خپل قرابات. (قرابت داری)

1012. *Charity begins at home.*

[The meaning is that one's first duty is to care for one's own family, or, that one's ties or responsibilities to family (or country, etc.) supersede all others. The word *qurābāt* (rhyming with *kheyrāt*) refers to one's kin or those with whom one has a relationship. Tair and Edwards translate the Pashto text in the words of a popular English proverb (perhaps based on a Latin text and / or an idea attributed to the Bible[48]) cited by a number of authors including John Wycliffe (1383), "Charity should begin at himself", and later by the 19th century novelist Charles Dickens, "Charity begins at home and justice begins next door." *LNB*]

خیراتونه مصیبتونه ژغوري.

1013. *Acts of charity drive away troubles and calamities.*

خیراتو کښې دي نقصان دے او ختمو کښې دي فائده ده.

1014. *In the giving of alms there is a financial loss, but in reading the Holy Qur'an there is profit for you.*

Used to disparage the person who seeks to avoid giving alms.

[This is a sarcastic comment. Recitation of the Holy Qur'an (*khatam*) brings religious benefit, but is not a susbtitute for charity and the social obligations associated with faith. *LNB*]

خیراتي اس غاښ ئي کتل.

1015. *To get a free horse and then to count its teeth.*

This is an expression similar to "looking a gift horse in the mouth."

[One assesses the age of a horse by inspecting his front teeth. If the horse is free, one should receive it with gratitude and not inspect the gift too closely. Cf. Proverb 1143. *LNB*]

خیښي په خوښۍ سورلي په رضا.

1016. *A meaningful relationship requires mutual love and riding requires mutual consent.*

د اباسین نه چي اوبۀ غواړې تږے نۀ ئي!

1017. *If you ask for water from "Abasin" it seems that you are not thirsty!*

In the North West Frontier Province of Pakistan, the Abasin or Indus River flows in rapids through deep gorges, making it almost inaccessible to man. This proverb applies to any man of means who is miserly and refuses to share his resources, [that is, his resources are similarly inaccessible. *LNB*]

د ارت لوتکي دي تش کوزبرې ډک راخيژي.

1018. *As with the Persian wheel, the full buckets rise while the empty buckets go down.*

The "Persian wheel" is an age-old device used throughout Central and Western Asia to irrigate land from wells. A system of wheels and cogs rotates a rope containing numerous buckets. As the full buckets rise to empty into a conduit, the empties go down to be refilled.

This proverb suggests the cycle of life, or perhaps the vicissitudes that make a person happy one day and sad the next.

د آس لته آس زغمي.

1019. *The kick of a horse can be borne only by another horse.*

Only a strong man can bear the onslaught of the strong.

د اور په بانه راغله د کور مېرمن شوه.

1020. *She came asking for fire and became mistress of the house.*

The Pakhtun villager commonly will borrow fire from a neighbor's hearth. The proverb refers to a person in an apparently harmless garb who is actually not at all harmless and ends up grabbing everything from you. This widely known proverb was used as a jibe at the British who came to India.

[This proverb is applied to any guest or friend who takes advantage of his / her host, or to any foreigners or so-called "guests" of a host country who exercise undue influence or control. For example, the British came to India for trade and ended-up as its rulers. Other "guests" may take advantage of hospitality to advance their own purposes. This is a classic example of the use of proverbs for political commentary. *LNB*]

د باچا زوئ ته چا وُوٸ چې قحط دے خلق د لوږې مري. وٻ ئي "غوړي وريژی ولې نۀ خوري!"

1021. *When a man informed a prince that there was a famine in the kingdom, he received the reply, "Why don't they eat butter oil and rice as I do!"*

The proverb will remind westerners of the famous reply attributed to Marie Antoinette, who when the mob clamoured for bread, responded "Let them eat cake!"

د باهر بدي ورکه شي. د کور بدي نۀ ورکېږي.

1022. *Differences outside the family can be resolved. Differences in the home drag on and on.*

This can be applied to nations as well as to individuals.

د بدې خبرې سل کاله عمر وي.

1023. *Bad words live for a hundred years.*

The impact of bad deeds lasts for a very long time.

[Proverbially, in Pashto "one hundred years" is shorthand for a long period of time. *See* Index for "hundred". *LNB*]

د بوډۍ نه سپي ډوډۍ يوړه وي ئې د خدای په نامه دې وي.

1024. *When the dog ran off with the bread, the old woman said, "Let it be in the name of God."*

When a thing is lost or taken by force, it should not be treated as alms, [which are normally given in the Name of God.]

د پښتو کاڼے په اوبو کښې نۀ ورستېږي.

1025. *The stone of* pakhtunwali *cannot be dissolved in water.*

The psychology of the Pakhtun requires that eventually one will take his revenge on an enemy, even though outwardly he may appear friendly.

It may also mean that the Pakhtun's word of honor does not grow old. ["One cannot escape the inevitable consequences of *pakhto*.]

د پېښې نه تېښته نشته.

1026. *One must accept those events that are bound to occur.*

د تُورې پرهار رغېږي. د ژبی پرهار نۀ رغېږي.

1027. *The wound of the sword will heal, but not that of the tongue.*

[A variety of images are used to describe the "tongue" in Pashto proverbs. Here the tongue is likened to a weapon inflicting wounds that do not heal. The proverb may instruct the young, and warn enemies: "Your words will not be forgotten." This is another stark reminder about the power of words. *LNB*]

د چونګبنو من نۀ پوره کېږي.

1028. *You can never weigh a* man *of frogs.*

A *man* is a weight of nearly eighty pounds [40 kilos]. Frogs will leap off the balance or scale.

[That is, the *man* will never be complete because leaping frogs cannot be weighed. *RWS*]

د خوار مُلا په بانگ څوک کلیمه نۀ وائي.

1029. *No one will recite the* kalima *at the call to prayers made by a poor mullah.*

The man of no authority is seldom taken seriously in matters of importance.

[There is a tradition among the Pashtun Muslims that after the call to prayer is finished they recite the *kalima. See* notes to Proverbs 35 and 291. *RWS*]

د دِيوِې د کونِي لاندِې تیارۀ وي.

1030. *There is always darkness underneath the lamp.*

This proverb is used by a person seeking something that lies near at hand but is not visible to him.

د زوراورو اوبۀ په لوړه خېژي.

1031. *The water of the powerful man flows uphill.*

The man in authority can do anything, just or unjust.

د سپو کور په کور بدي ده. خو فقیر ته یو دي.

1032. *Though the dogs fight among themselves the beggar is their common foe.*

[Though the dogs of different houses fight with each other, they unite against a beggar. *RWS*]

د سپي جوټه د سپي حق دے.

1033. *Any food or drink a dog tastes becomes his property.*

Nobody else likes to eat the food a dog has touched, as it is dirty.

[According to Islam, the dog is considered a *palit* or "defiled" animal. Whatever it touches or licks becomes unclean and spoiled. Also the dog is loyal to its master, but it is the enemy of its own species. *RWS*]

د سیک اصل په ویښتو وي.

1034. *The faithfulness and appearance of the Sikh are in his hair.*

A Sikh is a follower of an Indian religion which forbids a man [or woman] from removing hair on any part of his [/ her] head or body.

This proverb suggests that the outward appearance identifies a man.

[Hair is one of the five external symbols of the Sikh faith identifying a person as a member of the Khalsa brotherhood (Sikh faith). Long hair wrapped in a distinctive turban is a mark of Sikhism and Sikh identity. *LNB, RWS*]

د شپې کۀ لاړ نۀ شې د ورځې به وُنۀ رسې.

1035. *If you do not travel by night you will never reach your destination by day.*

د بنارہ وځه د نرخه ئي مۀ وځه.

1036. *You can leave the city but you should not disregard its prices.*

One cannot escape the tradition of the place where he was born and lived.

[Alternatively, "Leave the city but not its prices." *LNB, RWS*]

د عقل ورہے او د دنیا موږ چا نۀ دے لیدلے.

1037. *No one has ever seen a man who does not claim to be intelligent, or who claims to have enough wealth.*

Everyone claims to have enough intelligence but not enough wealth. That is, the desire to acquire wealth is greater than that of acquiring knowledge.

د غل په ږیره خس.

1038. *The thief has a straw in his beard.*

Three suspected thieves were one day brought before a *qazi* (judge). Having no evidence against any of them, the wise judge suddenly exclaimed, "The thief has a straw in his beard," whereupon the guilty man tugged at his beard and was caught. The meaning is that a guilty conscience cannot escape punishment.

د فقیر چې چرته بنه هلته شپه.

1039. *The beggar spends the night wherever it is convenient.*

د کالۀ کشر مۀ شې د کاروان مشر مۀ شې.

1040. *May you not be a youngster in a family or the head [leader] of a caravan.*

The youngster does the menial work about the home and the caravan master is plagued by the numerous problems of his followers.

[Everyone orders about the youngest child in a family; the elder or head of a caravan faces numerous hassles and annoyances. Both are unenviable positions. *RWS, LNB*]

د کريو جواب، کرسي!

1041. "Do something." "I'll do it" (is the proper reply for it).

[kar is a Hindi word meaning "do", and karsi means "it will be done"—the only proper answer (jawāb) to "do it". RWS, LNB]

د کوهي خاوره په کوهي تمامېږي.

1042. The clay excavated from the well is used in building the well.

The income of a family is used for the wellbeing of the family itself. The profit of a firm should be spent on its development.

د ګيدړ تر نازه د زمري څيرل بنۀ دي.

1043. It is better to be torn by a lion than to be loved by a jackal.

[Alternatively, "... by a lion, than by the whims of a jackal." RWS]

د لښکر په اخر څه د ماتې په سر څه.

1044. When the army moves into battle, it is better to be in the rear; when the army flees in defeat, it is better to be in the front.

The proverb is used to taunt cowards who in both cases fear for their own safety.

د ليوۀ لکۍ ده نۀ ئي پرېښنوے شی نۀ ئي تينګوے شي.

1045. It is like the tail of a wolf—one can neither let it go nor hold on.

This proverb describes the indecision of the man who was once in a jungle clinging to the tail of a wolf. Out of fear of being attacked by the wolf, he could not decide whether to hang on or let the wolf go. The story applies to any indecision caused by fear.

[When someone undertakes a job there can come a point where it is impossible to either abandon it or continue it. The purpose of catching the wolf's tail in the first place is to engage in a fight. By holding on to the tail the wolf cannot harm him, but it is tiresome work. Should he let go, the wolf will certainly attack. *RWS*]

د مابنام لوگے هر سرے آسمان ته وچتوي.

1046. *The smoke rises in the evening from every man's fire.*

د مجلس یاران دي څۀ شو په خاورو کښې وراستۀ شو.

1047. *Where are your bosom friends? They have turned into dust.*

د مسافر د شپو حساب مۀ کوۀ د سر خواست ئې کوه.

1048. *Count not the days [nights] of the traveler, but pray for his safety.*

د مغل زور په دهقان، د دهقان زور په زمکه.

1049. *The Mughal oppresses the landowner; the landowner presses the land.*

The Mughals probably collected exorbitant taxes from landowners. That is why the latter tried hard to get more produce from the land to pay the taxes.

د موزي په تومت څۀ شي لا ئې پرې زرۀ ښنۀ شي.

1050. *The coward will only laugh at ridicule. He does not mind it.*

[The coward or wicked person does not care about blame, rather he is happy to receive it. *RWS*]

د ميرهٔ يو لاس په خوارهٔ بل په چارهٔ.

1051. *The brave man has one hand on the bread [food] and the other on his dagger.*

د مېلمانهٔ په بيرهٔ د كالهٔ څه؟

1052. *What does the host care about the haste of his guest?*

د ناكسه اشنائي د خرهٔ سورلي.

1053. *Friendship with a low-bred man is like a ride on a donkey.*

د واورى رنځوران هم په پيتاؤ جنګونه كوي.

1054. *Those who have suffered from snow, fight for the sunlight.*

A man in straitened circumstances, when he finds favorable conditions, becomes bold.

[Alternatively, "Those who are sick or unwell in the snow are able to fight in the sunlight." *RWS*]

د ورور خور مي كړې محتاجه مي مهٔ كړې.

1055. *May I be the sister of my brother, but may I never need his help.*

د هغهٔ څخه زغله چې يو وار هو كړي بيا نه.

1056. *Always shy away from the person who once says "Yes" and then "No."*

Avoid a fickle-minded person.

د هغې بلا نه مهٔ ویریږه چي شپه ئي تر مینځ وي.

1057. *Fear not the calamity that would not arrive before night.*

One need not get nervous about something that has not yet happened. The delay gives time for self defence, [you have time to prepare for any calamity].

د هندو په هټ کښې شوې څيروه او د ما د مور دا لنډه لغړه ورځ څيروه.

1058. *Look at the bundles of cloth in the shop of the Hindu, while my mother goes about in rags.*

A young man from Waziristan once went to a bazaar where he saw a Hindu shop containing many bundles of cloth. Thinking of the poverty of his mother, he rushed inside and cried, "Look at the bundles of cloth in the shop of the Hindu, while my mother goes about in rags." He then took up a bundle of cloth and escaped with it. This may also be true of persons other than the Wazir. The Wazir are a Pashtun tribe.

[Years ago when Pashtun nomads traded their way from Afghanistan across northern India as far as Calcutta, the Hindus functioned as money lenders and cloth sellers. Pashtuns would buy cloth from Hindu shopkeepers on credit, and transport the cloth by camel caravan across the subcontinent, where they would sell it for profit. Among other negative images of the Hindu (see Index), Hindus have a proverbial reputation for being wealthy, tightfisted businessmen. *LNB*]

د وُنې سل کاله عمر دے. خو د مرغۍ پکښې يوه شپه ده.

1059. *The tree may live for a hundred years, while the bird will perch in it for only one night.*

د يار دپاره هندو د غوا غوښې خوړلي دي.

1060. *For the sake of his friend the Hindu has eaten the beef of the cow.*

No sacrifice is too great for the sake of friendship. The Hindu does not eat beef because the cow is a sacred animal in his religion.

[Here the otherwise scorned and idolatrous Hindu models the Pashtun ideal of sacrificial friendship. *LNB*]

د يو وطن خاوره د بل وطن دارو.

1061. *One country's soil is another country's medicine.*

Different soils and climates have different properties.

د يوی وُنې لرګے څه لوئی او کمکے.

1062. *Whether the piece of wood is large or small, it comes from the same tree.*

Those belonging to the same stock should not feel superior or inferior to their kith and kin [relative].

دا شل لږ زيات راومنډه چې زما دا هم در ورسي.

1063. *Thrust your spear further into my stomach so that my shorter spear can reach you.*

One should not leave his revenge to relatives, but must try to the very end to effect his own.

دا ګز دا ميدان.

1064. *This is the yardstick and this is the ground.*

A man is said to have returned from India with the boast that he had recently jumped twenty yards. Those sitting about had this suitable reply, "Ha! This is the yardstick and this is the ground. Prove it."

دریاب چې خۍ غورځنګ به خود لري.

1065. *When the river flows there should be waves.*

For example, when an army is on the move, there will be destruction.

دښمن دي کۀ په ګوړه مري په زهرو ئې مۀ وژنه.

1066. *If you can kill your enemy with* gur *(raw sugar) do not try to kill him with poison.*

دنیا داره چې دنیا د ډیرؤله سپین کفن دې یورو دغه نوره دې په چا وزپرموله.

1067. *Oh worldly wise! Of what use is all your accumulated wealth when you can take with you only a white shroud from this world.*

[Alternatively, "Oh worldly one! When you took with you only a white shroud (*kafan*) from all you gathered in this world, to whom did you leave the rest of your wealth? *LNB*]

دوست اشارې ته ګوري دښمن وارې ته ګوري.

1068. *A friend responds to a mere gesture, but an enemy seeks an opportunity to do his harm.*

دوست هغه دے چې په ځان دې ښۀ وي.

1069. *A friend is he who is good for you.*

[An alternative version of this text (Proverb 1175) replaces "friend" with the broader term "good": "Good is that which is good for you." Good things, like friends, do you good and lead to good. *RWS, LNB*]

دولت د لاس خيرې دي.

1070. *Wealth is the dirt on one's hand.*

One should not depend too much on wealth as it is likely to vanish at anytime.

دوه تُورې په يو تيكي كښي نه ځائيږي.

1071. *Two swords cannot be sheathed in a single scabbard.*

Two rulers cannot rule over one country. [*See* Proverb 449.]

ديوال چي مات شي هر سړے ترې نه گټه وُچتوي.

1072. *When the protective wall around the house is broken everyone takes away the stones.*

This proverb is used when a country or family develops a weakness; everyone will then seek the chance to attack it.

د

ډبره چي په ځای پرته وي درنه وي.

1073. *The undisturbed stone is heaviest.*

[If a stone is not lifted up, one cannot estimate its weight. Not all exposure is good, so it is better to leave the "stone" in the ground where no one really knows. *RWS, LNB*]

ډم په ډول نۀ شرمېږي.

1074. *The ḍəm or minstrel does not feel shy of beating the drum.*

The menial does not hesitate to perform his lowly duties. [*See* note to Proverb 615.]

ډم چي مرور شي د ځان نقصان ئې دے كلے چي مرور شي، د ډم نقصان دے.

1075. *If the ḍəm is annoyed with the villagers he is the loser. If the villagers are annoyed with him he is still the loser.*

[*See* note to Proverb 615.]

ډوډۍ خپله خوره عقل له بله زده كوه.

1076. *Eat your own bread but learn wisdom from others.*

دوډۍ راپسې راوړه د هندو لاندې مې شپه ده.

1077. *Bring my dinner to me; I am spending the night under the Hindu.*

The story is told of a quarrel between a Hindu and a Pakhtun. Somehow the Hindu overpowered his opponent and threw him to the ground. As he held the Pakhtun down, a man passed by and heard the Pakhtun say, "Bring my dinner to me, I must spend the night under the Hindu." The Hindu, seeing that he was in for a long night and fearing the strength of his opponent, sprang up and ran off.

This proverb is used when someone is saddled with a task requiring great stamina and patience. It also applies to one who, though temporarily strong, is afraid of the eventual thrust of his opponent.

دول دې په څنگ دے د وهلو ئې څه ننگ دے؟

1078. *When you have the drum at your side, why hesitate to beat it?*

When one approaches something undesirable, he might as well participate in it.

[Playing a drum is considered shameful for a Pakhtun. *LNB*]

دېرې خُلې دېرې خبرې.

1079. *Many mouths many words.*

[*See* variant proverb 815.]

دېرې مه وايه چې خطا کېږې نه.

1080. *Don't talk too much so that you do not go astray.*

This is similar in meaning to "Putting your foot in your mouth." It can also mean, be precise and concise. [*See* Proverb 804.]

راتله ئې خوند ئې ښۀ دے!

1081. *Weigh it for me, it's delicious!*

The proverb derives from an anecdote. A simple villager, upon seeing a display of sweets in a confectioner's shop, was invited by the shop owner "to have some." The villager, after sampling the sweets said, "Weigh it for me, it's delicious!" He spread his turban on the floor and watched the owner weigh out a quantity of the delightful confection. When the turban was full and the villager was preparing to leave, the owner asked for money. The customer said, "What money? I am your guest and you invited me to have some." While taking back his goods, the shopkeeper repeated bitterly, "Weigh it for me, it's delicious!"

راوله ورستي چې قدر راشي د ورمبي.

1082. *Oh God, let the later ones come so that the earlier ones may be appreciated.*

[This is, so that the true value of the earlier thing or person will be known. The words, "Oh God" are implied, not stated. *RWS, LNB*]

رائې چې آرا شي بلاؤ نه ترې په شا شي.

1083. *Once a proposal is accepted it will drive away all troubles.*

A united front is a protection against difficulties.

رګ هغه وهه چې وينه ترې وُخِي.

1084. *Cut that vein from which blood can be drawn.*

Always direct your energies toward that which gives a profit.

رنځور دې روغ شي د هر چا په دارو چې وي.

1085. *The patient should recover regardless of whose medicine is administered.*

In achieving one's objective one should exploit all sources.

روپۍ مې کتله پوزه مې بائيله.

1086. *In trying to save a rupee I lost my nose.*

A man once took his bent sword to a blacksmith to get it straightened. The smith offered to repair the damage for a *rupee*. When the man agreed to the price, the smith placed the blade across his head, and with a quick jerk straightened it out. Thinking this a simple process, the man asked the smith to return the blade to its earlier state, which was easily done. He returned to his home and tried to straighten it once more, but the blade slipped and cut off his nose. In agony he then cried, "In trying to save a *rupee* I lost my nose."

ربنتيا چې راځي دروغو به کلي وران کړي وي.

1087. *Before truth arrives, lies will have destroyed villages.*

[*See* Proverb 688.]

ربنتيا وئيل ښه دي خو د نۀ وئيلو برابر نۀ دي.

1088. *Truth is good; silence is better.*

[Speaking or telling the truth is good, but it is not as good as silence. An alternative version says, "Speaking good (*khə*) is good, but ..." (*See* Proverb 835.) *RWS*]

ړاندۀ ښځه په خدای سپارلې ده.

1089. *The blind man entrusts his wife to God's care.*

رُوند د خدایه څه غواړي دوه سترګي.

1090. *What does a blind man wish for mostly from God? Two eyes!*

رُوند یو ځل په موږي لوبږي رُوغ سل ځله.

1091. *The blind man will stumble on a peg only once, but the man with eyes will fall over it time and again.*

This proverb is often used in a figurative sense.

زامن خوارَه دي. غشی ئي کاږه دي.

1092. *Male children [sons] are sweet, but their arrows are bent.*

Bent arrows cannot be taken out of the body. The proverb communicates that having sons is most welcome, but to lose a son is unbearable.

زر په هغۀ گران وي چي کتل ئي په خپل ځان وي.

1093. *Money is precious to him who has earned it by the sweat of his brow.*

زرغونه به لنگبري. احمد شاه به ځني زبري.

1094. *No Zarghuna will ever again give birth to another Ahmad Shah.*

Zarghuna, an ordinary Pakhtun lady, was the mother of a celebrated monarch of the 18th century who conquered most of south and central Asia. The present state of Afghanistan is carved out of Ahmad Shah's empire.

This proverb means that great men are rarely born, or that great men are born of great mothers.

زړۀ ور يو ځل او بي زړۀ سل ځله.

1095. *The brave man dies only once; the coward dies many times.*

"Cowards die many times before their deaths, The valiant never taste of death but once."[49]

زړۀ ښائيست نۀ غواړي او خوب بالښت نۀ غواړي.

1096. The heart does not always seek beauty, just as the weary head does not require a pillow.

زړۀ نه زړۀ ته لار وي.

1097. One heart has a secret pathway to another heart.

[That is, "Love begets love." Cf. the Persian proverb, "There is a way from heart to heart." RWS, LNB]

زلمو د خندا نه موندلې ده.

1098. The laughing stock wins the race.

The unlikely man sometime plays the role of hero.

زما په سر منګے دے د بل په سر دې خُم وي.

1099. If I have a pitcher on my head, another should have a larger one on his head.

Since others do not share one's troubles, one is inclined to wish even more trouble for them.

[If a burden is on my head, I wish others would have an even heavier one than mine. RWS]

زما د سره تبره خدايه مۀ کړې دنيا ډېره.

1100. Since I must leave my worldly wealth behind me, Oh God, let it not be multiplied.

زما ميرهٔ او ستا ميرهٔ سره لښکر شي.

1101. *My husband and your husband make an army.*

When one woman asked another, "Just what is this army that marches against the enemy?" Her friend replied, "My husband and your husband make an army." The proverb pictures one courageous woman encouraging another.

زمرے د خپله زوره نهٔ دے خبر.

1102. *The lion does not know his own strength.*

When a man does something surprising, this expression is commonly used.

The proverb derives from an old Pakhtun myth that is still current. When Doomsday arrives and God wishes to destroy the earth, He will order the winds to blow on the mountains until they have disappeared. When the lion and the horse are in the path of the wind, they will cling tenaciously to the ground and will not be dislodged, even though they lose skin and flesh until they are nothing but skeletons. At that time they will cry out, "Oh God, had we known our own strength, we would have ruled over man as well as all other creatures."

[This proverb refers to a person who does not know his own ability or capacity. *RWS*]

زمري له خداے په هر ځاے کښې غوښي ورکوي.

1103. *God provides the lion with meat wherever he is.*

زور چې راشي د حساب ملا ماتوي.

1104. *When force is applied, the balance of assets and liabilities is upset.*

[Power is justice. *RWS*]

زور د اولس بد دے.

1105. *Public pressure is the most powerful force.*

زورور دې تر پامه کمزورے مۀ شۀ.

1106. *One should never underestimate the powerful man.*

[This proverb contrasts the powerful man (*zorawar*) and the weak man (*kəmzorey*)—one should not treat the former as if he were the latter. *LNB*]

زورور غوئ د غولي مینځ نیسي.

1107. *The powerful ox goes to the center of the courtyard.*

To show his superiority, the ox refuses to enter the stable or manger [and instead takes over the courtyard], signifying that the powerful man usually encroaches upon the rights of others.

[Alternatively, it can indicate that the best places are already occupied by those who are more able or more powerful. *RWS*]

زوم نۀ بالۀ شي نۀ شاړۀ شي.

1108. *The son-in-law is neither invited into nor ejected from the house.*

The father, always shy [embarrassed, uncomfortable] in the presence of his daughter's husband [i.e. his son-in-law], will never invite him to visit, but if he comes of his own accord, he will not be denied hospitality.

زوئ مې را مُلا کړه کډې مې ولاړې.

1109. *Hurry and make my child [son] a mullah for my caravan has already moved on.*

The story is told that a certain woman asked a mullah to teach her child so that he may become an educated man. In just a few days she returned in haste and said to the teacher "Hurry and make my child a mullah for my caravan has already moved on."

زویه رنگ به دې خداے کړي خوئ دې پخپله.

1110. *Oh my son, your fortune is from God, your character is your own effort.*

[The Pashto word translated "character" (*khwi, khəy*) may also refer to one's total conduct, habits and manner. *RWS*]

زۀ تاته وايم تۀ چا ته مۀ وايه.

1111. *I am telling it to you, you should not tell it to someone else.*

An ironic reference to the keeping of a secret.

زۀ د ادې مزدوره ادې د کلي مزدوره.

1112. *I am the maidservant of my mother and my mother is the maidservant of the entire village.*

Used by a person to signify his utter insignificance. Someone who is respected by his near and dear ones may not be shown the same respect by others.

[It also describes a person who is at the mercy of someone who in turn is at the mercy of others. *RWS*]

زۀ دې د پلار ویر کوم تۀ مې د خُلې پېښنې کوې.

1113. *While you mimic my expression, I am weeping for your father.*

Do not jump to conclusions if you do not know the real facts.

[Alternative translation: "I am weeping for your father and you are mimicking me." *RWS*]

زهٔ ستا د خُلُي قيصي کوم تهٔ زما د خُلُي پيښي کوې.

1114. *I am telling stories about your sweet tongue and you are laughing at my mouth.*

I am praising you and yet you mock me.

زهٔ وايم اورهٔ نشته تهٔ وائي پتيري پخي کړه.

1115. *I tell you there is no flour in the house, yet you are bent upon asking me to bake the bread without yeast.*

One cannot make something out of nothing.

[The proverb is used as an ironic rebuttal to someone who does not try to understand a situation. *RWS*]

زهٔ يو خوښنی دېرې.

1116. *I am alone and my pleasures are many.*

زهر څهٔ خروار خوړلي څهٔ مثقال.

1117. *A small amount of poison or a large amount, the result is the same.*

زير زير ګورې غوخکے تا بوؤلے دے.

1118. *You are staring at me, which means that you have driven off the bullocks.*

A farmer once lost his team of bullocks. While searching for them, he met another man and asked if he had seen a pair of bullocks passing by. "They went that way," said the stranger. The farmer went on until he saw another stranger staring at him suspiciously. Exhausted and unable to continue the search, the owner of the animals could only use a little psychology and cried out, "You are staring at me, which means that you have driven off the bullocks!"

ژاړه عمره ژاړه! اول دې نۀ خوړې هزار سوارخي اوس د خوار پلاؤ محتاج
شوې.

1119. *Weep! Weep, Oh Omer! Before this you objected to eating* hazar surakha *and now you get only this poor* palau.

According to the story, a young Pakhtun left his country for India where he worked for a Rajah as an attendant. He soon ingratiated himself to his employer, who offered him his pretty daughter as a bride. The young man happily joined the family, but after a time he became homesick and longed for his own country. His parents-in-law were shocked and insisted that he should not leave, for he had in their household all the comforts one could wish for and so it would be foolish to go away. One evening at supper, the discontented man began to sob with self-pity, moaning and saying, "Weep weep, Oh Omer. Before this you objected to eating *hazar surakha* [*hazār swārkha*] and now you get only this poor *palau*."

His wife had been watching from a distance and listening to his wailing. When she heard him praise the *hazar surakha*, she became curious and longed to taste it. So she informed her parents that if Omer left the palace she would go with him. Accordingly they left and went to his former home in the far away tribal area where his family lived in utter poverty.

To show her hospitality to the guests, Omer's mother often cooked *palau* and roasted chicken. However, because such dishes were not unusual in her parental home, the girl one day begged her mother-in-law to prepare *hazar surakha* for a change. This amazed the older woman, but the girl insisted and finally was served the "special dish." It was nothing but a simple barley bread which she found unpalatable and difficult to swallow, in contrast to *palau*, which is a dish made from rice and beef, mutton or chicken mixed with spices and fats.

This proverb reflects, as do many others, the Pakhtun's loyalty to his tribe and roots.

ژبه په دوو دېرشو غاښونو کښې ده.

1120. *The tongue is among thirty-two teeth.*

This proverb suggests that one should always hold his tongue. That is, a man should try to avoid all troubles, [especially those caused by careless talk. *RWS*]

ژرنده کۀ د پلار ده خو په وار ده.

1121. *Though the flour mill is owned by the father, the son must wait his turn.*

ژرنده ئې ښځې کړې ده او ښتپ د دۀ خر دے.

1122. *Although his wife ground the flour, the dust lies on his neck.*

This is used to ridicule the submissive, hen-pecked husband.

ژمے به څۀ وي خو دېر سارۀ؟

1123. *What does one remember about the winter except the bitter cold?*

Winter gives no trouble other than the cold.

[Literally, "What is winter but too much cold", that is, why praise winter when it is nothing but too much cold. *RWS*]

بۍغ د ملا امين د كلي.

1124. *The mullah prays; it's for the village to say, "Amen."*

It is the obligation of the mullah to call the prayer, but it is up to the people to respond. That is, everyone has his own duty to perform.

سازي مي څو وکړي چي پاتي ناسازي شوي.

1125. *Have I done enough constructive things that I may now concentrate on the destructive?*

سپر (ډال) هغه گرخوي، چي تُورو ته اوږه سموي.

1126. *Only he who can face the sword carries a shield.*

سپور (سور) دي داسي نۀ وائي چي پلے به نۀ شم او پلے دي داسي نۀ وائي
چي سپور (سور) به نۀ شم.

1127. *One who rides a horse should not claim that he will never walk, while the pedestrian should not claim that he will never ride.*

Change is inevitable.

سپوږمی کۀ په آسمان وي رڼا ئي په جهان وي.

1128. *Although the moon is in the far away sky, it casts its light upon the entire world.*

Great benefactors disregard distance. Everyone shares in what they give to humanity.

سپي ته نمړۍ غورځوۀ چې درته غاپي نه!

1129. *Throw a loaf of bread to the dog so it will not bark at you.*

Small, greedy persons can be satisfied with petty things.

[This is a reference to bribery. *RWS*]

سپي ته ئې ويل چې د چا د لاسه ئې په عذاب ئې ويل ئې د خپلو عزيزانو د
لاسه.

1130. *When someone asked the dog, "Who causes you all your troubles?"*
It replied, "My own kinsmen."

Mischief-mongers give trouble to their own kith and kin [relatives].

سپي ټامبړي (غپپړی) کاروان تېرېږي.

1131. *Though the dogs bark, the caravan moves on.*

This is similar to the English saying, "Time and tide wait for no
man." [*See* Proverbs 107 and 195.]

[Alternate meaning: a steady person does not care about the
comments of others. *RWS*]

سپے ډېر د خان د پاره غاپي لږ د مالک د پاره.

1132. *The dog barks more for himself and less for his master.*

Among servants, self comes first.

سپے ښۀ دے خو مثل ئې ښۀ نۀ دے.

1133. *The dog is welcome, the name of "dog" is not.*

سپے کۀ هر څومره بد شي خو بيا هم د څښتن کور ساتي.

1134. *No matter how vicious the dog becomes, he will still guard the house of his master.*

سپين ويل يا لېوني کوي يا زورور.

1135. *Frankness is the privilege only of the madman or the man of power.*

[Speaking the truth or being frank is a luxury only the mad or the powerful can afford. *LNB, RWS*]

سپيني پګرۍ سړو ته ښځو په سر کړي دي.

1136. *White turbans are given to the men by the women.*

White turbans among the Pakhtuns are a sign of respect in their society. This saying refers to the fact that some men owe their dignity to women.

سپيني وريژې نذر دين خوري او سپيني تُورې ئيل بوغ وهي.

1137. *The white rice is enjoyed by Nazar Din, the shining swords were borne by Yeel Bugh.*

Yeel Bugh typifies those who made sacrifices for their people in time of need, while Nazar Din represents those who have enjoyed the fruits of these sacrifices. That is, the credit due for one's achievements goes to others.

[Awal Bagh is a common Pashtun name. In the Bannuchi dialect it is pronounced "Yeel Bogh". *RWS*]

ست په ست به درته دري د خوشحال خټک خبرې.

1138. *Time and again you will recall the sayings of Khushal Khattak.*

This proverb is used when someone needs the advice of any wise man from the past [not just Khushal Khan Khattak].

ستا د خبره مې توبه شه خو دا سپي دې رانه کُرٍی کړه.

1139. *To hell with your alms, please call off your dogs.*

One day a beggar approached the *hujra* of a Khan, hoping to receive some help. When he asked for the Khan, he was insulted by the companions of the chief. While the beggar was being badgered, the Khan appeared and told a servant to give the fellow some alms and let him go. On hearing this the beggar exclaimed, "I have refrained from begging from you, but call off your dogs!"

ستا سپي زمونږ تبر خو نۀ دے راوړے؟

1140. *Has your dog not brought our axe (home)?*

The anecdote from which this proverb derives relates that a man, going next door to flirt with his neighbor's wife, was surprised to find her husband at home. In a state of utter confusion, the visitor blurted out, "Has your dog not brought our axe?"

سترګې د سترګو نه شرمېږي.

1141. *Eyes feel shy of other eyes.*

سخ د هغۀ چا چې ئې غم وي په بل چا

1142. *Fortunate is the man who has others to share his burdens.*

[It is good to have friends who share one another's griefs (*ghəm*) and burdens. *See* Proverb 769. *LNB*]

سخے چي دي په غوجل کبني لوئ شي غابن ئي مه ګوره.

1143. *When the calf grows to be a bullock under your shed, do not count
his teeth.*

When a person has been with you a long time, there is no reason to
subject him to testing. [*See* Proverb 1015.]

سر خرئیلي بنه ده نۀ مېرۀ شړلي!

1144. *It is better for a woman to suffer the shaving of her head than to be
cast out of the home by her husband.*

[To shave a woman's head is to shame her, but this is a lesser
disgrace than being thrown out of the house. *LNB*]

سر کال (کل) کړه پی غړپ کړه!

1145. *Shave your head and gulp the milk.*

Be shameless and then do anything you wish.

سر کۀ لاړ شي عادت نۀ خي.

1146. *One may lose his head but not his habits.*

This is similar to the saying, "Old habits die hard."

سړے په لوظ غوئ په سر بد لېږي.

1147. *A man may be judged by his words, an animal [cow] by his
appearance.*

سرے په نيت پر دے کارونه خدا ے کوي.

1148. *One must make up his mind and leave the rest to God.*

[Literally, "A man must have plans or intentions (*niyat*), but God's will prevails." *See* Proverbs 800 and 1006. *LNB*]

سرے تالا بنۀ دے خبره تالا نۀ ده بنۀ.

1149. *It is better to deprive a man of his belongings than to disrupt a discussion.*

سرے څۀ په يوه لوته سپيرۀ څۀ په سل لوتي.

1150. *What does it matter if a man dirties himself with one clod of earth or a hundred.*

سرے د غوړ په خبره ټربېږي او پټے د ډېران په سره.

1151. *A man puffs up with pride when taken into confidence, just as the earth becomes productive when covered by manure.*

سړي غرونه دي او ښڅي ئي ارمونه دي.

1152. *The men are the mountains, the women are their supports.*

Man cannot accomplish heavy endeavours without the help of women.

سستي او نېستي سره تړلي دي.

1153. *Idleness goes to poverty.*

Idleness and poverty are interlinked [literally, "tied together"; one leads to another. *LNB*]

سل بللي خُائبِړي يو نابللے نهٔ خُائبِړي.

1154. *A hundred invited guests can be accommodated, but not a single uninvited one.*

سل خرهٔ په يوهٔ سويه کبنې بنهٔ دي. نهٔ يو هندو په مرکه کبنې.

1155. *A single Hindu in a council is worse than a hundred donkeys under one shed.*

سل روپۍ بنې نهٔ دي يوه بنه خبره بنه ده.

1156. *A hundred rupees are not worth a single good word.*

[That is, "A single good word" is worth more than a hundred *rupees.*" *LNB*]

سوارهٔ ته چا وئيلي دي چې کور دې لرې دے.

1157. *Who is fool enough to say to a rider your house is far away.*

It should be obvious that a man who has the means can reach his destination.

سيکانو بنکته ګټه وکړه هندوانو دلته پګړۍ کړې کيبنوې.

1158. *The Sikhs won their battle far away, but the Hindus here cocked their turbans in pride.*

It is not appropriate for someone to take credit for the success of another, even if they are kinsmen.

[The Sikhs are noted for their martial prowess, but the Hindus are renound proverbially for their cowardice and impotency inn comparison with Sikhs—and of course, the Pashtun. *LNB*]

شاه د هغو چي شوګيري پسي کوی.

1159. *He who seeks his beloved (Shāh) must lie awake the whole long night.*

Here the term "beloved" (*shāh*) means the woman of his dreams, spiritually or in the flesh. It can also signify Almighty God.

[Those who pray the whole night will ultimately find what they long for. With the addition of a final syllable to the last verb, this proverb is identical to the second line of a *ṭappa*, which appears in its entirety in Proverb 993, an exhortation to vigilance and persistence. *RWS, LNB*]

[The picture is of one who pines and sits watching through the night for his beloved (*shāh* or commonly *shāh layla*). Alternatively, the initial word "*shāh*" can be understood and written without the letter "*he*", making the initial word a verb (and this is the form the text appears in Tair's larger collection of Pashto proverbs): "*shā də hagho che …*", with the wider meaning, "May it become theirs who stay awake the whole night for it."[50] *LNB*]

شپه چي په کور وي په ګور به نشي، چي په ګور وي په کور به نشي.

1160. *The night one must spend in the home will not be spent in the grave, and the night one is destined to spend in the grave cannot be spent in the home.*

Everything is preordained.

شرمخ هغه مېږه وري چي د رمي نه جدا شي.

1161. *The wolf carries [off] only the sheep that has strayed from the herd.*

[In unity there is strength. *RWS*]

شړۍ پرېږدم خو شړۍ ما نۀ پرېږدي.

1162. Though I want to toss off the blanket it clings to me.

Two men were once strolling beside a river when one of them spotted a black object floating on the surface. Thinking it was a blanket, he dove into the river and swam to retrieve it. As he grasped the object, it turned out to be a bear which promptly hugged him. As they struggled, the friend on the bank called out, "If you can't swim with it, leave it there." Whereupon the swimmer said. "Though I want to toss off the blanket, it clings to me."

This proverb is used when a person accepts something in good faith and then cannot get rid of it.

شل شاباسي که يو خاے کړې يو دمړے ترې نۀ جوړېږي.

1163. A score of "Well-done" would not make a penny.

This is an example [of a proverb using the language] of commercialism, which is rare in Pashto proverbs.

شناخت په ليدۀ شي او مينه په لقمه شي.

1164. Looks help in recognition, hospitality reflects love.

[That is, as acquaintance and familiarity comes through seeing a person, so love grows through the sharing of meals, literally, "through a bite or mouthful of food." *LNB*]

شېخه فريده خُله پټه بهتري ده.

1165. Oh, Sheikh Farid, it is better to keep quiet.

Sheikh Farid was a Pakhtun saint who lived in the Punjab (now a province of Pakistan) during the 13th century A.D. This is the proverbial advice, "Silence is golden". [*See* Proverb 835. *LNB*]

[This simple text illustrates the way the imagery used in proverbs reflects the interests and concerns of a society. Fariduddin Ganj-i Shakar (d. 1265), also called "Sheikh Farid" or "Baba Farid", was a Sufi poet-saint whose court (*dargah*) or spiritual center (*khānqāh*) and tomb is located near present day Pak Pattan on the River Sutlej. (He belonged to a noble family from Kabul; his grandfather took refuge in the Punjab during the invasion of Chengiz Khan.) Sheikh Farid was the disciple (*murid*) and spiritual successor (*khalifa*) of the pious Sheikh Qutbuddin Bakhtiar Kaki of the Chishtiyya Sufi order. In the 13th and 14th Centuries, Chishti Sufi saints were influential in spreading Islam throughout South Asia through their preaching and practice of the love of God and one's neighbor. Sheikh Farid was noted for his piety, service, spiritual excellence and asceticism. As his *dargah* was located on an important merchant caravan route linking Multan with Delhi, merchants, soldiers and nobles would stop there to invoke his blessing.

[Two details shed light on this Pashto proverb. One characteristic of the Chishtiyya assemblies is *samā* (literally "hearing"), the use of mystical dance and music used to heighten (or express) ecstasy (*wajd*). Muslim orthodoxy and more sober Sufi orders like the Naqshbandiyya (widespread in Central Asia) banned instruments, dance and listening to music. So it is plausible that the proverb, "Oh, Sheikh Farid, it is better to keep quiet", echoes the fierce controversy over Chishti practice, using him as a metaphor to teach the virtue of silence. Secondly, "Baba Farid" is revered by Sikhs as well as Muslims for his mystic poetry; several hymns and verses in Punjabi in the Sikh holy book *Guru Granth Sahib* are attributed to him. In this view, the proverb would be advising, in effect, "However beautiful your voice, silence is better." *LNB*]

ښار په ښهٔ خُلهٔ خوړے شي نهٔ په لنډۍ توره.

1166. *A city can be run better by a sweet tongue than by a sharp sword.*

[Literally, "A city can be eaten better by a sweet mouth (tongue) ..."
See Proverbs 385 and 418. *RWS*]

ښڅه د تن جامه ده.

1167. *Woman is the clothing of man.*

The wife glorifies her husband and adds grace and comfort to his being.

ښڅه د کور چراغ دے.

1168. *Woman is the lamp of the family.*

[Literally, "Woman is the lamp of the home or house." *RWS*]

[Proverbs 1167 and 1168 present a positive view of the woman and her role in relationship to her husband and family. Generally, in the proverb repertoires of most nations, the stereotype of women is negative, and this is the overall picture of women in Pashto proverbs as well. For examples of misogynous proverbs (expressing hatred or negativity toward women) *see* e.g. Proverb 873. Note that even these positive proverbs above serve to constrain the role of women and bolster male power. *LNB*]

ښڅه د وسواس په ورځ پيدا ده.

1169. *Woman was born on the day of suspicion.*

بنځه له اجاغه غواړه او لور خور و لمدبل ته ورکوه.

1170. If you wish to marry look for a poor girl; if you wish your
daughter[or sister] to marry find her a rich husband.

بنه په بنو به هر څوک وکړي مبرۀ هغه دے چې په بدو بنۀ وکړي.

1171. Doing good for good is normal, but the great man is he who does
good in return for evil.

[See Proverb 302 regarding the "Golden Rule". LNB]

بنۀ خوئ به دې سلطان کړي بد خوئ به دې حيران کړي.

1172. Good behavior will make you a king, while bad conduct will make
you worry.

بنۀ دوست په بد څا ے کښې معلوميږي.

1173. You can test a good friend in bad times.

[See Proverbs 877 and 911.]

بنه قصه بل ته کوه بنۀ خواړۀ خپل ته ورکوه.

1174. Tell a good story to an outsider, but give a good meal to your
kinsman.

بنۀ هغه دے چې په څان دې بنۀ وي.

1175. A good man is one who is good to you.

[Or, "A good thing is that which is good for your health." See Proverb
1069. RWS]

صبر د سپي ښهٔ دے خوراک د سړي ښهٔ دے.

1176. *The patience of a dog is praiseworthy and so are the eating habits of man.*

[Or alternatively, "... so are the manners of a man." *RWS*]

صبر د سړو لوئي هنر دے.

1177. *Patience is the key virtue of brave men.*

طبيب هغه چې په ځان ئې تېر وي.

1178. A doctor is one who has experienced it himself.

In times past a doctor learned only through personal experience. That is, "Experience is a good school, but its fees are heavy [or high]."

[There are many proverbs in English and other languages that illustrate the theme "one learns by experience" or "experience teaches". A good doctor (teacher, wise person) has much experience, but this may come at a cost as in the English proverb above, which appears in other forms as "Experience is a hard teacher" and as a "twisted proverb", for example, "Experience is a good teacher, but she sends in terrific bills," and "If experience is such a good teacher, why do I keep repeating the course?" *LNB*]

عاقلان بدي ورهٔ کوي بې عقلان په بدو ځان اخته کوي.

1179. *Wise men try to drive out mischief, fools only entangle themselves further in it.*

[The Pashto term translated "mischief" can also mean "enmity". RWS]

عثمانه کاڼے دي په سر پريوځه له اسمانه.

1180. *Oh Osman, a thunderbolt from heaven may fall on your head.*

The story is told that a man named Osman, living among the Yousafzais, commited a serious crime. When he was being carried in a procession through the bazaar on the way to his death by stoning, a Hindu shopkeeper cried, "Oh Osman, a thunderbolt from heaven may fall on your head." Upon hearing this Osman asked him, "Although these others have a right to punish me, what right have you?" The Hindu said, "Oh Khan, you have already fallen in the eyes of everyone else!"

[The phrasing of the Pashto is that of a curse, "Oh Osman, may a thunderbolt (literally "stone", *kāṇey*) fall ...!". The Hindu wishes that a "stone from heaven" be dropped on Osman's head—even as he is on the way to death by stoning! *LNB*]

عزرائيله وروره روغ رنځور پيژنه.

1181. *Oh the Angel of Death (Izrail), make a distinction between the ill and well.*

This proverb derives from a tale. One day an aged woman sat beside the bed of her young child who was seriously ill. She wailed and, in a moment of sympathy, prayed to God to take her instead of the child.

Meanwhile, a calf had broken its tether and wandered into the courtyard where it found a clay bowl (*qulpai*) containing the germinating flour. Pushing aside the lid, it thrust its muzzle into the heavy container. When it had eaten the flour and tried to withdraw its nose, it was caught fast. Confused, it entered the bedroom where the mother sat, wringing her hands. In the dark she could not recognize the strange being, and in her confusion she mistook it for Izrael, the archangel of death. The frightened woman revealed her weakness when she prayed, "Oh brother Izrail! Make a distinction between the ill and the well [the sick and the healthy]."

[The Muslim understanding is that at the hour of death (*see* Proverbs 72-74), Izrail, the "Angel of Death", comes to carry the soul away from the body; the pure soul to experience God's pleasure and pardon, the impure soul His wrath. In the Pashto text, as in the story, the woman addresses the supposed angel with the deferential greeting, "Oh brother Izrail ..." *LNB*]

عقل د بې عقلو نه زده كېږي.

1182. *Wisdom can be learned from fools.*

Someone once asked Luqman the Wise, "From whom have you learned such wisdom?" His answer was, "From fools." When asked how, he replied, "I merely refrained from doing what they would do." [For "Luqman" *see* Proverb 91.]

عقل د عزت يار دے كۀ عقل نۀ وي عزت خوار دے.

1183. *Wisdom is the true companion of honor; without wisdom, honor is lost.*

- 304 -

غاتر (قچر) ته ئي ويل چې پلار دې څوک دے ويل ئي اس غوندې ماما لرم.

1184. When the mule was asked who his father was, he replied, "My maternal uncle is a horse."

غر به در په سر کرم طاقت به درله در کرم.

1185. I will ask you to carry the mountain, but I will also give you strength to do it.

Man has the capacity to rise to great heights.

[The proverb in Pashto (*ghar ba dar pa sar kṛm tāqat ba dar la dar kṛm*) includes a number of poetic devices, including *rhyme* (/*ghar*/ *dar*/ *sar*/), *meter*, *repetition* (*dar*/ *kṛm*), *assonance* or repetition of the same vowel sound (/*a*/), and *colliteration* or the clustering of similar consonant sounds (/*b*/ *p*/). LNB]

غر په غر نۀ ورځي خوشحال خټک په سړي ورځي.

1186. A mountain will not beg for help from another mountain, but Khushal Khattak does!

A Yousafzai chief, while traveling to his own town, once stopped for the night at the *hujra* [the male social quarters or guest house] of the Khattak chief, Khushal Khan. While serving his guests their evening meal, the host remarked, "Eat, eat! A mountain comes to beg from another mountain, but Khushal will not."

Sometime later, when Khushal Khan was touring among the Yousafzai to solicit help against the Mughals, he spent the night with the Khan that he had formerly ridiculed by his remarks. Over dinner, the Yousafzai chief took his revenge by saying, "Eat, eat! A mountain will not beg for help from another mountain, but Khushal Khattak does so," whereupon Khushal Khan apologized for his earlier remark.

Khushal Khan Khattak was a celebrated warrior poet in the late 17th century. He wrote many prose works and much poetry in the Pashto language.

[An alternative version of this proverb says, "A mountain cannot go across to meet another mountain, but a man goes (can go) to another man (for example, for help)" That is, one mountain will not come to the aid of another mountain, but a man will. *RWS, LNB*]

غر که لوړ دے په سر ئي لار ده.

1187. *Though the mountain is high, it still has a path across its peak.*

[Similar to Proverb 406, this text avows that there is always someone of greater authority, strength or pride to whom one can appeal, or through whom one's purposes can be accomplished. The proud can always be defeated by someone prouder. A well-known variant (with the same meaning) uses Yusafzai (Pakistani) vocabulary and reads in Pashto: *kə ghar jəg* (or *lowī) day, no pə sar ye lār da. LNB*]

غشي ته چا وې چي ولې زغلې، وئيل ئي وروستو د لنيدې نه تپوس وکړه.

1188. *"Why are you flying so fast?" someone asked the arrow. Its reply was, "Ask the bow behind!"*

غل چي غلا کوي نور کور والا نۀ پُښتي.

1189. *When a thief is robbing a house he never asks the occupants for permission.*

غل سل کوره وران کړي يو خپل ودان نۀ کړي.

1190. *The thief despoils a hundred houses, yet he cannot furnish a house of his own.*

Stolen property does not benefit the thief.

غلبیل کوزي ته وائي تا کبنې دوه سوري دي.

1191. *The sieve taunts the water jar because it has two holes in it.*

The common water jar, like a teapot, has two openings. This proverb makes ironic reference to those who, while having many faults, ridicule others with fewer faults.

[The proverb is a sarcastic retort to a taunt, literally, "The sieve says to the water jar, 'You have two holes in you'," meaning "Who are you to criticise me!" *LNB*]

غم د پښتون جامه ده.

1192. *Sorrow is the dress of the Pakhtun.*

That is, Pakhtuns are not dismayed by adversity.

[The Pakhtun is always more worried about his honor than the cost (*ghəm*, "sorrow") associated with maintaining honor. For "sorrow" *see* Proverbs 102, 378 and Index. *LNB, RWS*]

غوا هم خدائ دے او پیپل هم خدائ دے (هندو ته).

1193. *The cow is a god, the "Pipal" tree is also a god, let them fight it out.*

It is said that a Hindu had planted a sapling of the *pipal* [*banyan*] tree. One morning, a Pakhtun came by and saw a cow briskly rubbing against the tree. When the Pakhtun pointed out to the Hindu the dangers of damage to the tree, the Hindu replied, "The cow is a god, the pipal is also a god; let them fight it out."

[In the abbreviated proverb text above, the final phrase associated with the story ("let them fight it out") is implied. This type of abbreviation is characteristic of many proverbs linked to well known stories. *LNB*]

- 307 -

غوائي چي سره بنکر په بنکر شي زيان د کانو بوټو دے.

1194. *When two bullocks fight, it is the shrubs and other plants that suffer.*

Two powerful enemies at war have little regard for the innocent [and weak; literally, "... the stones and shrubs lose (suffer loss)." *See* Proverb 528. *LNB, RWS*]

غوبنې او نوک نۀ سره جدا کېږي.

1195. *Flesh and fingernail cannot be separated.*

It is difficult to separate close relatives and friends.

غوبنې د هر چا خوبنې دي، خو پيشو پرې ايمان راوړے دے.

1196. *Everyone likes meat, but the cat worships it.*

[Literally, "... but the cat puts its faith (*imān*) in it"; the idiom "to put one's faith in" (something) is generally used with reference to God, for example, an unbeliever who converts, puts his faith in and worships (*imān rawṛəl*) the true God. *LNB*]

غوئ چي د غوبل په وخت موندۀ شي ورک ئي مۀ بوله.

1197. *If the strayed bullock is found at the time of threshing, he is not lost.*

[Or alternatively, "... he should not be considered lost." *RWS*]

فقر څۀ صلاح غواړي يو لکړه واخله او ورخۀ.

1198. *Learning to beg requires no instructions; just take a stick and begin.*

[Literally, "Begging (or poverty) needs no training ..." *RWS, LNB*]

فقيره کور دې چيرې؟ ويل ئي هر چيرې!

1199. *Someone asked a* faqir *(beggar), "Where is your home?" The reply was, "Everywhere!"*

[Structurally, the proverb is in the form of a question and answer dialogue: a direct address, "Oh *faqir,* where is your home?" (*see* Proverb 1200) and a brief retort, "He said, 'Everywhere.'" *See* Proverb 797. *LNB*]

فقيره نه دې کور سهي دے نۀ دې ډېره چې چرته دې ښنه هلته دې شپه.

1200. *Oh* faqir, *neither your* hujra *nor your home is known to others because you spend your nights wherever convenient.*

ق

قچر ته ئي وئيل چي څملي ولې نه وئيل ئي په ولاړه مي څه وخوړل چي
لا څملم.

1201. *Someone asked the mule, "Why are you not lying down?" It replied,
"I have not eaten enough in all my life while standing up, so why
should I lie down?"*

[This is another dialogue proverb with the common question and
answer structure, *see* Proverbs 797, 1199 and Index. *LNB*]

قلم دې کۀ باچا نۀ کړي د باچا تر څنګه خو به دې کښېنوي.

1202. *The pen may not make you a king, but it will certainly make you his
courtier.*

This is a reference to the acquisition of knowledge.

قيامت به هله شي چي پښتون له ننګه پرېوځي.

1203. *Doomsday will arrive when the Pakhtun says goodbye to his "nang"
(that is, code of honor).*

nang is an exclusive term for standing on the side of justice,
righteousness, and chivalry [and other notions associated with honor
as understood by Pakhtuns *LNB*]. It is the quality of *pakhtunwali* to
which every Pakhtun aspires. It is also called *pakhto* or *pashto*. [*See*
Proverb 341.]

[In Islamic, Christian and Jewish traditions, God's final judgment of
individuals and humankind ("the Last Judgment", *qiāmat*, here
translated "Doomsday") takes place at the end of the world. The
proverb underlines the Pashtun's extreme devotion to *pakhtunwali*
honor. The world will end before a Pashtun forsakes his honor. *LNB*]

كار تيار دے، يو نعل وشو خو يو اس او درې نعله پاتې دي.

1204. *All is ready. I have found a horseshoe, all I need now is a horse and three more shoes.*

With little in hand one aspires for large things.

كار چې بې وخته شي بې بخته شي.

1205. *When work is delayed, it loses its value.*

[This is a rhyming proverb: "Work that is *be-wakhta* (delayed, late) becomes *be-bakhta* (without blessing or value)." *LNB*]

كارغه هوښيار دے غُل خوري کتے کم عقل دے پۍ خوري!

1206. *The wise crow eats excreta, the stupid calf eats milk!*

[Literally, "The crow is wise (because) it eats excreta (crap); the calf is stupid (because) it eats milk." In Pashto, "stupidity" is crudely and idiomatically called "eating excreta (crap)". But the proverb is ironic, because although the crow is called "wise", it actually eats excreta, while the so-called "stupid" calf is drinking milk. *RWS, LNB*]

كاروان بندېږي د خلقو خولې نۀ بندېږي.

1207. *You can stop a caravan, but you cannot shut the mouths of people.*

[This proverb paints a picture of the unstoppable power of gossip and the impossibility of silencing the tongue. In Pashtun society, "What people say" (or "What people might say") about one's behavior (real or perceived) can destroy one's reputation and that of one's family.

A caravan of camels can be stopped by the caravan master, but no one can stop gossip from being passed on, one to another to another. *See* Proverbs 207, 738 and Index for "mouth", "tongue" and "honor". *LNB*]

کاږهٔ وري منزل ته نهٔ رسي.

1208. *The tilted load will not reach its destination.*

[A tilted or unbalanced load, for example, on a donkey or camel, won't reach its destination, because] it will fall off on the way. That which is basically wrong cannot be set right [or cannot succeed. Another version is, "A crooked load (*kog bār*) ..." *LNB*]

کالي چې اوبو يوړو سوبارے ما وريسې پريښنوو.

1209. *"When the stream carried away my laundry," said the woman, "I tossed the paddle in after it."*

What is the paddle when the clothes have been washed away.

کږه خُله په سُوک سمبږي.

1210. *A crooked mouth can be set right by a punch.*

Wicked people deserve severe punishment.

کښنلي ښهٔ وي کهٔ په زړهٔ منلي ښهٔ وي.

1211. *Which is preferable, beauty or that which the heart desires?*

[What is most "beautiful" is that which the heart has chosen or longs for. *RWS, LNB*]

كله مې په سوېري اوچوله كله مې په غرمو.

1212. Sometimes I dried it in the shade and sometimes in the sun.

A peasant once carried a hide to the market to sell it. The first leather merchant asked him how he had dried it. "In the shade", he said. The merchant said that he did not need the hide and no sale resulted. In the second shop the man was asked how had he dried the pelt? "In the sun," he promptly replied. Again he made no sale. When he entered the third shop, he was wiser. Again he heard the same question, but this time his reply was, "Sometimes I dried it in the shade, and sometimes in the sun."

كم عقل هغه چې نۀ خپله ورځي او نۀ د بل مني.

1213. Stupid is the man who neither knows himself nor accepts advice from others.

كور كول آسان دي خو اور بلول گران دي.

1214. It's easy to own a house, but difficult to keep a fire in it.

Maintaining a house and supporting a family are difficult tasks.

[Carrying on a job or work is one thing, but taking the initiative in something is more difficult, literally, "... to light a fire is difficult." *RWS*]

كورې شه سپيۀ دا سړے چې څه وائي هغه كوي.

1215. Be gone, Oh dog, whatever this man says, he means.

The proverb terminates another tale. Once a passing guest was invited by an acquaintance to stop and share a meal. "We will have a simple meal of cornbread, onions and whey," promised the host. They sat beside the house and the host brought forth everything exactly as he had promised—nothing special. While they were eating, a dog appeared and began to stare at them. Annoyed by the animal, the host made obscene threats, whereupon the guest added to the host's remarks, saying, "Be gone, Oh dog! Whatever this man says he means."

[A host may politely apologize to a guest for serving a humble meal, however, the meal itself often turns out to be more than generous. In this case, however, the host was true to his word: the guest anticipated more, but no special foods were served. The final comment is sarcastic, literally, "... Whatever this man says he does." *LNB*]

كول (كال) خو به تېر شي خو دا ستا سوے پتون به مي هېر نۀ شي.

1216. *The year will pass but I will never forget your burnt buttocks.*

During a famine, a man, worried about his sister who was married and living in a nearby village, decided to visit her and see how she was weathering the food shortage. As he approached her home, he saw from some distance his sister baking, and she also saw him. Recognizing him as her brother, which meant she would have to share the scarce bread, she quickly put the steaming loaf beneath her and sat upon it.

The brother politely refrained from indicating that he had seen what had transpired until he was about to leave. Then with a broad grin he said, "The year will pass, but I will never forget your burnt buttocks."

كوڼ دوه ځله خاندي.

1217. *The deaf man laughs twice.*

He laughs once when he sees others laugh, and again when he discovers what they are laughing about.

كوهے مۀ كنه د بل سرې په لار كښنې چرې ستا به د كوهي په غاړه لار شي!

1218. *Don't dig a well in the pathway used by others because you may someday fall into it yourself.*

One who lays a trap for others might fall into it himself one day. [*See* Proverb 597.]

[This proverbial truth is actually a verse from a *ghazel* of the Pashtun mystic poet, Abdur Rahman Baba. A *ghazel* is a lyric love poem in the Persian style, for example, with a rhyming letter that ends each line; an author's poems were often written and collected into a book called a *diwan*. A similar truth to this is expressed in an ancient poetic psalm (song) written by King David "He who digs a hole and scoops it out falls into the pit he has made. The trouble he causes recoils on himself; his violence comes down on his own head."[51] *RWS, LNB*]

كۀ بادشاهي غواړم نو نۀ ئي مومم او كۀ فقيري غواړم نو كند كچكول تيار دي.

1219. *If I long to be a king, it can never be, but if I wish to be a beggar, the begging bowl and the rags are ready.*

It is difficult to become rich, but much easier to become poor.

[The proverb compares the futile desire for a lofty kingdom (*bādshāhi*) with the reality of poverty (*faqiri*), the life of a beggar, marked by the begging bowl (*kachkol*) and rags which are always near at hand. *LNB*]

كه باران وي كه ږلى مېلمه غواړي بنه نمړى.

1220. *Whether it rains or hails the guest should be shown the hospitality he deserves.*

[That is, whatever the condition of the house, the guest wants or expects good food. *RWS, LNB*]

كه په خپل وطن كښې خان ئي په بل وطن حېران ئي.

1221. *Though you are a prosperous man in your own country, in another land you are completely dependent upon others.*

[Though a *khān* (chief, prosperous man) in your homeland, you are *hayrān* (literally, "surprised"), that is, a nobody and dependent on others, in a foreign country. *LNB*]

که تهٔ نازو شې خو میروس خان به څوک زیږ وي؟

1222. *Though you may be named Nazo, who will give birth to Mirwais Khan?*

    Merely having the name Nazo does not mean a woman can give birth to a great man such as Mirwais Khan Ghalzai, whose mother was Merman Nazo. Mirwais Afghan was the ruler of Qandahar who defeated the Iranians.

[The Ghalzai (Ghilzai) chief Mirwais (d. 1715) of the Hotak clan defeated the Safawid Persian Empire at Qandahar in 1709, providing a base for the founding of an autonomous and independent Afghan state (really a confederation of tribes and khanates) in 1747 under King Ahmad Shah Durrani, which stretched from Herat in the west to the Indus River in the east. *LNB*]

که ځې ځې ابازو له به راځې.

1223. *No matter where you journey, you will always return to Abazai.*

    The proverb signifies that a man's loyalties are always with his place of origin. [*See* Proverb 634.]

که چاړه د سرو شي خو په خپته د منډلو نهٔ ده.

1224. *Though the dagger may be of gold it is not meant for stabbing oneself with.*

    A precious thing, if not handled properly, may cause you harm. [*See* variant Proverb 544.]

[A harmful thing may be valuable, but nevertheless it is still harmful. *RWS*]

که خر مري خو هندو به وړي.

1225. *Even if he dies from the effort, the donkey must carry the Hindu.*

    The cruel master never has mercy for his servants.

که د فتح خان باندې ئې خو حال مې در معلوم دے. که نۀ وي نو در باندې در غم.

1226. *If you belong to Fatheh Khan Banda (village) then you know me very well. If not, be prepared to receive my attack.*

The proverb refers to a habitual criminal who used to sit an arrow's distance from the road and challenge passersby with this statement. As he was a cripple, the inhabitants of Fatheh Khan Banda would only laugh. Those who were strangers would fear his words and lay down their belongings there and then.

This proverb is similar to the truism, "Barking dogs seldom bite." [*See* Proverbs 43, 511 and 685.]

که د ورو نه لنگېدے نو کوڅې به ډکې وي.

1227. *If boys could cause pregnancy, the streets would be littered with offspring.*

If everyone could do difficult tasks, there would be no need for specialists.

که زر پاک وي نو د اوره ئې څه باک وي.

1228. *If the gold is pure it has no fear of fire.*

That is, it glitters all the more.

[This proverb can mean that a person with a clear conscience need not worry, or that a person's true character will be revealed. *LNB, RWS*]

که زۀ مرم خو وار خو به تېروم.

1229. *Even if I am to die I still want my turn.*

The story is told of a Muslim with two wives. He shared his time equally between them, inviting one each night. Once when he was to visit wife number one, she was ill. The second wife seeing that her rival was unable to receive the master, gathered up his bedding and was about to carry it to her own bedroom, when the indisposed wife said, "Even if I am to die, I still want my turn." (In the household, each person customarily has only one quilt, mattress and pair of sheets for his personal use.) [See Proverbs 3, 684, 1229 and 1334.]

که سل کشمیره راکړې خراسان به پرې ورنکړم.

1230. *I would not trade my Khurasan for a hundred Kashmirs.*

Khurasan is the former eastern province of the Abbasid Caliphate [749 – 1258 A.D.], covering the whole area in which the Pakhtuns live today. The present day eastern province of the same name, located in Iran, is but a segment of the original Khurasan [which is associated with the Afghanistan of today. *LNB*]

The disputed territory of Jamu and Kashmir to the north of Pakistan is regarded by Persian poets as the Earthly Paradise.

[This text is similar in meaning to the English proverb, "East or West, home is best." *See* Proverbs 445 and 634. *RWS*]

که کم عقل نۀ وے نو هوښیار به مشري په چا کوله.

1231. *If there were no stupid people in the world, over whom would the clever rule.*

که لنډے غوئے په بدی کښې قبلوې نو پلور (پلار) دې مو وژله ده.

1232. *If you will accept this puny bullock as blood money, then I have killed your father, otherwise I am not the culprit.*

A man was murdered by an unknown assailant. When his sons were seeking the murderer to carry out their revenge, a man from the community appeared at their door leading behind him an emaciated bullock. Addressing the eldest son of the deceased he said, "If you will accept this puny bullock as the blood price, then I have killed your father; otherwise, I am not the culprit."

Sometimes the murderer can atone for his crime with the payment
of blood money, if it is accepted by the aggrieved party (the family of
the one murdered).

كه مشر مشرتوب غواړي نو كشر هم د دُنيا دود غواړي.

1233. *If the elders demand respect, the youngsters also deserve the
traditional courtesy.*

كه نۀ وے بې رامئی په هر چا به ابادۍ وے خپلۍ ببسيى.

1234. *Were it not for natural calamities, everyone would feel secure in his
village.*

[Or, "If there were no disloyalties among relatives, everyone ..."
RWS]

كه ورور دې خپل وي خو چې په راز د بل وي دشمن ترې بنۀ دے.

1235. *An enemy would be better than a brother who has made an alliance
against you with others.*

[Though one may be your own brother, if he makes an alliance with
another, such a traitor is worse than an enemy. *RWS*]

ک

كته بې ستړيا نه كېږي.

1236. *Without wearing himself out no one can become wealthy.*

There is "No gain without pain."

كته ئې د مزدور غوندې، خوره ئې د خُښتن غوندې.

1237. *Earn it like a laborer, eat it like a master.*

گډې كه لم دې لوئ دے خپله كونه دې پرې پټه ده.

1238. *Oh sheep, though your tail is big it covers your backside.*

A wealthy man should not boast of his riches, which profit only himself.

[The "big tail" covers only his own backside. The fat-tailed sheep is common in Pakistan and Afghanistan. *LNB, RWS*]

گل سره ازغي وي.

1239. *Every rose has thorns.*

[The common proverb found in a number of European languages "Every rose has its thorn" or "There is no rose without thorns" teaches a basic fact of life and of human nature, viz. there is always something to diminish life's pleasures, nobody is perfect, and every joy in our lives brings or foreshadows its own sorrow. *See* Proverb 390. *LNB*]

- 320 -

گور کۀ گران دے خو د مړي ناکام دے.

1240. *Though lying in a grave is unwelcome, the dead have no choice.*

گوره ورته کبِرده مچ دے باندې کښینی به.

1241. *Place brown sugar in front of him and like the fly he will land on it.*

[A greedy person can be trapped by offering him something that he likes. *RWS*]

ګیدړ د اوښ په سوېري تلو وېل ئې دا زما دے!

1242. *The jackal, walking in the shade of the camel, pretended that the shadow was his own.*

The image is of one who indulges in tall talk, [who exaggerates or makes false claims; literally, "The jackal, walking ... said, 'This (shadow) is mine'" *LNB, RWS*].

ګیله له یاره ده نه له اغیاره!

1243. *One can complain about his friend, but not about outsiders!*

[Or, "A complaint can be made by a friend, but not by an outsider." *RWS*]

ل

لاس چي مات شي غاړي له ځي.

1244. *When the arm is broken it hangs in a string from the neck for support.*

When a person alienated from his family gets into trouble, he will return to his kin for help.

[A person in trouble will ultimately ask for help from his relatives. *RWS*]

لاس دې اووينځه له ژونده که غلط شوې د دشمن په خوشامنده.

1245. *Wash your hands of your life if you have been deceived by the flattery of an enemy.*

لټ د دوبي سوبرے غواړي، د ژمي پيتاوے!

1246. *The lazy man longs for the sunshine in winter and the shade in summer.*

لرګي تراشه سړي ځنې جوړوه.

1247. *Chisel wood and from it make human beings.*

This suggests that wild people can be turned into civilized beings through training.

[This also may be an ironic expression about people today who are not equal to the standard of manliness of the old days. *RWS*]

لږ خوره طبیب ته به نۀ ئې اړ.

1248. *Eat less and you will not need a doctor.*

لک پتي نۀ دے بنۀ اوپتی بنۀ دے.

1249. *Better a dependable friend than a millionaire.*

لکه جاله ئې ویني که داسې جاله وان لیدے نو زړۀ به ئې چاودے وو.

1250. *The raft feels the turbulent waters; if the raftsman could also sense the danger, he would have collapsed there and then.*

[Feeling everything out of control, literally, "... his heart would have exploded," an idiom meaning that he was so overwhelmed with such emotion and alarm that he could have "collapsed". *LNB*]

لکه د شرمخ ګډوري ته وائي چې دا اوبه ولې خړوې.

1251. *The wolf said to the lamb, "Why are you muddying the water?"*

This proverb refers to a folk tale. A lamb was drinking water from a stream when a wolf emerged from the forest and began to drink upstream. Seeing the lamb and taking him for an easy prey, the wolf sought an excuse [to challenge and attack him] and called out, "Why are you muddying the water?" "How can my drinking offend you," said the lamb, "when I am downstream?" The wolf, pretending he thought the reply arrogant, said, "But your father had insulted me before you were born." The lamb answered, "But that was my father, not I!" The wolf ate the lamb anyway, calling him insulting and rebellious.

لکه د شېخ چلي د خپلې ناستې بناخ پرېکوې.

1252. *Like Sheikh Chili he sits on a branch and saws off his perch.*

According to an old story told to children, a simple man named Sheikh Chili was sawing off a large branch on which he sat, when a passer by told him, "Do not cut the branch or you will fall." The simpleton inquired, "Are you a foreteller [fortune-teller] that you know so much?" "Yes," he said and started off. A few more cuts with the saw and the foolish fellow crashed to the ground and bloodied his nose. Leaping up he ran after the other man and said, "You must be a holy man. You told me the truth. Now tell me when I am going to die?" He learned that he must die two days later. Weeping he went to his house and told his wife what had happened. (The remainder of the story does not apply to this proverb.)

The proverb is used to teach that one should not be disloyal to one's supporters.

لکۍ که ډېرې وي سر يو بنۀ وي.

1253. *Though there may be many tails there should be but one head,*

The proverb derives from a popular myth concerning two snakes in a jungle. One had a hundred tails but only one head. The other one had one tail and a hundred heads. When the jungle caught fire, the single-headed serpent followed a straight course and escaped, but the other could not decide between a hundred different opinions and was consumed by the flames.

The application is to [the value of having] one recognized leader of any group or government.

لند کلونه اوږدۀ ئې پيغورونه.

1254. *The years are short, the insults are long.*

Insults are never forgotten. [*See* Proverb 375.]

لنديه غوايۀ په لوړه اوخيژه څار وکړه، چې نور عالم څه کوي هاغسې تۀ کړه.

1255. *Oh puny ox, climb to the upland, watch what your brothers are doing and imitate them.*

[This is similar to the proverb, "When in Rome, do what the Romans do." *See* Proverbs 89, 631 and 885. *RWS*]

لور چې ښه شي د مور کوڅی ئې په پښه شی.

1256. *When the daughter proves that she is well behaved she steps into the shoes of her mother.*

[Obedient children follow their parents. *RWS*]

لونده ژبه هر خوا اوړي.

1257. *A wet tongue can twist in any direction.*

Words can be given many meanings.

لویو وکړه نو وړو ترې زده کړه.

1258. *The elders did it, the children copied them.*

Set a good example to children, who will act accordingly due to their impressionable age.

له سياله سره سيالداري کړه له همزولي سره راز داري کړه.

1259. *Compete with your rival, confide in your friend.*

[The term "rival" (*siyāl*) can also be translated "equal". One's ideal competitor or adversary is equal in power or status; similarly, marriages are usually arranged with a *siyāl*, a family who is equal in status, for example, the father's brother's son / daughter. The term translated "friend" (*hamzoley*) means someone of the same age, a peer or contemporary, for example, a classmate. *LNB*]

له کم عقله سجنه هوښنیار دشمن ښه دے.

1260. *An intelligent enemy is preferable to a foolish friend.*

لېوۀ ته ئې نصیحت اوکړو په هغه ورځ ئې شل ودارل.

1261. *Though someone advised the wolf to show mercy to other animals,*
        he killed twenty that day.

The English proverbs "The leopard cannot change his spots" or
"You can't teach an old dog new tricks" have a similar meaning.

[The proverb can also mean that good advice given to a mean-spirited
person can have a reverse reaction. *RWS*]

[The English axiom, "A leopard cannot change his spots" is based on
the ancient words in the Bible, "Can an Ethiopian change the color of
his skin? Can a leopard take away its spots? Neither can you start
doing good, for you always do evil."[52] In a similar way, the wolf
ignored advice to show mercy but instead acted according to his true
character. *LNB*]

ماته مه گوره خو دې پورې اديرې ته گوره.

1262. *Don't look at me, look at the graveyard yonder.*

This is a reference to the inevitability of death.

[When someone requires or insists on the truth about a situation from an apparent pretender, he may use this proverb, in effect asking the person to swear on his grave and in the light of eternity. *RWS, LNB*]

مار زخمي کړه مېږو ته ئي پرېږده.

1263. *Wound the snake and leave it to the ants.*

مار وژلې ښهٔ دے تربور وهلې ښهٔ دے.

1264. *It is better to kill a snake and humble [beat] a* tarbur *(cousin).*

An enemy (snake) should be eliminated, but a cousin may be useful if kept in a subservient role. [*See* Proverbs 485, 486 and 716.]

مال خوږ دے خو د اولاد نه خوږ نهٔ دے.

1265. *Wealth is not dearer than one's children.*

مال دې لاړ شي سر دې لاړ شي پت دې نهٔ ځي.

1266. *A man may lose his wealth and his head, but not his honor.*

[This is one line of a poem by Khushal Khan Khattak: "A man may lose his life and wealth, but not his honor, because the sole value of a person is in keeping his honor." In the Afghan dialect, this proverb appears in the form, *sar de drumi māl de drumi pat de nə zi. RWS*]

[Note that the boundary between genres like proverbs and poetry is often less than clear. The perception of proverbiality is sometimes determined by usage, traditionality or "truth value", rather than structural differences. Thus, lines from classical poetry (as here) or folk poetry (*ṭappa*) can be associated with proverbs (*mataluna*). *See* Proverb 106 and Index for "proverbs:folk poem:*ṭappa, landəy". LNB*]

ماهي وئيل ما به خبرې کړې وے. مگر خله مې د اوبو ډکه ده.

1267. *The fish said "I would have spoken if I had not had a mouth full of water."*

مچ ويل که د پيغلې په مخ ومرمه مړ نۀ يم.

1268. *The fly said "If I die on the cheek of a pretty damsel I will have died happy."*

[Literally, "If I die on the cheek of a young woman (that is, a woman of marriageable age) I am not dead." *LNB, RWS*]

مخکښېنۍ ځه خو بېرته هم گوره.

1269. *Move forward, but also look backward.*

Don't forget your past.

مرگ په بانه دے دولت په هيله دے.

1270. *Death requires a cause, wealth requires an effort.*

مرګ يو ځل دے.

1271. *Death comes only once.*

مريئ ته ئي وئيل رانيسم دې وئيل ئي ستا اختيار!

وئيل ئي تښتئ خو به نه؟ وئيل ئي زما اختيار.

1272. *A man said to the slave, "I want to catch you." The slave replied, "Whatever you wish." "Won't you run away?" the man asked. The slave said, "That is for me to decide!"*

[This is another example of a dialogue proverb, in this case with a four-part structure ABCB$_1$, revolving around the clever slave's pithy replies "... Your wish (*stā ikhtiyār*) ... My wish! (*zmā ikhtiyār*)" and a word play involving *ikhtiyār* (will, wish, choice, decision; in other contexts, authority) and the deferential idiomatic expression, "As (whatever) you wish." *LNB*]

مړي مړۀ شي او ژوندي خپل روزګار کوي.

1273. *The dead pass away, the living continue their routine lives.*

مشر د خرو هم شته.

1274. *Even the donkeys have a leader.*

ملا ځنګل ته نۀ ځي او بلا جمات ته نۀ ځي.

1275. *The mullah does not go to the jungle and the ghost does not go to the mosque.*

ملا واخله اورې راکړه نۀ اورې.

1276. *The mullah listens to "Take it" and not "Give it."*

[For proverbial steroeotypes of the mullah, *see* Proverb 85 and Index for "mullah". *LNB*]

منرِکانو ګینګړي جوړ کړل ویل ئې د پیشو په غاړه کښې به ئې څوک اچوي؟

1277. *The rats made alarm bells, but who was there to tie them around the cats neck?*

That is, "Who will bell the cat?"

[This proverb is associated with the fable of the old mouse who suggested they hang a bell on the cat's neck to warn all mice of her approach. A wise young mouse answered, "Excellent, but who will do the job?" Anyone who risks his own life or encounters personal hazard for the sake of others undertakes to "bell (hang a bell on) the cat." Some people are full of good advice, but are unwilling to take the necessary risks. *LNB*]

منګے په یو ځل ماتېږي.

1278. *The pitcher breaks only once.*

A weak man cannot bear constant troubles.

مور او لور جنګ وکړو کم عقلو پرې باور وکړو.

1279. *The mother and daughter had a quarrel, but the foolish ones assumed that the two women had become enemies.*

Word duels [that is, arguments] between two close kinsmen do not necessarily lead to enmity.

[A fight between a mother and her daughter isn't all that serious. *RWS*]

[However, (literally) "... the foolish believed it" was serious! The term *jang* used in the proverb can refer broadly to conflicts ranging from a minor argument, quarrel or disagreement to a feud, battle or war. The "foolish" lack the wisdom to discern the difference between "fights" and thus the critical social skills needed to manage them. *LNB*]

مور ئې رنگ ګوري ښحهٔ ئې څنګ ګوري.

1280. *The mother searches his face , the wife searches his pockets.*

[The mother is concerned about his wellbeing (*rang*, associated with the color of his face), while his wife is interested only in what he has brought with him (*tsang*). *LNB*]

مونږه غلهٔ سهي خو تا دې خداے جوړ کړي.

1281. *True, we may be thieves, but we wish you a speedy recovery from your insanity.*

One day a man was sleeping on the *chārpay* [cot] when he was surprised by a band of thieves. They robbed him of his goods, tied him securely to his bed, and carted him off.

When he saw people passing he cried for help and announced that he was being kidnapped. But when the passersby attempted to help him, the abductors would say to their victim, "True we may be thieves, but we wish you a speedy recovery from your insanity."

[The final phrase is in the form of a blessing, "... but may God make you well," ("from your insanity" is implied by the story associated with the proverb). *LNB*]

مه داسې خوږ شه چې تبر دې کړي، مه داسې تریخ شه چې قی دې کړي.

1282. *You should not be so sweet that you will be swallowed, nor so bitter that you will be vomited.*

One should avoid extremes.

[This is also advice for negotiating the demands of *pakhtunwali*: one must demonstrate generosity, kindness and friendship without appearing soft, naive, or weak, and likewise demonstrate strength without arrogance or a feud-provoking belligerence. *LNB*]

مېړانه د مېړو جوهر دے.

1283. *Bravery is the essence of noble men.*

میړنی همیشه د خندنی د لاسه مري.

1284. *The hero is usually destroyed by a ridiculous person.*

[Literally, "The courageous or brave-hearted man is killed by a laughable person (*khandani*) or "fool". *See* Proverb 926, 985 and 1260 and other proverbs regarding the "fool" or "foolish, stupid" people. *LNB*]

میړو ته ګوره برخې وېشه.

1285. *Look for the superiority in men before distributing shares.*

[*See* Proverb 609.]

میړونه مري اؤ مېړانه ئې پاتې کېږي.

1286. *Noble men die, their noble deeds survive.*

مېلمه د کوره شړلې بنۀ دے نۀ په ګېډه نهر.

1287. *It is better to drive a guest from the home than to deprive him of hospitality.*

نابلده غلو جمات مات کړے دے.

1288. *The ignorant thieves broke into the mosque.*

They could not differentiate between a mosque and a house.

ناوې جينۍ راغله نوے دود ئي راوړو.

1289. *A new bride has brought new traditions.*

This proverb is used sarcastically when a person assumes a new role and seeks to make changes.

نښتر چي زړېږي غوړ ئي پېخ ته لوېږي.

1290. *When the pine grows old the pitch runs downs into the lower trunk.*

نن په ما صبا په تا.

1291. *Today I am in trouble, tomorrow you will face it.*

[Today it happened to me, but tomorrow it could be your turn. Literally, "Today (it is) on me, tomorrow on you." *LNB, RWS*]

نوم د ډيوې کېږي سوزي تبل.

1292. *It is the oil that gives light, the lamp takes the credit.*

Sometimes credit is not given to the one who deserves it.

[Literally, it is "the oil (that) burns", and so gives the light, but this is not acknowledged—the "lamp gets the name." *LNB*]

نوے نوکر په منډه هوسۍ نيسي.

1293. *The new servant catches the deer by running after it.*

[When a person starts a new job he is enthusiastic. *RWS*]

نۀ پردی دېره نۀ خپله اديره.

1294. *One's family cemetery is better than another man's hujra.*

In other words, an individual, however reluctantly, would prefer to spend his time in the family graveyard rather than in another's social center. The *hujra* is an all male social center for the Pakhtuns.

[That is, one feels more relaxed in one's home, even if it is not comfortable. *RWS*]

نۀ د بې مالګي خوړو مزه شته، نۀ د پردي زويه ګيله شته.

1295. *Food without salt is tasteless, [so is a] complaint from another's son.*

As food is tasteless without salt, so another man's son may not be as good as you want him to be.

[Food without salt has not tasty, nor is complaining about another man's son. *RWS*]

نۀ سرے هندو دے، نۀ څناور خر دے!

1296. *The Hindu cannot be considered a man as the donkey cannot be considered an animal.*

[This proverb is also known with a slightly different word order (*nə hindu saṛay dey, nə khar zanāwər dey*) but with the same meaning. *RWS*]

نۀ غل يم نۀ د غلو مل يم!

1297. *I am neither a thief nor their companion.*

نياتى (دوست) به دې وژړوي اؤ دشمن به دې وخندوي.

1298. *A friend will make you weep and an enemy will make you laugh.*

A friend will tell you the truth about yourself and an enemy will misguide you while feigning to do you good.

[For example, a friend will show you your weaknesses with good intentions, while the person who is not a friend will try to hide them from you. *See* Proverb 857. *RWS, LNB*]

نېستي د سړي سترګي ړندويى.

1299. *Poverty makes one blind.*

Poverty compels a man to do anything [literally, "blinds a man's eyes."]

و

وادهٔ اسان دے خو تک توک ئې گران دے.

1300. *Marrying is easy, but the preparations are difficult.*

[In Pakhtun society, marriage preparation involves many cultural requirements and financial expectations, making it demanding and costly. *LNB, RWS*]

واوري اوبهٔ شوې خو سارهٔ ئې کم نهٔ شو.

1301. *The snow has melted, yet it is cold.*

That is, old habits or characteristics die hard. [Literally, "... its coldness did not decrease." *RWS*]

وران رباب ئې د مجلس خوند خرابوي.

1302. *You are like a* rabab *that is out of tune and spoils the concert.*

The *rabāb* is a popular Pakhtun musical instrument that resembles a guitar.

[The *rabāb* is shaped more like a lute; the body (about 8 inches deep) and tuning pegs are usually made of mulberry (*tut*) wood, with a goatskin face, three plucked gut strings, gut frets, two or three "drone" strings and ten to fourteen other steel strings that vibrate sympathetically when the main strings are plucked, together producing a deep resonant sound—when all the strings are in tune! However, the *rabāb* is difficult to tune and keep tuned, as temperature and humidity affect the wooden pegs, face and strings over the course of a "concert". If one's life and manner are " out of tune," you ruin the atmosphere for everyone around you. *LNB*]

ورور ته بې زويه مهٔ شي دشمن ته بې وروره مهٔ شي.

1303. *May you not be without a son against a brother, or without a brother against an enemy.*

A man with property may be hated by his brother's family if he has no heir. They will wish his death so that they may inherit his property. Therefore, your brother would like you to remain without a son so that he can inherit your property after your death. Nevertheless, this very brother, if you are alive, will help you against your enemy.

ورور چې ننگيالے شي د خور په سر تکرے شي.

1304. *When the brother becomes a man of prowess, his sister basks under his protection.*

وروري خوري به کوؤ، حساب تر مينځه.

1305. *True, we are brother and sister, but we must still be accountable to one another.*

وزی که پټ وي په راشه به څرګند شي.

1306. *Though the measuring cup is stored away, it will appear when the harvest is to be apportioned.*

Although something may appear useless at the moment, it will prove useful at the appropriate time.

[In alternative versions, *uzay* (measuring cup) is replaced by *wazay* ("hungry man", or "ear of corn"): "The unseen hungry man will emerge at the time of crushing (for his share)", or "The ear of corn, though hidden, will come out at the time of crushing." *RWS*]

وزې وئيل چي که زۀ نۀ وايم زما دا ګډه پښه به اووئي.

1307. *The goat said, "If I don't tell the story, my broken leg will!"*

The Pakhtuns have a folk tale to which this proverb refers. The village herdsman, who leads the goats and sheep out to pasture each day, was once annoyed by a balky goat. In anger he threw a stone at her and broke her leg. Since he was responsible for the damage, he approached the goat and begged her not to tell her owner how the injury had occurred. The animal replied. "If I don't tell the story, my broken leg will!"

وسله هغه ده چي په لاس دي راغله.

1308. *Anything which is in your own hand can be used as a weapon.*

ونه ګوره سوپري لاندي ئي کښېنه ، سړے ګوره سوال ترې کوه.

1309. *Look at the tree, and sit in its shade,*
      Look at the man and ask him for help.

Seek assistance from one capable of rendering it.

ویر به دي هله وُکړم چي ښېګړه دي په زړۀ کړم.

1310. *I will weep over your death only if I can recall some kindness you have shown me.*

[*See* Proverb 148.]

ﻫﺎﺗﻲ ﻛﻪ ﻟﻪ ﺗﻨﺪﯤ ﻣﺮﻱ ﻫﻢ ﭘﻪ ﮐﭙﺪﻩ ﮐښﯥ ﺋﻲ ﻳﻮ ﺯﻧﮕﻮﻥ ﺍﻭﺑۀ ﻭﻱ.

1311. *Though the elephant may be dying of thirst, the water in his stomach will still be knee deep.*

The meaning is that a rich man may declare bankruptcy when his holdings are still sufficient to support the man of average income.

ﻫﺮ ﭼﺎ ﺗﻪ ﺧﭙﻞ ﺯﻭﺉ ﺷﻬﺰﺍﺩﻩ ﺩﮮ.

1312. *To every man his own child [son] is a prince.*

The story is told that a king, in a jolly mood, once said to a palace sweeper, "Go and bring me the handsomest boy in the kingdom!" The poor man considered the request for some time, then brought his own son to the ruler. The king looked at the scruffy lad and said, "What! This ragamuffin? Bring me a handsome boy." The sweeper replied. "Your majesty, this is my own child, and let me remind you, to every man his own child is a prince." The king smiled.

ﻫﺮ ﺧﻮﮎ ﺑﻪ ﺣﺴﻴﻦ ﻭﮮ ﺧﻮ ﮐﻪ ﻧۀ ﻭﮮ ﮐﺮﺑﻼ ﭘﮑښﯥ.

1313. *Everyone would be a Hussain had there been no Karbala.*

Hussain, a grandson of the Prophet Mohammad (PBUH) accepted martyrdom at Karbala rather than bow to Yazid the undeserving caliph.

The meaning of the proverb is that it is easy to call oneself great without facing trials and tribulations [or, if there are no trials and tribulations to face].

هر څۀ له ګوکنده سره حسابوي!

1314. *"Oh you fool, you compare everything to Gokand."*

Two travelers were passing through Gokand to their own territory in the Kohistan area of Swat in Pakistan. The area is famed for its natural beauty. The two becoming tired, lay down under a large fig tree beside a stream where one of them promptly fell asleep. As he snored his jaw opened wide and a juicy fig dropped directly into his mouth. He leapt up in surprise and tasted the fruit, "Will Paradise be like this?" he asked his friend. Since there is a legend in the Muslim world indicating that in Paradise any wish will be immediately satisfied, the friend saw the comparison clearly and thinking that no place can equal Gokand, blurted out, "Oh you fool! You compare everything with Gokand!"

This proverb suggests that to each man his own homeland is superior to Paradise itself. [*See* Proverbs 445, 876 and 1230.]

هر سړے د ژمي اور څان ته راکاږي.

1315. *In winter everyone likes to draw the fire nearer to himself.*

هر وطن هر ئي دستور.

1316. *Every country has its own customs.*

[*See* Proverb 325.]

هسې مۀ کوه انسانه چې زوئ ګران کړې لور ارزانه.

1317. *Oh sons of Adam, never discriminate between a son and a daughter.*

[The word translated "sons of Adam" refers to human beings and humankind. *RWS*]

هغه دروغ مهٔ وايه چې سبا رښتيا کېږي.

1318. *Do not tell today a lie that will prove false tomorrow.*

[Literally, "... a lie that tomorrow will become truth." This is a warning similar to the English sayings, "The truth will out" and "Time brings truth to light." *LNB*]

هغه مچۍ د سوات دي چې غُل ئې شات دي.

1319. *Only in Swat can one find bees that excrete honey.*

The common belief of the Pakhtuns is that honey is the product of the bees' excretion.

هله به بېګا کړم چې ستا روزی پېدا کړم.

1320. *Only when you have earned your bread will I bring the night, says God.*

God gives sustenance to all his creatures.

[God, the ultimate Provider, though not mentioned explicitly, is implied as being the speaker in this proverb. *LNB*]

هم ودېږي هم رقصيږي!

1321. *The bride was being married and dancing at the same time.*

Pakhtun brides do not do this.

[A Pakhtun bride does not dance, or even smile, at her own wedding, as she is to exhibit sadness over leaving her father's house and family. *LNB*]

هندو اور د دنيا دپاره قبول کړے دے.

1322. *The Hindu has accepted fire for worldly wealth.*

A dead Hindu is burned in fire [cremated] and a Muslim is not. A Hindu would prefer to be rich, rather than to accept Islam in order to escape burning [both temporal and eternal—the fire can refer to the fires of hell *RWS, LNB*].

هندو غلا کوي خو د سپو نه ويرېږي.

1323. *Although the Hindu would like to commit theft he is afraid of dogs.*

He is too much of a coward for a dangerous act.

هوسۍ هوا د غرۀ خوري اؤ وابنۀ د سمي خوري.

1324. *The deer enjoys both the cool air of the mountain and the bush shrubbery of the valley.*

Some people are fortunate enough to enjoy all bounties wherever they are found.

یا به دهقان وهي یا به کلال وهي.

1325. *You will punish either the plowman or the potter?*

The story is told that a man had two daughters, one married to a farmer and the other to a potter. During a drought he visited the former's wife and upon his leaving her home she begged him to pray for rain so that the seeds her husband had sown would sprout. Then he visited his other daughter and found that she and her husband, because of the drought, had been able to prepare a large quantity of pottery. Since the pottery needed drying in the sun before it could be baked, and since she saw dark clouds forming on the horizon, she begged her father to pray that the rain would not come for some days. The poor father, caught in a dilemma, knelt and prayed, "Oh God, you will punish either the plowman or the potter."

یا به هئ شي ساروان یا به هئ شي کاروان.

1326. *The camel drivers must lose either their lives or the caravan.*

The drivers must stay with the caravan or it will be robbed by bandits. This proverb applies to any leader of a tribe or country who must remain vigilant to safeguard his followers and his territory.

[Alternatively, "Either the camel driver will move or the caravan." That is, when the bandits attack, they reason that either the camel driver (*sārwān*) will run away or the caravan (*kārwān*). The "caravan" is the whole line of camels that is looked after by a driver. *RWS*]

یا دې مۀ وے پوهه کرے یا دې مۀ وے پیدا کړے.

1327. *(Oh God!) Either you should not have created me or you should not have given me this wisdom.*

The suffering and misery of the world are too much to bear for the wise, conscientious man.

[Often sensitive and thoughtful people experience the greatest mental anguish over the suffering they see around them. In a sense, "Ignorance is bliss." The appeal to God is implied. *LNB, RWS*]

يا نر شه يا د نر چا کر شه.

1328.   *Be either a man of courage or a follower of the brave man.*

يار مې دې هندکے وي خو خوراک مې دې کيچرے وي.

1329.   *I would accept a Hindkai as a friend if I could have rice for my daily meals.*

The Hindkai are non-Pakhtuns living in the Indo-Pakistan subcontinent, who were looked down upon. The meaning is that in exchange for getting some benefit, one would not mind being in unsavory situations.

[Speakers of Hindko, sometimes called "Punjabi Pathans", are settled throughout the North West Frontier Province, and have now intermingled and intermarried with Pashtuns. They comprise the most significant linguistic minority in the province. *LNB*]

يو به مړ نۀ شي بل به موړ نۀ شي.

1330.   *If one man does not die, the other man does not enjoy prosperity.*

يو په وينو ورسره ژاړي بل په اوبنکو ورسره نۀ ژاړي.

1331.   *Though one weeps blood for his friend, the other does not even shed a tear in return.*

This proverb refers to the marked difference between a sincere and an insincere friend. [*See* Proverb 643.]

يو د لوبِّ مري بل ئي سر ته پراتي گوري.

1332. *While one is dying of hunger, the other is searching for a "parāṭa"
under his pillow.*

Often a poor man is erroneously considered to be wealthy. A *parāṭa*
is a rich bread made from fine wheat flour cooked in butter oil and
served as a delicacy.

[The picture is of someone vainly searching for a *parāṭa* (meaning,
riches) "under his (that is, the poor man's) pillow" on the assumption
that he is wealthy. *LNB*]

يو غر بل غر ته او درېدے شي يو سرے بل سري ته نۀ شي اودرېدے.

1333. *One mountain can withstand another mountain, but one man cannot
withstand another man.*

A mountain can bear the pressure of a larger neighboring mountain
that presses against it, but a Pakhtun will forgive a blood enemy if he
seeks pardon or asylum.

[In Pashtun culture, the resolution of conflicts and blood feuds,
forgiveness, and reconcilitation, can be brokered by a *jirga* or council
of elders, or by the traditional practice of *nanawāti*, "begging
forgiveness", and this proverb may be a reference to this practice. The
nanawāti ritual provides a way for the offender to humble himself and
seek pardon from the family of the one he has injured, and involves
the sacrifice of a sheep. Forgiveness can be granted without loss of
honor. Unlike the unmoved and unforgiving mountain, a Pashtun will
give way under the pressure of someone sincerely seeking forgiveness
or asylum. *LNB*]

يو لرگے به اور وُنه کړي دوه ښځي به کور وُنۀ کړي.

1334. *One lone log cannot burn in the fire place, and two women cannot
live together in the same house.*

Two wives usually quarrel among themselves. This proverb speaks
against polygamy among the Pakhtuns, which is still not uncommon
in their society [*see* Proverb 1229.]

[Alternatively, "One log by itself cannot catch fire ..." *RWS*]

یو وائي مریے دې یم ، بل دې فکر وکړي چې په څو مې اخستے دے.

1335. *If one says "I am your slave", the other should think of the amount paid for him.*

This is an ironic reference to the person who takes advantage of a friend's complete sincerity.

[Out of sincerity someone may offer all that he has, but the other person should still think carefully about it before accepting the offer. *RWS*]

یو ئې خوري بل ورته کوري!

1336. *One is eating, the other is watching him.*

The situation described in the proverb is against the Pakhtun traditions of hospitality. Pakhtun society believes in sharing a meal with anyone who is present.

یو ئې درمن ته نۀ پریږدي ، بل د دړی نه کم نۀ اخلي.

1337. *He is not permitted even to approach the threshing place, yet he demands not less than a bagful.*

The unworthy man often makes unreasonable demands.

[Alternatively, the proverb can be used humorously when there has been a misunderstanding. *RWS*]

یو ئې سر وهي بل ئې پلې.

1338. *One hits [beats] him on the head, another on the ankles.*

The notion is of causing someone double suffering.

[This proverb refers to a person caught between two enemies: one that is seen and one that is hidden. *RWS*]

یو ئې غلوي بل ئې اوښان د لارې اړوي.

1339. *While one distracts his attention the other robs him of his camels.*

یو ئې ګټي سل ئې خُتي.

1340. *One earns it and a hundred enjoy it.*

یوه خُلهٔ په زرو ډکه شي، ډیرې خُلې په خاورو نهٔ ډکیږي.

1341. *One mouth can be filled with gold, but many mouths cannot be filled with earth.*

This is a criticism of large families and overpopulation.

یوه شپه په ژرنده کښې هم تېربدے شي.

1342. *A night can be spent even in a flour mill.*

Even where there is a lot of noise, one should bear the hardship for some time.

[Or, one should at least be able to bear occasional hardships. *RWS*]

یوې د غمه ژړل، بلې د خوشۍ نه پورې خندل.

1343. *One wept out of grief, another laughed at her out of pleasure.*

Some people are not affected by another's grief.

یوې زده کړه بیا ئې مهٔ کړه.

1344. *Learn plowing, even though you may never plow a single furrow.*

It is better to learn a skill even if one does not need it.

[Literally, "Learn plowing and then don't do it." *RWS*]

یوې زۀ کوم پولې دے توروي.

1345. *I do the plowing while he builds the dikes.*

This proverb means that one person does the actual spade work, but another puts on the finishing touches; or, one does the heavy job and another the light one.

یه د توري غوا مبرمنې ، چې غوا لوشلے نۀ شې ترې نه پاسه متراونې.

1346. *Oh mistress of the black cow, if you are unable to milk it stay away from it.*

This proverb is used as a reprimand for any person too stupid to perform a simple act.

یه ملا، یه ملا! پلار به دې ملا وي!

1347. *"Oh, mullah!" one said. The mullah replied, "Your father will be a mullah!"*

In the late 19th century, during the reign of Amir Abdur Rahman of Afghanistan, when the agreement was signed that established the Durand Line between British India and modern Afghanistan, the northern side of the division separated the Kafiristan territory into two parts. The major portion of the territory went to Afghanistan. The Amir, fearing that the British were unreliable, sent a number of mullahs as missionaries to convert the Kafirs, already in his domain, to Islam. The native people rejected the attempt and killed many of the religious intruders. This in turn caused fear among the mullahs and led to their refusal to accept the title of "mullah".

Hence, when someone might call out, "Oh, mullah," [in the Pashto text, the words are repeated: "Oh, mullah! Oh, mullah!"] the holy man would reply, "Your father will be a mullah!", meaning, "Don't call me a mullah!"

يه وروره کافره، يه خوري بي شرمي.

1348. *Oh brother the infidel! Oh sister shameless.*

The girl is not ashamed of her brother's carelessness and lack of attention, though she would always worry about him.

[These are idiomatic rebukes. The expression, "Oh, shameless sister!" (*be-sharme khori*) is used to scold an immodest, shameless, or brazen woman, that is, one who fails to exhibit modesty in her dress, public behaviour and demeanour, for example, not covering her head or face properly, wearing tight clothes, walking ahead of her husband, talking openly with men. Shame and modesty are closely related concepts. Social etiquette generally involves a woman censuring another woman, a man another man, or his own wife, daughter or sister. *LNB*]

يې خو يې خو پينځه روپۍ نيشته.

1349. *Although you are what you are, I don't have five rupees with me.*

According to an early anecdote, a king levied a fine of five *rupees* on any man who would call another person a *dayus*, an insulting term that means "henpecked". One day, a man, during a quarrel, wished to insult his opponent, but could not afford the fine, therefore, he exclaimed, "Although you are what you are, I don't have five *rupees* with me."

يش (اوښ) وطن وينى خر قدم وينې.

1350. *The camel sees the world around him, the donkey sees only his hooves.*

This proverb suggests the difference between the man of destiny and the unintelligent person or fool.

END NOTES

[1] Proverb 14: *Luke* 10:7.

[2] Proverb 54: *Sura* Seba XXXIV.

[3] Proverb 91: *Sura* 31 (12, 27).

[4] Proverb 120: *Hadith*, al-Bukhari 4:52:72.

[5] Proverb 138: *Proverbs* 10:13 and 26:3.

[6] Proverb 148: *Taurat (Exodus)* 21:24.

[7] Proverb 173: *Zabur (Psalm)* 51:6, 7, 10.

[8] Proverb 195: Horace, *Odes* I, xi,8.

[9] Proverb 216: *James* 3:5.

[10] Proverb 302: *Luke* 6:31.

[11] Proverb 310: *Book of Proverbs* 13:24.

[12] Proverb 315: *Book of Proverbs* 21:9 and 17:1.

[13] Proverb 322: Cicero, *Tusculaneae Quaestiones* (Tusculan Disputations).

[14] Proverb 328: *Dictionary of Islam: Being A Cyclopaedia of the Doctrines, Rites, Ceremonies, and Customs, together with the Technical and Theological Terms of the Muhammadan Religion*, Thomas Patrick Hughes, First Published 1885, Cosmo Publications, New Delhi 1986, p. 648.

[15] Proverb 358: John Heywood, *A dialogue Conteynyng the Nomber in Effect of all the Proverbes in the Englishe Tongue*, London Berthelet, 1549, reprinted as *The Proverbs of John Heywood*, ed. Julian Sharman, Darby, PA:Folcroft Library Editions, 1972.

[16] Proverb 389: *Brewer's Dictionary of Phrase and Fable*, p. 371.

[17] Proverb 389: *Isaiah* 22:13.

[18] Proverb 398: Desiderius Erasmus, *Moriae Encomium* (The Praise of Folly), 1509.

[19] Proverb 398: John Skelton, *Why come ye not to Courte?*, 1522.

[20] Proverb 398: H. G. Wells, in *The Penguin Book of English Short Stories*, ed. Christopher Dolley (Middlesex, England: Penguin Books, 1967), pp. 103-128.

[21] Proverb 445: From the first two lines of a poem ("Home, Sweet Home") by John Howard Payne, which was set to music by Henry R. Bishop.

[22] Proverb 452: John Heywood, *A dialogue Conteynyng the Nomber in Effect of all the Proverbes in the Englishe Tongue*, London Berthelet, 1549, reprinted as *The Proverbs of John Heywood*, ed. Julian Sharman, Darby, PA: Folcroft Library Editions, 1972.

[23] Proverb 492: William Shakespeare, *Henry V*, 4.4, 1599.

[24] Proverb 521: Thorburn, S. S. (1978 [1876]). *Bannu: Our Afghan Frontier.* Lahore: Sang-E-Meel Publications. Originally published, London: Trubner & Co.

[25] Proverb 539: Alexander Pope, *An Essay on Criticism* (Fr.III), 1711.

[26] Proverb 576: *Aesop's Fables*, 'The Fox and the Grapes'.

[27] Proverb 582: *The Philosopher's Stone*, 1859.

[28] Proverb 611: From the *Diwan* of Rahman Baba.

[29] Proverb 612: From the *Diwan* of Rahman Baba.

[30] Proverb 630: From the *Diwan* of Rahman Baba

[31] Proverb 645: *Galatians* 6:7

[32] Proverb 645: From *Sow Flowers: Selections from Rahman Baba The Poet of the Afghans*, translated into English by Robert Sampson and Momin Khan, InterLit Foundation, reprinted 2004, p.5.

[33] Proverb 659: *Ecclesiates* 4:9-10

[34] Proverb 705: *Matthew* 7:7.

[35] Proverb 705: *Book of Proverbs* 8:17

[36] Proverb 726: From Chaucer's *Prologue to the Monk's Tale* (1387-1400).

[37] Proverb 726: *Book of Proverbs* 16:18.

[38] Proverb 726: *2 Samuel* 1:19.

[39] Proverb 747: John A. Subhan, *Sufism: Its Saints and Shrines*, Lucknow: Lucknow Publishing House/Kessinger Publishing, 2003, pp.244-45.

[40] Proverb 800: For Sufism and mysticism in Islam *see* e.g. Annemarie Schimmel, *Mystical Dimensions of Islam*. Chapel Hill: University of North Carolina Press, 1975; *Deciphering the Signs of God: A Phenomenological Approach to Islam*. Albany: State University of New York Press, 1994.

[41] Proverb 834: *Proverbs* 17:28.

[42] Proverb 846: *Genesis* 3:19.

[43] Proverb 846: The words of the burial or funeral service are found in the Anglican *Book of Common Prayer* first published in 1662.

[44] Proverb 852: William Shakespeare, *Hamlet* II, ii, 95.

[45] Proverb 877: Ennius, *Scaenica* 210.

[46] Proverb 914: *Deuteronomy* 6:4.

[47] Proverb 968: From William Shakespeare's, *Much Ado About Nothing*, 1598/9.

[48] Proverb 1012: Terence (185-159 B.C.), *Andria*; *1 Timothy* 5:4, 8.

49   Proverb 1095: William Shakespeare, *Julius Caesar* II, ii.

50   Proverb 1159: *Rohi Mataluna:Pashto zarbul amsal bumgha Urdu tarjuma* (*Rohi Mataluna: Pashto proverbs with Urdu translation*), Mohammad Nawaz Tair, Pakhto Academy, Peshawar University, First edition, 1975, Volume II, p. 108.

51   Proverb 1218: *Zabur* (Psalm) 7:15, 16.

52   Proverb 1261: *Jeremiah* 13:23.

SELECTED READING

Bartlotti, Leonard N. (2000). *Negotiating Pakhto: Proverbs, Islam and the Construction of Identity Among Pashtuns.* Ph.D. Thesis. University of Wales. (Publication forthcoming.)

Caroe, Olaf. (1985) *The Pathans: 550 B.C.-A.D. 1957.* 4th Edition. Karachi: Oxford University Press.

Denny, Frederick M. (1994). *An Introduction to Islam.* 2nd Edition. New York: McMillan Publishing Co.

Elphinstone, Mountstuart. (1992 [1815]). *An Account of the Kingdom of Caubul. Volume I & II.* Karachi: Indus Publications.

Enevoldsen, Jens. (2004) *Sound the Bells, O Moon, Arise and Shine!.* Peshawar: InterLit Foundation.

Enevoldsen, Jens. (1993) *The Nightingale of Peshawar: Selections from Rahman Baba.* Peshawar: InterLit Foundation.

Grima, Benedicte. (1993) *The Performance of Emotion among Paxtun Women: "The Misfortunes Which Have Befallen Me".* Karachi: Oxford University Press.

Heston, Wilma L. & Nasir, Mumtaz (1988). *The Bazaar of the Storytellers.* Islamabad: Lok Virsa.

Hughes, Thomas Patrick. (1979 [1885]) *Dictionary of Islam.* Safat, Kuwait Islamic Book Publishers.

Lindholm, Charles. *Generosity and Jealousy: The Swat Pukhtun of Northern Pakistan.* New York: Columbia University Press.

Sampson, Robert & Khan, Momin (2004). *Sow Flowers: Selections from Rahman Baba, The Poet of the Afghans.* Peshawar: InterLit Foundation.

Schimmel, Annemarie (1994). *Deciphering the Signs of God: A Phenomenological Approach to Islam.* Albany: State University of New York Press.

Schimmel, Annemarie (1975). *Mystical Dimensions of Islam.* Chapel Hill: University of North Carolina Press.

NOTES ON CONTRIBUTORS

DR. LEONARD N. (LEN) BARTLOTTI, PH.D., a consultant to organizations engaged in development work in Afghanistan, Pakistan and Central Asia. Founder and former Executive Director of the InterLit Foundation. "Dr. Len" lived in Peshawar, Pakistan for 14 years (1985-1999), and is noted for his research on Pashtun culture and oral literature. After completing his Ph.D. in Islamic Studies at the University of Wales (2000), he served as a Lecturer and Research Tutor in Oxford, UK, and is currently Associate Professor of Intercultural Studies at Biola University, La Mirada, California, USA.

PROF. THOMAS C. EDWARDS Assistant Professor of the Humanities Department, College of Engineering at the University of Michigan. He worked with Professor Tair to translate the proverbs from Pashto to English.

PROF. DR. RAJ WALI SHAH KHATTAK, PH.D. University of Peshawar, 1985, Director of the Pashto Academy from 1995 until 2005 and Editor-in-chief of the monthly journal *Pashto* from 1995 to July, 2004. Raj Wali Shah Khattak was born in the village of Dak Ismail Khel, District Nowshera in 1952. He graduated from the University of Peshawar in 1975, and in 1977 received his Masters in Pashto, plus the Gold Medal for the top student in the Province. Dr. Khattak has more than 60 research articles to his credit, plus over 100 critical reviews, and is well-known as a writer and poet. He is also a resource person for national and international radio and television, and an authority on the new script for the Pashto language.

PROF. MUHAMMAD NAWAZ TAIR, University Professor in Pashto Language and Literature. Born in 1934, Nawaz Tair was educated in Islamia College Peshawar and Government College Lahore. He took his Master's Degrees in Geography, Persian and Pashto from the University of the Punjab and Peshawar. A poet of great merit, Prof. Tair has introduced new themes and forms into Pashto poetry. Appointed as Junior Research Officer in the Pashto Academy, University of Peshawar in 1958, he made extensive research in Pashto language, literature and culture. In addition to publishing more than 100 research papers, he is also the author of more than 50 books in Pashto, Urdu, Persian and English. He was the Director of the Pashto Academy from 1979 to 1994. He was also the Editor of *Pashto*, the monthly journal of the Pashto Academy, from 1977 to 1992.

INDEX

Abasin (Indus River), 55, 233, 583, 622, 803, 1017. *See also* 177
Abazai, 634, 1223
Abdur Rahman Baba. *See also* 164, 421, 461, 611, 612, 630, 645, 1218
Abdur Rahman, Amir. *See also* 1347
ablution, 586
Abraham. *See also* 332
abyss, 992
accusation, 86. *See also* 76, 375, 627, 738. *See* word
Adam, 5, 1317
Adam Khan, 6, 7, 514
addict (*charsi*), 555
advantage, 304, 485, 990. *See also* 266, 288, 346, 556, 562, 616, 820, 832, 1020, 1335
advice, 746, 803, 1213, 1261. *See also* 106, 143, 154, 301, 306, 421, 452, 517, 747, 804, 883, 885, 905, 1004, 1027, 1138, 1165, 1277, 1282
Aesop. *See also* 576
Afghani, 849
Afghanistan. *See also* 49, 177, 236, 413, 567, 608, 1004, 1058, 1094, 1222, 1230, 1238, 1347
Afridi. *See also* 1, 305
agree, 479, 693. *See also* 403
Ahmad Shah, 1094. *See also* 1222
air, 1324
Akbar Pura, 150
Akbar, Emperor, 150
Akhund, 85, 86, 87, 88, 89, 90. *See* mullah
alive, 658, 697, 701, 790. *See also* 71, 1303
Allah. *See* God
alms, 1014, 1139. *See also* 1024
alone, 78, 397, 420, 450, 659, 784, 1116. *See also* 155, 164, 643, 821
alphabet: *alef*, 154, 155
    lām, 154
    heh. *See also* 106
Amen, 1124
Amritsar, 159

Amruddin Lala, 68
amulet, 635
ancestor, 740
angel. *See also* 147, 289, 539
Angel of Death (Izrail), 1181
anger, angry, 61, 654, 836, 897. *See also* 101, 206, 480, 530, 584, 1307
animals, 605, 801, 1147, 1296. *See also* 577, 747
    ass, 164, 953, 956, 958. *See also* 138
    bear. *See also* 1162
    buffalo, 446, 637, 672
    bullock, 528, 777, 885, 1118, 1143, 1194, 1197, 1232
    calf, calves, 98, 432, 446, 637, 700, 777, 823, 1143, 1206. *See also* 1181
    camel, 203, 236, 237, 238, 239, 240, 241, 242, 243, 650, 802, 1242, 1339, 1350. *See also* 416, 1001, 1058, 1207, 1208
    cat, 59, 470, 471, 472, 473, 474, 475, 735, 934, 1196, 1277. *See also* 941
    cattle, 135. *See also* 637
    cobra, 506
    colt, 117
    cow, 159, 396, 424, 698, 700, 823, 907, 1060, 1147, 1193, 1346. *See also* 204, 236
    deer, 1293, 1324
    dog, 119, 128, 144, 208, 253, 320, 430, 488, 502, 575, 646, 752, 761, 780, 791, 801, 802, 832, 837, 919, 933, 959, 961, 1024, 1032, 1033, 1129, 1130, 1131, 1132, 1133, 1134, 1139, 1140, 1176, 1215, 1323. *See also* 43, 206, 208, 396, 444, 511, 680, 685, 702, 1226, 1261
    donkey, 18, 21, 23, 29, 32, 134, 135, 219, 220, 347, 376, 482, 486, 498, 810, 864, 917, 923, 925, 926, 927, 928, 929, 930, 931, 932, 933, 934, 935, 936, 937, 938, 939, 940, 941, 946, 947, 948, 950, 951, 952, 954, 955, 957, 985, 1053, 1155, 1225,

1274, 1296, 1350. *See also* 416, 444, 811, 1208
duck, 263
elephant, 69, 70, 71, 758, 1311
fish, 523, 824, 1267. *See also* 191, 475
fox, 488. *See also* 576
frog, 48, 781, 1028
goat, 324, 537, 687, 708, 1307. *See also* 236
horse, 10, 11, 12, 13, 14, 15, 16, 17, 18, 19, 20, 21, 22, 23, 24, 25, 26, 27, 28, 29, 30, 31, 32, 33, 34, 48, 117, 306, 331, 347, 372, 737, 1000, 1015, 1019, 1127, 1184, 1204. *See also* 138, 444, 467, 524, 687, 689, 709, 739, 948, 1102
jackal, 265, 274, 291, 400, 576, 577, 618, 780, 829, 959, 1043, 1242
lamb, 52, 221, 437, 1251
leopard, 762. *See also* 6, 1261
lion, 206, 265, 473, 618, 649, 735, 829, 1043, 1102, 1103
lizard, 531, 571, 644, 703, 794
monkey, 221
mouse, mice, 470, 472, 474, 986. *See also* 158, 379, 1277
mule, 16, 23, 938, 1184, 1201
ox, 700, 1107, 1255. *See also* 482
ram. *See also* 332
rat, 735, 1277. *See also* 747
sheep, 437, 1161, 1238. *See also* 236, 396, 424, 1307, 1333
snake, 90, 364, 571, 703, 732, 1263, 1264. *See also* 181, 1253
swine, 735
water buffalo. *See also* 444
wolf, 279, 1045, 1161, 1251, 1261
See birds; insects
ankle, 1338
ant, 382, 897, 1263. *See also* 54
anticipation, 481. *See also* 76, 85
Apollo. *See also* 159
appearance, 159, 421, 636, 1034, 1147. *See also* 49, 173, 557, 798, 1005
apple. *See also* 202, 206, 424, 702
April, 778
arena, 969
Aristotle. *See also* 924
arm, 509, 722, 1244. *See also* 289

armpit, 407, 408
army. *See also* 1065
    lashkar, 351, 1044, 1101
arrogance, 921
arrow, 510, 1092, 1188. *See also* 1226
ash, 841, 843, 845. *See also* 842
asil. See noble
ass, 164, 953, 956, 958. *See also* 138. *See* donkey
assembly, 638. *See also* 442
Asu, month of, 121, 122, 123
August, 533
aunt, 473, 487
autumn, 123
Awal Bagh. *See also* 1137
axe, 456, 517, 923, 1140
Azo Gul, 116
Babar, 268
Baboo Jan (Babu Jan), 444
back, 32, 802. *See also* 284, 624
    shā, 293, 506, 535
backbiter, 715, 858
backside, 1238
bad, 439. *See also* 129, 178, 284, 397, 424, 444, 588, 854
    bad behavior. *See also* 151
    bad character. *See also* 466
    bad company. *See also* 310, 947
    bad condition. *See also* 662
    bad conduct, 1172
    bad deeds. *See also* 59, 94, 1023
    bad effect. *See also* 36
    bad habit. *See also* 93, 160. *See* habit
    bad intentions, 1005. *See* crooked
    bad loser. *See also* 370
    bad purpose. *See also* 291, 882
    bad quality. *See also* 80
    bad son, 922
    bad times, 1173
    bad way of life. *See also* 282
    bad words, 1023. *See also* 283. *See* taunts
    See evil; wicked
Badabera, 339
Badi, 284, 289
bag, 218, 360, 371, 533, 1337
Bajaur, 95, 482
Bakhtyar, 572
Bala Manrai, 275

bald, scurvy-headed, 225, 718, 920
Balkh, 721
Bannu, Bannuchi, 305, 551. *See also*
305, 487, 708
Bara River, 273
barber, 395. *See also* 615
Barbotai, 319
barley, 218, 219, 220, 532, 594. *See also*
932
barn, 533, 695. *See also* 77, 709
basket, 106, 547, 884. *See also* 409, 416,
533
battle, 686, 1044, 1158
jang, 372, 528, 628
See fight; war
bear. *See also* 1162
beard, bearded, 1038. *See also* 79, 470.
See sheikh
beat, beating, 69, 92, 147, 209, 293, 305,
497, 498, 554, 573, 574, 613, 682,
713, 762, 765, 807, 883, 1074, 1078,
1264, 1338. *See also* 17, 309, 444.
See drum
beauty, 1096, 1211. *See also* 159, 344,
445, 499, 1314
beauty mark (*khāl*), 39
bed, 336. *See also* 1181, 1281
beef. *See also* 1119
bees, 1319
beg, beggar, begging, 119, 343, 772,
789, 1186. *See also* 1139
char, 795
faqir, 1032, 1039, 1199, 1219
faqr, 1198
malang, 673
begging bowl (*kachkol*), 1219
behavior, 1172. *See also* 91, 92, 148,
151, 340, 375, 549, 572, 633, 738,
765, 950, 975, 1207
bell, 1277
belly. *See* stomach
belongings, 861, 1149. *See also* 516,
766, 1226
beloved, 153. *See also* 6, 504, 748
shāh, 993, 1159
yār, 611, 630
See friend
benefit, 129, 405, 563, 675, 1008. *See*
also 787, 820, 823, 1014, 1190, 1329

Benét, Stephen Vincent. *See also* 195
berries, 507, 530
betrayed, 480
Bible, Holy. *See also* 14, 216, 782, 905,
1012, 1261
birds, 156, 297, 960, 1059. *See also* 75,
162, 433, 489, 804, 945
chick, chicken, 557, 558, 559, 560,
562, 563, 564, 565, 566, 567, 577,
832. *See* hen; rooster
crane, 584
crow, 526, 1206
hawk, 434
hen, 117, 556, 563, 565, 566, 567,
568, 569, 570. *See also* 577.
See chicken; rooster
lark, 374, 942, 943, 960
parrot, 442
partridge, 499
robin. *See also* 924
rooster, 82, 278, 556, 561, 563. *See*
also 437, 577. *See* chicken; hen
wren, 434, 546, 816
See animals
birth (social status). *See* noble
bismillah, 93
creed, 160. *See also* 291
bitch. *See* dog
bitter. *See* sour
black, 444, 476, 503, 504, 505, 511, 698,
761, 1346. *See also* 547, 625, 627,
1162. *See* accusation
blacksmith, smith. *See also* 1086
blame, 221, 540. *See also* 15, 59, 86, 99,
266, 1050
blanket, 978, 1162
blessing, 652. *See also* 67, 291, 459, 501,
635, 747, 757, 914, 991, 1006, 1165,
1205, 1281
barakat, 301, 906. *See also* 294, 295
nemat, 199, 577, 667
blind, 320, 398, 766, 824, 1089, 1090,
1091, 1299
blood, 36, 513, 626, 1008, 1084, 1232,
1331. *See also* 182, 425, 663, 858,
875, 889, 1252, 1333
blood enemy, blood feud. *See* feud;
enemy
blood money (*badǝy*), 1232
blow, 345, 409. *See* punch

boast, boaster, 360, 619. *See also* 30, 38,
  117, 134, 255, 268, 298, 416, 428,
  432, 451, 541, 546, 587, 620, 668,
  771, 781, 902, 984, 991, 1064, 1238
boat, 322, 323, 391, 395. *See also* 650,
  677
bone, 104
book, 608
  Bible, Holy. *See also* 14, 216, 782,
    905, 1012, 1261
  Guru Granth Sahib, 1165
  Qur'an, Holy. *See also* 54, 91, 106,
    608, 635 1014
borrow, borrowed, 146, 331. *See also*
  336
boulder, rock, 167, 490, 603, 644, 794,
  853. *See also* 194, 650, 1004
bounty. *See* blessing
bow, 1188
bowl, 55, 113, 469, 583, 817. *See also*
  204, 492
  begging bowl (*kachkol*), 1219
  kandol, 972
  qulpai. *See also* 1181
boy, 1227. *See also* 96, 284, 622, 312
bracelets, 447
braggart, 541
branch. *See also* 1252
brave, bravery, noble deed, 382, 1283,
  1286. *See also* 115, 536, 577, 735
brave, courageous man, 90, 587, 619,
  1051, 1095, 1177, 1328. *See also* 149,
  361, 536, 663, 735, 1284
bread, 33, 85, 106, 119, 193, 204, 212,
  227, 228, 229, 349, 429, 884, 1024,
  1051, 1076, 1077, 1115, 1129, 1320.
  See also 259, 795, 1021, 1216
  cornbread. *See also* 1215
  daily bread (*rozi*). *See also* 914
  hazar surakha, 1119
  maize bread, 428
  parāṭa, 1332
breath, 591. *See also* 404
bribery. *See also* 1129
bride, 674, 1289, 1321. *See also* 283,
  622, 841, 1119. *See* girl
bridge, 197. *See also* 189, 273
bridle, 948
brother, 51, 342, 696, 742, 825, 959,
  995, 1006, 1055, 1235, 1255, 1303,

1304, 1305, 1348. *See also* 485, 997,
  1003, 1181, 1216, 1259
brother-in-law. *See* in-laws
brush, 579. *See also* 424
bucket, 1018
buffalo, 446, 637, 672
bull's-eye, 497
bullet, 375
bullock, 528, 777, 885, 1118, 1143,
  1194, 1197, 1232
bully, 309
Bunir, Buniri, 661. *See also* 305, 458,
  460, 656
burden, 769. *See also* 271, 530, 564, 937,
  957, 1000, 1099
  bār, 346
  See load; sorrow
burgled. *See* theft
butcher, 324, 396. *See also* 181
butter, 244, 672, 907
butter oil, 1021. *See also* 60, 1332
buttermilk, 307
buttocks, 19, 1216
cake. *See also* 1021
calamity, trouble, 130, 231, 293, 294,
  295, 537, 548, 604, 741, 787, 877,
  882, 985, 1006, 1013, 1057, 1083,
  1130, 1234, 1291. *See also* 62, 192,
  206, 208, 213, 216, 217, 263, 311,
  324, 438, 498, 499, 502, 558, 588,
  599, 657, 702, 720, 722, 726, 732,
  786, 797, 804, 821, 837, 845, 856,
  911, 943, 951, 962, 1099, 1120, 1123,
  1244, 1278. *See* sorrow
Calcutta. *See also* 1058
calf, calves, 98, 432, 446, 637, 700,
  777, 823, 1143, 1206. *See also*
  1181
camel, 203, 236, 237, 238, 239, 240,
  241, 242, 243, 650, 802, 1242,
  1339, 1350. *See also* 416, 1001,
  1058, 1207, 1208
camel driver, 1326
canal. *See* sluice
cannon, 431
cap, 701, 788. *See also* 409
  ṭopal. *See also* 843
caravan, 1040, 1109, 1131, 1207, 1326.
  See also 58, 240, 271, 776, 1058,
  1165

care (*elāj*), 72
cargo. *See* burden; load (*bār*)
carpenter, 201
cash. *See* money
cat, 59, 470, 471, 472, 473, 474, 475,
    735, 934, 1196, 1277. *See also* 941
cattle, 135. *See also* 637
caution, 75. *See also* 127, 214
cemetery, 1294. *See* grave
censure. *See also* 549
chaff, 496, 629. *See also* 782
chair (*dholī*). *See also* 622
character, 139, 309, 919, 1110. *See also*
    103, 138, 143, 145, 168, 234, 257,
    340, 444, 466, 477, 508, 520, 725,
    877, 927, 1228, 1261
characteristic, 799. *See also* 80, 147,
    473, 960, 1301
chārbayta (folk poem). *See also* 275
charity, 837, 1012, 1013. *See also* 1014.
    See alms
Charsadda, 129
Chaucer. *See also* 577, 726
cheap, inferior, 105. *See also* 29, 238,
    339, 509, 518, 788, 928, 1062
cheek. *See* face
Chengiz Khan. *See also* 1165
chew, 250
chick, chicken, 557, 558, 559, 560, 562,
    563, 564, 565, 567, 577, 832. *See also*
    566, 1119. *See* hen; rooster
chickpea. *See also* 706
chief. *See* elder
child, children, 258, 310, 501, 505, 585,
    671, 727, 825, 957, 1092, 1109, 1258,
    1265, 1312. *See also* 52, 54, 92, 98,
    101, 200, 260, 278, 531, 549, 684,
    712, 739, 1040, 1181, 1252, 1256.
    rat children (*chudā*). *See also* 747
childhood, 768
chowkidār (watchman). *See also* 480
Christian. *See also* 5, 846, 914, 1203
Chung, 838
churning skins, 677
Cicero. *See also* 322
circumcision, 751. *See also* 96, 615
city, 385, 418, 598, 1036, 1166
clap, clapping, 521. *See also* 67
clay, 842, 1042. *See also* 841, 843, 1181.

See dirt; dust; earth
clean, 158, 173, 466. *See also* 224, 562,
    853
clever. *See* foolish; wise
clod (of earth), 1150. *See also* 781
cloth, 1058. *See also* 42, 788, 814
clothes, clothing, 140, 141, 146, 304,
    636, 805, 998, 1011, 1167, 1192,
    1209. *See also* 80, 152, 332, 650, 941,
    1348
cloud, 44, 46, 289. *See also* 511, 1325.
    See sky
club, 138, 182, 509, 762. *See also* 204
clump. *See* handful
cobra, 506
cock, cockrel. *See* rooster
code of honor, 341. *See also* 247, 341,
    608, 629, 668
    nang, 1203
    See pakhtunwali
colander. *See* sieve
cold, 1301
collar, 775
color. *See also* 1280
colors
    black, 444, 476, 503, 504, 505, 511,
        698, 761, 1346. *See also* 547, 625,
        627, 1162
    brown. *See also* 282
    gray, 959, 960, 961
    green, 932. *See also* 567, 871
    red, 936
    scarlet, 663
    white, 444, 511, 698, 954, 1067, 1136,
        1137. *See also* 173
    yellow, 839
colt, 117
community, 84, 403. *See also* 92, 120,
    526, 740, 1232
companion. *See* friend
compete, competition, 286, 619, 1259.
    See also 198, 629, 943, 969, 982.
    See rival
complain, complaint, 243, 530, 621,
    952, 978, 1243, 1295. *See also* 77,
    242, 480, 559, 672, 706, 759, 805,
    820, 884
comrade. *khpəl*, 868, 877
    mal, 784
    See friend

conclusion, 855
conscientious man. *See also* 1327
constructive, 1125
contemporary, 714
   hamzoley. See also 1259
corn, 433, 941. *See also* 305, 629, 949, 1306
costly. *See* precious
cotton, 200, 352, 413, 533
cough, 912
council, 1155. *See jirga*
country, 163, 636. *See also* 91, 176, 259, 403, 449, 708, 1012, 1020, 1071, 1072, 1119, 1326
   watan, 325, 445, 876, 1061, 1221, 1316
   See world
courage, 20, 536, 1328. *See also* 103, 115, 508, 1101
   ghayrat. See also 935
court, 158, 169. *See also* 479, 1165
courtesy, 1233. *See also* 254, 806.
   See custom (*dud*)
courtier, 1202
courtyard, 1107. *See also* 1181
cousin. *tarbur*, 485, 486, 716, 1264
   See rival
cow, 159, 396, 424, 698, 700, 823, 907, 1060, 1147, 1193, 1346. *See also* 204, 236
coward, 309, 529, 737, 1050, 1095. *See also* 90, 265, 291, 369, 382, 400, 488, 536, 628, 735, 738, 1044, 1323
crane, 584
credit (commendation), 514, 566, 1292. *See also* 1137, 1158
credit (financial), 512, 1006
creed. *See also* 91, 651
   bismillah, 160. *See also* 291
   kalima, 35, 291, 1029
   See pray
cremation. *See also* 1322. *See* fire
criminal. *See also* 221, 1226
cripple. *See also* 1226
crooked, 1210
   kog, 401, 1005. *See also* 1208
crop, 528. *See also* 123, 157, 174, 176, 289, 352, 371. *See* harvest
crow, 526, 1206

cunning, 723. *See also* 49, 261, 942,
cunning man. *See also* 49
curse, cursed, 1, 24, 129, 212, 239, 420, 953, 980. *See also* 47, 501, 826, 1006, 1180. *See* proverbs
custom, tradition. *See also* 1, 31, 52, 92, 148, 233, 236, 341, 405, 409, 485, 486, 608, 609, 620, 622, 629, 673, 740, 787, 806, 849, 1029, 1036, 1229, 1266, 1336
   dastur, 325, 1316
   dud, 1233, 1289
   See way
dagger, 407, 408, 544, 614, 1051, 1224. *See* knife
dam. *See* sluice
damsel. *See* girl
dance, dancing, 1321. *See also* 1165
   atan, 66, 67, 68
danger, dangerous, 279, 1250. *See also* 5, 73, 82, 90, 153, 214, 216, 340, 346, 486, 544, 578, 740, 762, 835, 882, 961, 1006, 1193, 1323
darkness, 1030
darling, 2, 958, 997
date, 945. *See also* 291
Daudzai, 357
daughter, 148, 387, 799, 1170, 1256, 1279, 1317. *See also* 148, 283, 357, 622, 941, 997, 1108, 1119, 1259, 1325, 1348
daughter-in-law. *See* in-laws
David, King. *See also* 1218, 726, 173
day, days, 65, 259, 448, 657, 1035, 1048, 1169, 1261. *See also* 78, 106, 195, 332, 962, 1109, 1252, 1325
   old days. *See also* 63
   See Judgment Day
deaf, 1217
death, dead, die(s). *See also* 102, 195, 341, 389, 615, 846
   dead (person, body). *See also* 162, 284, 1322
      maray, 439, 443, 570, 891, 904, 995, 1240, 1273. *See also* 62
   death, 259, 1181, 1310. *See also* 148, 215, 378, 558, 874, 1180, 1303
      ajal, 72, 73, 74
      marg, 96, 324, 393, 394, 438, 681, 733, 1270, 1271

zankadan, 94, 968
die(s), 54, 396, 524, 662, 1008, 1095, 1229. *See also* 694, 889, 1252
mәṛ, 71, 697, 734, 764, 933, 989, 1268, 1330
mri, 617, 658, 1066, 1225, 1268, 1286, 1311, 1332
See grave; kill
debt, 353, 354, 355, 356, 512, 602, 1006. *See also* 966
badal. See exchange
deceit, deceive, 416, 1245. *See also* 125, 173, 282, 992
declaration. *See* creed
decorate, 545. *See also* 77
deer, 1293, 1324
defame, 724
defeat, defeated, 268, 734, 1044. *See also* 669
defiled (*palit*). *See also* 1033
degrade, degraded. *See also* 772, 917. *See* insignificant
Delhi. *See also* 1165
demon. *See jinn*
dependence, 404, 983
Dera Ismail Khan. *See also* 374
desert, 582
desire, 15, 111, 288, 397, 760, 975, 1211. *See also* 31, 48, 173, 248, 252, 347, 471, 656, 971, 1037, 1219
destination, 1035, 1208. *See also* 366, 622, 954, 1157
destroy, 356, 412, 688, 738, 889, 983, 1087, 1284. *See also* 275, 289, 375, 737, 787, 1102
destructive, 153, 1125. *See also* 765
devil. *See also* 762, 323, 314
shaytān, 168
dhikr (*zikәr*), *See also* 291. *See* Sufi
dialogue proverbs. *See* proverbs
diamond. *See also* 234
Dickens, Charles. *See also* 1012
Dickenson, Emily. *See also* 924
died, dies. *See* death
difficult, difficulty, 10, 143, 207, 296, 317, 1214, 1300. *See also* 35, 94, 154, 217, 226, 235, 242, 291, 294, 334, 395, 444, 454, 758, 769, 941, 996, 1083, 1119, 1195, 1219, 1227, 1302

dignity, 304, 441. *See also* 414, 460, 785, 788, 936, 1136
dike, 184, 781, 1345
dinner, 90, 281, 1077. *See also* 1186
dirt, 468, 1070. *See also* 842
disciple, discipleship, 459. *See also* 461
discipline. *See* punishment
discussion, 254, 855, 1149. *See also* 939
disgrace, 375, 738. *See also* 328, 487, 713, 858, 867, 870, 936, 1144. *See* shame; taunts
dishonor. *See also* 1, 148, 902, 1006,
dispute, 933. *See also* 253, 485, 850
distribution, 583. *See also* 55, 90, 667, 805
distrust. *See* suspicion
Diwana Baba, 460, 656
doctor, 748, 1178, 1248
dog, 119, 128, 144, 208, 253, 320, 430, 488, 502, 575, 646, 752, 761, 780, 791, 801, 802, 832, 837, 919, 933, 959, 961, 1024, 1032, 1033, 1129, 1130, 1131, 1132, 1133, 1134, 1139, 1140, 1176, 1215, 1323. *See also* 43, 206, 208, 396, 444, 511, 680, 685, 702, 1226, 1261
donkey, 18, 21, 23, 29, 32, 134, 135, 219, 220, 347, 376, 482, 486, 498, 810, 864, 917, 923, 925, 926, 927, 928, 929, 930, 931, 932, 933, 934, 935, 936, 937, 938, 939, 940, 941, 946, 947, 948, 950, 951, 952, 954, 955, 957, 985, 1053, 1155, 1225, 1274, 1296, 1350. *See also* 416, 444, 811, 1208. *See* ass
Doomsday. *See* Judgment Day
door, 668, 758, 990. *See also* 77, 204, 709, 1232
dough, 83, 223, 465. *See also* 229, 367
downfall, 109. *See also* 5, 241
dowry, 357
drake. *See* duck
dress. *See* clothes
drink. *See* syrup
shәrbat, 199, 813
drowning man, 175, 358
drum, drummers, 69, 305, 442, 573, 682, 883, 1074, 1078

dry, 55, 83, 201, 202, 203, 204, 583, 588, 1212. *See also* 174, 1004, 1325
duck, 263
dung pat, 942
dunghill, rubbish heap, 503, 552, 556, 557, 844
Durand Line. *See also* 1347
Durkhanai. *See also* 6, 7
dust, 493, 586, 667, 843, 845, 936, 1047, 1122. *See also* 842, 846. *See* clay; earth (*khāwra*); ground
duty. *See also* 1124, 1012, 561, 51
   compulsory duty (*farz*), 979
   optional duty (*sunnat*), 979
ear, 305, 433, 452, 453, 801, 928. *See also* 231
earn, 33, 116, 361, 381, 441, 602, 1093, 1237, 1320, 1340. *See also* 380, 414, 923
earth, 40, 47, 341, 586, 846, 1150, 1151. *See also* 54, 696, 846, 961, 1102
   khāwra, 646, 1341, 842, 841, 259
   See dust; ground; world
eat, eating, 14, 26, 170, 199, 204, 205, 221, 230, 248, 323, 339, 428, 481, 591, 594, 646, 658, 667, 739, 757, 772, 806, 860, 932, 941, 966, 980, 991, 999, 1000, 1001, 1021, 1060, 1076, 1119, 1176, 1201, 1206, 1237, 1248, 1336. *See also* 5, 291, 507, 775, 998, 1033, 1166, 1186
echo, 171. *See also* 98
educated man. *See also* 1109
effort, 64, 276, 527, 1110, 1225, 1270. *See also* 157, 201, 248, 380, 444, 526, 648, 650, 705, 905, 906, 912, 988, 1011
egg, 56, 117, 263, 569. *See also* 409
eggplant (*brinjal*), 63
Egyptian, 678
Eid, 76, 77, 78, 79, 332, 334
elder, chief, 1258. *See also* 15, 53, 92, 253, 526, 758, 1186,
   khan, 349, 620, 836, 837, 838, 839, 1221. *See also* 409, 1139, 1180
   məshər, məshrān, 1233
elephant, 69, 70, 71, 758, 1311
embarrassment. *See* shame
encourage, encouragement, 405. *See also* 15, 25, 195, 284, 650, 705

enemy, 1032, 1279. *See also* 82, 173, 279, 369, 488, 502, 506, 517, 530, 604, 618, 652, 668, 732, 1025, 1033, 1101, 1194, 1264, 1333, 1339.
   dukhman, dushman, 50, 494, 664, 911, 1003, 1006, 1066, 1068, 1235, 1245, 1260, 1298, 1303. *See also* 617, 857
   See feud
engagement. *See also* 252, 378, 615
enmity, 354. *See also* 283, 910, 1179, 1279
   tarburwali. *See also* 486
enough, sufficient (*bas*), 87, 564. *See also* 760
equal, unequal, 477, 612. *See also* 209, 620, 805, 939, 982, 1247, 1314
   siyāl, 3, 910. *See also* 928, 1259
   See rival
Erasmus, Desiderius. *See also* 398
Eve. *See also* 5
evening, 868, 1046. *See also* 1119
event, 1026. *See also* 426
evil, 160, 383, 581, 596, 1171. *See also* 91, 287, 299, 311, 401, 474, 577, 597, 757, 941, 986, 1261. *See* bad; wicked
exchange, reciprocate, 113, 222. *See also* 148, 1329
   badal, 247. *See also* 283, 940
excreta, crap, stool, 525, 752, 753, 757, 858, 1206, 1319. *See also* 298. *See* relieve
expect, expectation, 491, 518, 602, 731, 769. *See also* 92, 147, 301, 388, 458, 469, 512, 549, 572, 582, 642, 700, 1220, 1300
extinguish. *See* kill
eyes, 41, 44, 45, 112, 263, 398, 720, 766, 860, 942, 962, 966, 1006, 1090, 1091, 1141. *See also* 106
fable. *See* story
face, 212, 225, 660, 717, 1280. *See also* 8, 948, 1348
   face-to-face, 293, 774
   məkh, 41, 221, 293, 455, 488, 535, 798, 868, 1268
faith. *See also* 35, 340, 344, 1014
   imān, 335, 681, 1196
faithful, unfaithful, 94, 729, 1034. *See also* 115, 126

fallen, 328, 365. *See also* 726, 1180

family, families, 97, 136, 151, 571, 776, 1022, 1040, 1294. *See also* 52, 143, 144, 283, 318, 332, 341, 356, 440, 444, 455, 473, 485, 486, 487, 567, 622, 720, 738, 799, 841, 849, 859, 910, 938, 990, 1010, 1012, 1042, 1072, 1119, 1207, 1214, 1232, 1244, 1303, 1321, 1333, 1341

khpǝl. See also 312, 858, 859

kor, 88, 315, 1168. *See also* 530

mina, 627

siyāl. See also 1259

See house

famine, 1021. *See also* 1216

fan, 350

faqir. See beggar; holy man

farm, 277. *See also* 257

farmer. *See also* 8, 105, 121, 122, 1118, 1325

fast (*rozhǝ*), 657. *See also* 76, 332, 800, 945

fat, 60, 85, 100, 428, 471. *See also* 1119.

ghee. See also 282

See butter oil

fate, 495, 603, 721, 750. *See also* 73, 157, 171, 317, 420, 448, 582, 651, 653, 657, 811, 985. *See* God's will,

Fatheh Khan Banda, 1226

father, 51, 52, 53, 54, 95, 97, 106, 118, 267, 351, 369, 431, 525, 601, 736, 849, 918, 925, 1113, 1121, 1184, 1232, 1347. *See also* 233, 480, 485, 585, 622, 796, 799, 1003, 1108, 1251, 1259, 1321, 1325. *See* in-laws

father-in-law. *See* in-laws

favor. *See* kindness

fear, 511, 668, 1057, 1228. *See also* 54, 73, 96, 213, 289, 400, 415, 479, 539, 591, 608, 681, 733, 747, 874, 892, 955, 975, 999, 1044, 1045, 1077, 1226, 1347

feet. *See also* 645, 677

feud. *See also* 89, 839, 889, 1279, 1282, 1333. *See* enemy

fever, 62, 438

field, 176, 277, 580, 778. *See also* 8, 122, 157, 196, 305, 371, 583, 609, 871. *See* earth

fig. *See also* 1314

fight, quarrel, 124, 142, 255, 427, 514, 669, 1032, 1193, 1194. *See also* 3, 67, 82, 128, 191, 192, 270, 278, 334, 375, 448, 521, 528, 792, 797, 939, 1045, 1077, 1334, 1349

jang, 265, 315, 332, 377, 530, 531, 624, 684, 716, 829, 1054, 1279

See battle; war,

filth, filthy, 298, 423

finger, fingers, 66, 223, 477, 478, 720, 767, 807. *See also* 282, 284

fingernail, 251, 920, 1195

fire, 198, 210, 211, 214, 215, 216, 217, 533, 588, 589, 616, 786, 996, 1020, 1046, 1214, 1228, 1315, 1322, 1334. *See also* 272, 324, 367, 540, 593, 625, 1253

hell fire, 1006. *See also* 1322

fish, fishing, 191, 523, 824, 1267. *See also* 475, 941

fist, 251

flattery, 1245. *See also* 577, 992

flesh, 886, 980, 1195. *See also* 182, 1102, 1159

flood, 51

flour, 83, 221, 222, 224, 360, 427, 796, 1115, 1121, 1122, 1342. *See also* 54, 121, 466, 1181, 1332

flour mill. *See* mill

flower, 167, 504, 757, 839, 887, 888. *See also* 106, 499, 645

fly, 672, 1241, 1268. *See also* 424

foe. *See* enemy

food, meal, 113, 254, 323, 338, 339, 681, 753, 775, 859, 981, 998, 1033, 1051, 1174, 1295, 1329. *See also* 158, 317, 318, 332, 394, 457, 533, 557, 625, 650, 828, 1164, 1215, 1216, 1336

mṛai, 199

nmṛai, 1129. *See also* 1220

apple. *See also* 5, 202, 206, 424, 702,

barley, 218, 219, 220, 532, 594. *See also* 932

barley bread (*hazar surakha*), 1119

beef. *See also* 429, 551, 1119

berries, 507, 530

bread, 33, 85, 106, 119, 193, 204, 212, 227, 228, 229, 349, 429, 1024, 1051, 1076, 1115, 1129, 1320,

1332. *See also* 259, 795, 914, 1021, 1119, 1216
   maize bread, 428
butter, 244, 672, 907
butter oil, 1021. *See also* 60, 1332
buttermilk, 307
cake. *See also* 1021
chicken. *See also* 429, 551
chickpea. *See also* 706
corn, 433, 941. *See also* 305, 629, 949, 1306
cornbread. *See also* 1215
daily bread. *See also* 157
date, 945. *See also* 291
egg, 56, 117, 263, 409, 569
eggplant (*brinjal*), 63
fat, 60, 85, 100, 428, 471
   ghee. See also 282
fig. *See also* 1314
fish. *See also* 941
flour, 83, 221, 222, 224, 360, 427, 796, 1115, 1121, 1122, 1342. *See also* 54, 121, 466, 1181
garbanzo bean. *See also* 706
garlic, 591
grain, 14, 219, 427, 706. *See also* 371, 629, 778
grape, 170. *See also* 576
jujube berries, 339
maize, 176, 528, 646
meat, 248, 475, 1103, 1196. *See also* 471, 941
melon, 454, 819, 944
milk, 59, 178, 232, 244, 759, 1145, 1206. *See also* 156, 189, 637
millet, 305, 338, 981
mulberry, 170, 501, 553
mutton. *See also* 1119
nut. *See also* 650
oil, 520
onion, 428, 457, 770. *See also* 1215
plum, 576
porridge, 100, 244, 245, 246, 968. *See also* 744
radish, 414
raisin, 390
rice, 157, 1021, 1137, 1329
   palau, 429, 551, 1119
   sangroba, 551
salt, 568, 1295
sesame seed, 520

soup, 87, 281, 816
spinach, 963, 972
sugar, 388, 617, 643, 813, 819, 1066, 1241
tomato. *See also* 63
turnip. *See also* 425
walnut. *See also* 421
wheat, 5, 518, 695, 711, 821
   wheat bread, 85. *See also* 193
   wheat flour. *See also* 1332
whey, 878. *See also* 1215
fool, foolish, 79, 397, 780, 811, 1157, 1179, 1182, 1260, 1279, 1314. *See also* 138, 305, 492, 539, 563, 613, 835, 926, 927, 932, 935, 951, 956, 954, 955, 968, 985, 1119, 1252, 1284, 1350. *See* stupid
foot, feet, 48, 101, 347, 348, 367, 391, 515, 550, 571, 578, 585, 625, 755, 812, 814, 982. *See also* 77, 804
forbidden, 901. *See also* 5, 210, 291, 1034
   harām, 381, 828. *See also* 562
force, 11, 286, 403, 438, 559, 587, 826, 907, 1049, 1104, 1105. *See also* 6, 15, 20, 68, 120, 258, 361, 490, 492, 549, 1024
forehead, 277, 599, 663, 954. *See also* 613
forest, 213. *See also* 216
forgiveness. *See also* 300, 517, 1333
fort, 882
fortunate man. *See also* 750
fortune, luck, 262, 276, 277, 317, 322, 971, 1110, 1142. *See also* 572, 694, 1002, 1324
forward, 1269
fox, 488
friend, companion, 368, 484, 1249, 1260, 1331. *See also* 9, 36, 115, 164, 204, 332, 407, 459, 461, 530, 562, 584, 604, 605, 622, 637, 722, 784, 792, 793, 817, 839, 877, 888, 937, 1002, 1020, 1101, 1142, 1162, 1195, 1314, 1335
   ashnā, 125, 126, 127, 128, 129, 130, 131, 132, 864
   dost, 664, 910, 911, 1068, 1069, 1173, 1298. *See also* 857
hamzoley (peer, of the same age), 1259

insincere. *See also* 643, 1331
khpəl, 215, 417
mal, 302, 710, 872, 900, 901, 905, 1297
malgərey, 256, 899
yār, 82, 642, 660, 729, 730, 746, 769, 770, 893, 1047, 1060, 1183, 1243, 1329. *See also* 26
See beloved; comrade; friendship; partner
friendly, unfriendly. *See also* 82, 898, 1025
friendship, 599, 1053. *See also* 126, 164, 257, 302, 355, 457, 483, 484, 521, 643, 718, 763, 769, 806, 886, 910, 1009, 1060, 1282
yār, 447
See friend
frog, 48, 781, 1028
frying pan, 557. *See also* 272, 324,
fuel, 963. *See also* 367
Fullonius, William. *See also* 398
gain, profit, wealth, 291, 1014. *See also* 191, 433, 615, 694, 706, 752, 1042, 1084, 1236, 1238
game, 840. *See also* 248
  angay. See also 171
  gambling. *See also* 278
  marbles, 370
garbanzo bean. *See also* 706
garlic, 591
generation, 719
generosity, 84. *See also* 85, 318, 375, 425, 457, 622, 757, 842, 844, 1009, 1215, 1282
gentleman, 136, 140. *See* noble man
ghazel. See also 1218
Ghazni, 464
ghəm. burden, 746, 1142
  grief, 378, 1343
  mourning, 102
  sorrow, 183, 611, 1192
  trouble, 333, 334, 728
  worry, 625, 890
ghost, 1275. *See also* 463
giantess. *See also* 540
gift, 85, 896. *See also* 28, 113, 119, 247, 283, 332, 392, 457, 684, 972, 1015
girl, maiden, damsel, 357, 1170. *See also* 106, 622, 1119, 1348

jinəy, 39, 84, 1289
peghla, 476, 964, 1268
glass house, 264
goat, 324, 537, 687, 708, 1307. *See also* 236
God, 399, 577, 1082, 1320, 1327. *See also* 35, 49, 54, 72, 159, 164, 173, 199, 291, 332, 389, 415, 459, 461, 495, 501, 583, 643, 645, 705, 735, 924, 945, 979, 1102, 1159, 1165, 1181, 1196, 1203, 1325
Allah, 157, 158, 450. *See also* 91
habib, 748
khoday, 50, 98, 274, 296, 301, 302, 303, 420, 458, 472, 480, 572, 614, 649, 650, 651, 652, 653, 654, 655, 656, 667, 668, 694, 802, 805, 818, 827, 847, 850, 891, 892, 893, 894, 895, 896, 897, 898, 899, 900, 901, 902, 903, 904, 905, 906, 908, 909, 910, 911, 912, 913, 914, 915, 916, 918, 919, 920, 921, 922, 923, 926, 991, 1006, 1024, 1089, 1090, 1100, 1103, 1110, 1148, 1193. *See also* 1281
mawlā, 747
rab, 1
Rahman, rahmān, 168, 299
God's will, 650, 818. *See also* 495, 748, 802, 991, 1148
Gokand, 1314
gold, 544, 1224, 1228, 1341. *See* money
good, 128, 134, 140, 179, 246, 344, 439, 461, 526, 871, 918, 1069, 1088. *See also* 178, 284, 299, 444, 588, 706, 709, 924, 969, 1073, 1162, 1261, 1295, 1298
  good advice. *See also* 1261
  good behavior, 1172
  good character. *See also* 143, 520
  good deed, 419, 1171. *See also* 94, 113, 945
  good example. *See also* 1258
  good family, 136. *See also* 144
  good food, 1174. *See also* 1220
  good fortune. *See also* 694
  good friend, 1173
  good habit, manner. *See also* 91, 205, 645
  good impression. *See also* 49

good intention, purpose, 280. *See also* 882, 1298

good luck. *See* fortune

good man, 947, 1175

good name. *See also* 1

good quality, 80, 835. *See also* 499

good reward. *See also* 359

good school. *See also* 1178

good story, 1174

good things. *See also* 22, 90, 568, 672, 907, 932, 1175

good word, 1156

good works. *See also* 117

See noble

good-hearted man. *See also* 832

grain, 14, 219, 427, 706. *See also* 371, 629, 778

grandfather. *See also* 134

grandmother, 1008

grandson, 1008

grape, 170. *See also* 576

grass, 26, 237, 932. *See also* 42, 567, 871

grate, 212

grave, graveyard, 147, 388, 483, 484, 500, 873, 874, 1160, 1240, 1262. *See also* 151

gray, 959, 960, 961

great, significant man, 1171. *See also* 241, 620,1222, 1094, 1004, 924, 902, 698, 653, *See* man

greed, greedy, 487. *See also* 85, 99, 268, 339, 478, 507, 712, 1241

greedy man. *See also* 88, 472, 643, 677, 866, 931, 942, 1129

green, 932. *See also* 567, 871

grief. *See* sorrow; weep

ground, 99, 218, 460, 595, 817, 935, 966, 1064. *See also* 20, 47, 54, 846, 1073, 1077, 1102, 1252

guest, 368, 1154. *See also* 1, 204, 254, 323, 457, 494, 566, 638, 1020, 1081, 1119, 1186, 1215

melma, 318, 319, 330, 681, 1052, 1220, 1287. *See also* 103

guest house (*hujra*). *See also* 1139, 1186 *dera*, 1200, 1294

guilt, guilty, 284. *See also* 86, 223, 261, 581, 734, 782, 1038

Gujar. *See also* 637

Gujrat. *See also* 747

gun (*topak, boṟay*), 361

gutter, 272

gypsy, 547, 548

habit, manner, 160, 904, 1146, 1176. *See also* 18, 60, 91, 93, 127, 645, 959, 1010, 1110, 1301

Hadith, 651. *See also* 120, 650, 873

hail, 1220

Hajj, Hajji. See pilgrim

hand, 67, 111, 156, 226, 364, 392, 433, 434, 435, 436, 454, 465, 468, 521, 547, 677, 696, 766, 801, 806, 870, 881, 888, 1051, 1070, 1245, 1308. *See also* 8, 72, 77, 85, 106, 162, 204, 229, 224, 313, 350, 367, 456, 1181

empty handed, 493, 494

handful, 170, 220, 360, 949. *See also* 838

handmill. *See* mill

happy, happiness, 9, 126, 836, 1268. *See also* 373, 378, 389, 397, 446, 553, 598, 615, 1018, 1050

hard-hearted man. *See also* 425

harm, 563, 596, 1068. *See also* 345, 604, 807, 1045, 1224

harmless. *See also* 1020

harvest, 176, 1306

hashish (*chars*), 555

haste, hasty, 75, 320, 321, 1052. *See also* 107

hasty man, 496

hate, hatred. *See also* 106, 310, 1303

Hatemai, 213

hawk, 434

hay, 307, 633

Hazara District. *See also* 622

head, 149, 188, 328, 348, 406, 409, 603, 614, 664, 698, 701, 702, 703, 718, 731, 756, 775, 801, 843, 869, 905, 938, 1096, 1099, 1144, 1145, 1146, 1180, 1253, 1266, 1338. *See also* 42, 234, 350, 476, 553, 613, 746, 966, 1009, 1034, 1086, 1218, 1348

headache, 613. *See also* 459

healthy, well, 1181. *See also* 789

heap, large amount, 949, 1117

heart, 173, 383, 384, 400, 402, 543, 550, 611, 670, 783, 865, 997, 1002, 1096, 1097, 1211. *See also* 106, 231, 258, 401, 425, 444, 492, 640, 648, 832, 842, 844, 924, 1250

hearth, 625, 916. *See also* 1020

heavens. *See* sky

heavy, 490, 778, 1073. *See also* 42, 346, 1152, 1178, 1181, 1345
drund, 902

hell, 461, 837, 1006, 1139. *See also* 1322

help, 1, 51, 111, 256, 1055, 1164, 1186, 1309. *See also* 60, 77, 236, 242, 312, 540, 553, 577, 582, 722, 837, 869, 905, 939, 1139, 1152, 1186, 1244, 1281, 1303

helpless, 975. *See also* 1008

hen, 117, 556, 563, 565, 566, 567, 568, 569, 570. *See also* 577. *See* chicken; rooster

henna, 77

henpecked. *See also* 1349

Herat. *See also* 1222

herd, 135, 432, 1161

herdsman, shepherd, 6. *See also* 236, 637, 1307

heritage, 1010. *See* inherit

hero, 1284. *See also* 6, 7, 361, 504, 514, 1098

hide, leather. *See also* 1212

Hindkai, 1329

Hindko (language). *See also* 1329

Hindu, 35, 210, 553, 652, 830, 1058, 1060, 1077, 1155, 1158, 1225, 1296, 1322, 1323. *See also* 1180, 1193

hit. *See* beat

hole, 251, 467, 1191. *See also* 370, 1218

holy man. *See also* 420, 1252, 1347
faqir, 119, 933, 1199, 1200. *See* beg
pir. See saint

home. *See* house

homeland. *See also* 177, 608, 876, 1221, 1314

honey, 1319

honor, honorable, 724, 1007, 1203. *See also* 1, 3, 58, 106, 115, 144, 247, 318, 328, 341, 375, 387, 494, 608, 620, 629, 668, 738, 859, 873, 889, 935, 938, 1006, 1009, 1025, 1192, 1203,
1207, 1333
izzat, 870, 1183
nang, 1203
pat, 1266
See pakhtunwali

honorable man. *See also* 340, 494

hope, 311, 643. *See also* 308, 351

Horace. *See also* 195

horn, 926, 934. *See also* 204, 824

horn (trumpet). *See also* 23

horse, 10, 11, 12, 13, 14, 15, 16, 17, 18, 19, 20, 21, 22, 23, 24, 25, 26, 27, 28, 29, 30, 31, 32, 33, 34, 48, 117, 306, 331, 347, 372, 737, 1000, 1015, 1019, 1127, 1184, 1204. *See also* 77, 138, 444, 467, 524, 687, 689, 709, 739, 948, 1102

horseman, horse rider. *See* rider

horseshoe, 1204. *See also* 48

hospitality, 236, 1164, 1220, 1287. *See also* 113, 247, 254, 318, 375, 494, 1020, 1108, 1119, 1336. *See* guest

host, 1052. *See also* 318, 323, 457, 1020, 1186, 1215

Hotak. *See also* 1222

hound. *See* dog

house, home, 536, 542, 681, 709, 841, 951, 1012, 1072, 1108, 1115, 1140, 1144. *See also* 27, 56, 83, 169, 445, 476, 500, 567, 598, 609, 634, 668, 726, 754, 775, 820, 841, 1040, 1086, 1119, 1215, 1216, 1220, 1230, 1252, 1288, 1294, 1321
kara, 324, 349, 569, 699, 809
khāna, 442
khuna, 1009
kor, 103, 106, 131, 307, 309, 330, 356, 382, 416, 427, 428, 429, 430, 431, 483, 484, 522, 530, 627, 665, 675, 726, 873, 887, 954, 1020, 1022, 1134, 1157, 1160, 1189, 1190, 1199, 1200, 1214, 1287, 1334. *See also* 315, 1032, 1168
mina, 440

household. *See also* 4, 56, 283, 627, 684, 1119, 1229
kor, 117
See house

housewife. *See* wife

Hughes, Thomas. *See also* 328
Hukam Chand, 830
human, human being, 300, 1247. *See also* 276, 311, 380, 444, 501, 785, 924, 1128, 1203
 ensān, 167, 168, 1317
 See man
hundred, 220, 247, 330, 411, 412, 1023, 1059, 1150, 1154, 1155, 1156, 1190, 1230, 1340. *See also* 444, 684, 1253
hunger, 88, 231, 393, 1332
 hunger strike, 488
hungry man, 227, 228, 229, 230, 287. *See also* 231, 1306
hunt, 248, 291, 618, 752
hurt, 369, 455, 886. *See also* 214, 613
husband, 44, 76, 148, 797, 1101, 1144, 1170. *See also* 635, 836, 847, 1004, 1122, 1140, 1167, 1168
Hussain, 1313
hybrid, 601
hypocrisy, hypocrite. *See also* 85, 384, 401, 407, 408, 474
idleness, 314, 1153
Ilam (mountain), 458
ill-bred, 936. *See* rogue
impolite proverbs. *See* proverbs
India, Indian, 976. *See also* 177, 210, 305, 547, 620, 622, 863, 1020, 1058,1034, 1064, 1119, 1347
Indus River. *See also* 1222. *See* Abasin
inexperienced man. *See* undisciplined
infant, 759
inferior. *See* cheap; insignificant
infidel, 898, 1348. *See* non-believer (*kāfir*)
influence, 133. *See also* 226, 294, 556, 1020
inherit, inheritance. *See also* 1003, 1303
 mirās, 162
in-laws
 brother-in-law, 84
 daughter-in-law. *See also* 990
 father-in-law, 841. *See also* 622
 mother-in-law. *See also* 106, 990
 sister-in-law, 84
 son-in-law, 1108
innocent man. *See also* 591
insects. ant, 382, 897, 1263. *See also* 54

bee, 1319
fly, 672, 1241, 1268. *See also* 424
worm. *See also* 54, 75, 829
insignificant, degraded, light. *See also* 45, 66, 103, 117, 317, 546, 570, 962, 968, 972, 1112
 spǝk, 902, 1007
insignificant, weak, 278, 777. *See also* 35, 202, 309, 492, 553, 579, 749, 975, 1194, 1282
insignificant, weak man. *See also* 45, 89, 103, 198, 349, 409, 528, 546, 672, 698, 734, 780, 816, 845, 943, 962, 1029, 1106, 1278
insult. *See also* 1349. *See* taunts
intelligent. *See* foolish; wise
intention, 280, 800, 1005. *See also* 173, 401, 1148, 1298
interference, 534, 679, 743. *See also* 479
intoxicant, 389
inward, 401. *See also* 173, 640. *See* outward
Iran, Iranian. *See also* 1222, 1230
iron, 234, 235
Islam, Islamic, 120. *See also* 5, 35, 54, 291, 381, 415, 461, 586, 608, 651, 654, 740, 914, 979, 1033, 1165, 1203, 1322, 1347
 See forbidden; lawful; religious law, code; *shariah*
jackal, 265, 274, 291, 400, 576, 577, 618, 780, 829, 959, 1043, 1242
Jamu and Kashmir. *See* Kashmir
jar. *See* pitcher
Jerusalem. *See also* 54
Jesus Christ. *See also* 302, 705
Jewish. *See also* 5, 914, 1203
jihad. See also 120
jinn. See also 54, 459
 periyan, 463, 464
jirga, 526. *See also* 903, 1333. *See* council
job. *See* work
Job. *See also* 158
John Heywood. *See also* 358
journey, 634, 1223. *See also* 240, 251, 283
joy, joyful, 378, 733, 916. *See also* 106, 250, 259, 334, 683, 717, 970, 1239

judge, judging, 257, 421, 1147. *See also* 6, 47, 86, 557, 767, 782, 800, 949
qazi, 479. *See also* 1038
Judgment Day, Doomsday. *See also* 82, 147, 891, 1102
qiāmat, 753, 1203
jujube berries, 339
July, 533
June, 533
jungle, 17, 402, 530, 1275. *See also* 577, 1045, 1253
justice, 169. *See also* 472, 572, 645, 850, 1012, 1104, 1203
Kabul, 366. *See also* 1165
Kabul River. *See* Landai, Landi
Kafiristan. *See also* 1347
Kalabat, 622
Kamalai, 12
Kandahar, Qandahar, 567. *See also* 1222
Karbala, 1313
Kashmir, 445, 781, 876, 1230
Khachana, 224
Khan Abdul Ghaffar Khan. *See also* 924
Khattak, 890. *See also* 305, 923
Khost, 608
Khurasan, 1230
Khushal Khan Khattak, 1007, 1138, 1186. *See also* 177, 1266
kick, 40, 587, 807, 1019. *See also* 204
kill, killed, 32, 90, 166, 284, 364, 470, 562, 617, 703, 935, 1066, 1232, 1261, 1264. *See also* 489, 603, 696, 945, 1284
mər, 198, 369, 867
See death
kin, kith and kin. *See* kinsman
kindness, favor, 61, 296, 426, 1310. *See also* 60, 134, 168, 182, 296, 302, 388, 517, 645, 652, 817
king, 259, 269, 414, 1172, 1219. *See also* 412, 449, 1312, 1349
bāchā, 169, 278, 327, 398, 1202
kinsman, relative, 850. *See also* 332, 382, 443, 696, 722, 737, 742, 868, 1012, 1062, 1063, 1112, 1195, 1234, 1244
khpəl, 312, 856, 857, 858, 862, 863, 867, 875, 1130, 1174. *See also* 417
kinsmen, relative. *See also* 1158

kiss, 600
knead, 367. *See also* 83
knife, 558. *See also* 181
knowledge, 137. *See also* 787, 1202
Kohistan. *See also* 1314
labor. *See* work
laborer, 1237. *See also* 14, 95
Lachai, 752
ladle, 744
lady. *See* woman
lamb, 52, 221, 437, 1251
lamentation, 195, 756. *See also* 494
lamp, 1030, 1168, 1292
Landai, Landi (Kabul River), 177
landəy (folk poem). *See* ṭappa
landowner, 1049. *See also* 620
large hearted man. *See also* 842
lark, 374, 942, 943, 960
laugh, laughter, 495, 683, 840, 857, 964, 965, 970, 1050, 1114, 1217, 1298, 1343. *See also* 54, 98, 106, 1226
laughing stock, 1098
laundry. *See* clothes
law. *See also* 148, 526, 560, 608, 645, 696
  Islamic. *See also* 415, 586, 654
  See Shariah
lawful, 396.
  halāl. *See also* 381, 396, 562, 828
  See Islam; *Shariah*
laziness, 707. *See also* 56, 171, 224
lazy man, 1246. *See also* 482
leader. *See also* 103, 152, 526, 565, 586, 758, 787, 788, 838, 892, 1253, 1326
  bāchā, 398
  khan, 633
  malək, 271, 566, 809. *See also* 620. *See* lord
  məshər, məshrān, 1040, 1274
  See elder; king; master; religious leader
learn, 252, 851
leaven, 466. *See also* 259
leech, 425
leg, 546, 1307. *See also* 204, 814
leopard, 762. *See also* 6, 1261
letter. *See* alphabet
lid, 859. *See also* 1181

lie, liar, 688, 827, 1087, 1318. *See also* 889

life, lives, 148, 404, 523, 904, 912, 1201, 1245, 1273, 1326. *See also* 1, 72, 75, 94, 153, 171, 195, 312, 322, 341, 346, 347, 350, 359, 378, 389, 403, 459, 494, 603, 645, 653, 672, 717, 745, 750, 846, 872, 889, 924, 954, 957, 1009, 1219, 1266, 1277, 1302
   cycle of life. *See also* 259, 1018
   way of life. *See also* 636, 658, 841, 940, 974

light. *See* insignificant

lightning, 289

lion, 206, 265, 473, 618, 649, 735, 829, 1043, 1102, 1103

lizard, 531, 571, 644, 703, 794

load, 237, 240, 242, 953, 1208. *See also* 42, 416, 746, 940
   bār, 270, 271, 810, 930, 931, 957, 1001. *See also* 1208
   See burden

log. *See* wood

Lord (*khāwand*), 847

lord (*malək*), 542. *See also* 271.
   See leader

loss, 295, 1014. *See also* 51, 54, 102, 153, 181, 294, 447, 515, 548, 564, 603, 677, 709, 764, 933, 1194, 1333

love, 148, 258, 340, 355, 457, 610, 627, 635, 639, 803, 1016, 1043, 1164. *See also* 106, 275, 302, 310, 385, 457, 461, 524, 705, 782, 958, 1009, 1097, 1165

lowborn. *See* rogue

loyal, loyalty, 136. *See also* 94, 114, 770, 1119, 1223

luck, lucky. *See* fortune

luggage, 58, 809

lungi. See also 329, 553

Luqman. *See also* 91, 1182

madman, 965, 1135

maiden. *See* girl

maidservant, 165, 1112

maize, 176, 528, 646. *See* bread

Makkah, 927. *See also* 827

man, men, mankind, 33, 78, 143, 157, 168, 296, 297, 298, 299, 301, 302, 303, 304, 366, 403, 410, 421, 570, 578, 585, 649, 655, 717, 802, 896, 909, 919, 964, 965, 1056, 1136, 1142, 1147, 1149, 1150, 1151, 1152, 1176, 1207, 1296. *See also* 572, 606, 705, 835, 846, 924, 1148, 1185
   See human

manliness. *See also* 1247

manners, 1010. *See also* 205, 1176, 1302
   adab, 91, 92, 310
   See habit

Manu, Manuzar, 666

manure, 844, 1151. *See also* 367

March, 777, 778

Mardan. *See also* 58

mare. *See* horse

Marie Antoinette. *See also* 1021

marriage, marry, 357, 373, 387, 718, 1170, 1259, 1300, 1321. *See also* 106, 459, 479, 615, 622, 910, 997

Marwat, 193. *See also* 329

master, 15, 20, 103, 134, 257, 575, 646, 790, 791, 930, 954, 1132, 1134, 1237. *See also* 27, 266, 337, 847, 1033, 1225, 1229. *See* leader

matter (*khabəra*), 233

Maududi. *See also* 91

May, 533

Mazo Gul, 116

meal. *See* food

mean-spirited man. *See also* 1261

measuring cup, 1306

meat, 248, 475, 1103, 1196. *See also* 291, 396, 471, 562, 941

medicine, 1061, 1085

melancholy, 4

melon, 454, 819, 944

menial, 615. *See also* 57, 395, 615, 625, 682, 838, 839, 1040, 1074. *See* servant,

Mero, 7, 514

merry making, 359, 389, 754. *See also* 305, 694, 999

milk, 59, 178, 232, 244, 759, 1145, 1206. *See also* 156, 189, 637

mill, 224, 362, 427, 796, 820, 821, 1121, 1342. *See also* 195, 520. *See* flour

mill owner (*āsiyāwān*), 49

millet, 305, 338, 981

millionaire, 1249

mimic, 1113

minister, 259
Mirwais Khan Ghalzai, 1222
mischief, 1179. *See also* 284.
See enmity
mischief-monger, 93, 282, 595, 601. *See also* 168, 1130
miser, miserly. *See also* 85, 323, 430, 726, 757, 860, 1017. *See* greed
misfortune, 353, 537
mistake, 6. *See also* 110, 300
mistress, 1346
modesty. *See* taunts
Mohammad Akbar Khan, 275
money, 258, 467, 468, 469, 515, 622, 687, 1001. *See also* 105, 116, 174, 283, 318, 361, 414, 425, 459, 494, 524, 853, 1081
gold, 689, 690, 691, 1093
pice, kāsirə, 238
See blood money; *rupee*
monkey, 221
month, 65, 121, 122, 352, 533. *See also* 76, 350
moon, 1128. *See also* 106
morning, 868. *See also* 637, 1193
Moses (*Musa*). *See also* 914
mosque. *See also* 152, 787
jumāt, 1275, 1288
mother, 56, 57, 58, 59, 60, 61, 62, 63, 94, 95, 96, 97, 98, 99, 100, 101, 102, 103, 108, 505, 525, 538, 573, 736, 742, 759, 773, 799, 849, 958, 1058, 1112, 1256, 1279, 1280. *See also* 200, 224, 260, 284, 289, 585, 941, 990, 1094, 1181, 1222. *See* in-laws
mother-in-law. *See* in-laws
mountain, 51, 64, 129, 213, 451, 467, 668, 670, 689, 708, 1152, 1185, 1186, 1187, 1324, 1333. *See also* 98, 194, 234, 361, 458, 811, 968, 1102
mourning, 443. *See* sorrow
ghəm, 102
mouse, mice, 470, 472, 474, 986. *See also* 158, 379, 1277
mouth, 221, 280, 384, 386, 478, 577, 585, 649, 772, 858, 860, 889, 966, 967, 984, 991, 1079, 1114, 1207, 1210, 1267, 1341. *See also* 181, 401,

418, 609, 804, 815, 834, 1015, 1080, 1166, 1314. *See* tongue
mud, muddies, 191, 192, 606, 824, 956, 996, 1251. *See also* 196, 754.
See water
Mughal, 863, 1049. *See also* 150, 1186
mulberry, 170, 501, 553
mulberry wood, 201. *See also* 1302.
See wood
mule, 16, 23, 938, 1184, 1201
mullah, 133, 152, 267, 635, 787, 1029, 1109, 1124, 1275, 1276, 1347. *See also* 89, 90, 147, 407, 608
See Akhund
Mullah Akbar, 90
Multan. *See also* 1165
murder, 570, 696. *See also* 1232
music, 674. *See also* 102, 305, 615, 1165
musical instruments. *See also* 1165
drum, 69, 305, 573, 682, 883, 1074, 1078. *See also* 615
rabāb, 1302
musician (*dəm*), 1074, 1075. *See also* 615, 682
Muslim, 384, 652. *See also* 35, 49, 210, 291, 407, 787, 979, 1029, 1165, 1181, 1229, 1314, 1322
mustard seed, 435
mutton. *See also* 1119
myself, self, 90, 130, 249, 540, 785. *See also* 476, 524, 1132
myth. *See also* 289, 735, 1102, 1253.
See story
naked, 287, 288
name, 1, 847, 1024, 1133, 1222. *See also* 49, 52, 93, 213, 224, 291, 305, 460, 532, 572, 620, 838, 1024, 1137, 1292.
See credit
nanawāti. See forgiveness
narrow, 500, 874, 1002
Nazar Din, 1137
Nazo, 1222
neck, 243, 722, 1122, 1244, 1277. *See also* 152, 492
needy man. *See* poor
neighbor, 59, 151. *See also* 83, 103, 1020, 1140, 1165
Neki. *See also* 284
nephew, maternal (*khora'ay*), 731, 1003

niece, 997

night, 272, 324, 336, 448, 946, 993, 1035, 1039, 1048, 1057, 1059, 1077, 1159, 1160, 1200, 1320, 1342. *See also* 289, 637, 1186, 1229

nightmares, 581

noble, well-bred man, 132, 137, 138, 139, 141, 142, 143, 144, 789, 826, 1283, 1285, 1286. *See also* 21, 117, 165, 275, 473, 620, 819, 938, 1007

noise, 492, 559, 792. *See also* 1342

non-believer (*kāfir*), 344, 384

North West Frontier Province. *See also* 1329, 1017, 813, 233

nose, 1, 261, 604, 662, 751, 761, 1086. *See also* 41, 1181, 1252

nut. *See also* 650

obedience. *See also* 332, 415, 580, 1256. *See* manners

obligation, 102, 222. *See also* 440, 494, 586, 966, 979, 1014, 1124

obscene proverbs. *See* proverbs

oil, 520, 1292

old, 633, 890, 1290. *See also* 1008, 1025
old age, 81, 692, 768, 773
old days. *See also* 1247
old device. *See also* 1018
old dog, 253. *See also* 1261
old fool. *See also* 954
old habit. *See also* 160, 1146, 1301
old mare, 306
old mouse. *See also* 1277
old myth. *See also* 1102
old story. *See also* 1252

old man, woman, 598, 1024. *See also* 134, 289, 480

Old Testament. *See also* 148, 310, 315, 705, 726

Omer, 1119

one hundred thousand (*lāk*), 426. *See also* 71

one-eyed man, 398

onion, 428, 457, 770. *See also* 1215

opium eater, 489

Orakzai. *See also* 1

orchard, 274

origin, 145. *See also* 1223

orphan, 751

Osman, 1180

outcast (*shaṛəl*), 903

outward, 401, 421, 640. *See also* 49, 173, 557, 940, 959, 1025, 1034. *See* inward

oven, 465

owner, 12, 271, 985. *See also* 30, 52, 236, 257, 637, 790, 847, 884, 1081, 1118, 1307. *See* master

ox, 700, 1107, 1255. *See also* 482

paddle, 1209

paisa. See rupee

Pak Pattan. *See also* 1165

Pakhpulla. *See also* 540

Pakhto, Pashto (language). *See also* 1, 7, 14, 27, 35, 49, 75, 82, 104, 106, 120, 129, 138, 148, 152, 154, 155, 171, 182, 195, 213, 231, 233, 252, 275, 282, 283, 291, 302, 305, 313, 332, 339, 357, 396, 406, 416, 425, 429, 433, 437, 473, 444, 445, 454, 460, 477, 517, 521, 532, 609, 631, 651, 664, 705, 708, 725, 726, 804, 846, 863, 865, 873, 877, 920, 941, 989, 1001, 1009, 1012, 1023, 1027, 1110, 1159, 1163, 1168, 1179, 1180, 1181, 1185,1186, 1187, 1206, 1347

Pakhtun folklore. *See also* 102, 284

Pakhtun tribes
Afridi. *See also* 1
Ashnaghar. *See also* 129
Babar, 268
Bannuchi, 305. *See also* 1137
Buniri. *See also* 661
Daudzai, 357
Hotak. *See also* 1222
Khattak, 890. *See also* 305, 923
Marwat, 193. *See also* 329
Orakzai. *See also* 1, 275
Wazir. *See also* 361, 1058
Yousafzai, 58. *See also* 609, 1009, 1180, 1186

Pakhtun, Pashtun, 247, 340, 341, 342, 343, 344, 345, 346, 980, 1192, 1203. *See also* 6, 35, 39, 52, 56, 63, 67, 75, 85, 86, 94, 102, 106, 113, 115, 129, 143, 147, 148, 171, 176, 177, 224, 233, 236, 249, 254, 259, 268, 278, 284, 305, 312, 318, 328, 341, 361, 378, 387, 405, 421, 425, 454, 457, 460, 485, 486, 494, 503, 504, 526, 553, 572, 583, 608, 609, 615, 620,

629, 684, 689, 696, 712, 738, 740,
806, 849, 859, 863, 873, 876, 889,
890, 892, 910, 935, 973, 975, 990,
997, 1003, 1006, 1009, 1020, 1025,
1029, 1058, 1060, 1077, 1078, 1094,
1102, 1119, 1136, 1137, 1158, 1165,
1193, 1203, 1207, 1218, 1230, 1294,
1300, 1302, 1307, 1319, 1321, 1329,
1333, 1334, 1336

pakhtunwali, pakhto (code of honor), 341,
629, 1025. *See also* 1, 340, 341, 387,
583, 608, 873, 935, 1203, 1282

Pakistan. *See also* 177, 233, 413, 656,
747, 1004, 1017, 1165, 1230, 1238,
1314

Palsgrave, John. *See also* 1540

pannier, 433, 929, 940. *See* saddle bag

Paradise, 5, 376, 527. *See also* 120, 311,
445, 876, 1230, 1314

parrot, 442

partner. *See also* 278

   mal, 171

   See friend

partridge, 499

Pashakal, 65

Pashtun. *See* Pakhtun

pass away. *See* death

path, pathway, 287, 1097, 1187, 1218.
See also 234, 299

patience, 919, 1176, 1177. *See also* 159,
900, 1077

patient, 1085

payback. *See* exchange

peace. *See also* 517

peace, peaceful, 94, 153. *See also* 147,
315, 407

pedestrian, 1127

peg, 579, 939, 1091. *See also* 1302

pen, 1202

penny, 1163

performance, 895. *See also* 497, 700,
969

permission, 419, 1189. *See also* 83

persecution, 856

Persian. *See also* 49, 152, 454, 849,
1097, 1218, 1222, 1230

Persian wheel, 1018

person. *See* human; man

persons

Abdur Rahman Baba. *See also* 164,
421, 461, 611, 612, 630, 645, 1218

Abraham. *See also* 332

Adam, 5, 1317

Adam Khan, 6, 7, 514

Afghani, 849

Ahmad Shah, 1094. *See also* 1222

Akbar, Emperor, 150

Amruddin Lala, 68

Apollo. *See also* 159

Awal Bagh. *See also* 1137

Azo Gul, 116

Baboo Jan (Babu Jan), 444

Badi, 284, 289

Bakhtyar, 572

Benét, Stephen Vincent. *See also* 195

Chaucer. *See also* 577, 726

Chengiz Khan. *See also* 1165

Chung, 838

Cicero. *See also* 322

David, King. *See also* 173, 726, 1218,
1218,

Dickens, Charles. *See also* 1012

Dickenson, Emily. *See also* 924

Diwana Baba, 460, 656

Durkhanai. *See also* 6, 7

Erasmus, Desiderius. *See also* 398

Eve. *See also* 5

Fullonius, William. *See also* 398

Hatemai, 213

Horace. *See also* 195

Hughes, Thomas. *See also* 328

Hukam Chand, 830

Hussain, 1313

Izrail (Angel of Death), 1181

Jesus Christ. *See also* 302, 705

Job. *See also* 158

John Heywood. *See also* 358

Kamalai, 12

Khachana, 224

Khan Abdul Ghaffar Khan. *See also*
924

Khushal Khan Khattak, 1007, 1138,
1186. *See also* 1266

Luqman. *See also* 91, 1182

Manu, Manuzar, 666

Marie Antoinette. *See also* 1021

Maududi. *See also* 91

Mazo Gul, 116

Mero, 7, 514

Mirwais Khan Ghalzai, 1222

Mohammad Akbar Khan, 275
Moses (*Musa*). *See also* 914
Mullah Akbar, 90
Nazar Din, 1137
Nazo, 1222
Neki. *See also* 284
Omer, 1119
Osman, 1180
Pakhpulla. *See also* 540
Palsgrave, John. *See also* 398
Pir Baba, 458, 460, 653. *See* Sayyed
  Ali Tirmezi
Qamer, 338
Qazi Ghulam, 134
Saul, King. *See also* 726
Sayyed Ali Tirmezi. *See also* 460
Shah Dawla, 747
Shah Zaman, 569
Shahai. *See also* 504
Shakespeare, William. *See also* 14,
  492, 968
Sheikh Chili, 1252
Sheikh Farid, 1165
Sheikh Mir, 892
Sheikh Qutbuddin Bakhtiar Kaki. *See*
  also 1165
Shiva. *See also* 159
Skelton, John. *See also* 398
Solomon, King (*Bacha Suliman*). *See*
  also 54, 310, 315, 659, 705, 726,
  835
Tor Dalai, 504
Tor Mullah, 507
Tora, 625
Torai, 512
Wells, H.G. *See also* 398
Yazid. *See also* 1313
Yeel Bugh, 1137
Zarghuna, 1094
Zazi, 512
perverted man, 282
Peshawar. *See also* 65, 150, 275, 622,
  634
pestle, 594
phylactery. *See* amulet
pick-axe. *See* axe
pilgrim, pilgrimage. *See also* 656, 795
  Hajji, Hajj, 827. *See also* 332, 800
pillow, 1096
pine tree, 1290

pious man. *See also* 892
pious, piety, 474, 692. *See also* 49, 827,
  1165
  sheikh, 470
pipal (tree), 1193
pir. *See* saint
Pir Baba, 458, 460, 653. *See* Sayyed Ali
  Tirmezi
pitch, 1290
pitcher, 492, 792, 1099, 1191, 1278. *See*
  also 842
places
  Abazai, 634, 1223
  Afghanistan. *See also* 1058, 1230,
    1238
  Akbar Pura, 150
  Amritsar, 159
  Badabera. *See also* 339
  Bajaur, 95, 482
  Bala Manrai, 275
  Balkh, 721
  Bannu, 305, 551. *See also* 487, 708
  Barbotai, 319
  Bunir, 661. *See also* 458, 460, 656
  Calcutta. *See also* 1058
  Charsadda. *See also* 129
  Delhi. *See also* 1165
  Dera Ismail Khan. *See also* 374
  Diwana Baba (shrine), 460, 656
  Fatheh Khan Banda, 1226
  Ghazni, 464
  Gokand, 1314
  Gujrat. *See also* 747
  Hazara District. *See also* 622
  Herat. *See also* 1222
  Ilam (mountain), 458
  India, 976. *See also* 210, 620, 622,
    863, 1020, 1058, 1064, 1119, 1347
  Iran. *See also* 1230
  Jamu and Kashmir. *See also* 1230
  Kabul, 366. *See also* 1165
  Kafiristan. *See also* 1347
  Kalabat, 622
  Kandahar, Qandahar, 567. *See also*
    1222
  Karbala, 1313
  Kashmir, 445, 781, 876, 1230
  Khost, 608
  Khurasan, 1230
  Kohistan. *See also* 1314

Makkah, 927. *See also* 827
Mardan. *See also* 58
Multan. *See also* 1165
North West Frontier Province. *See also* 233, 813, 1017, 1329
Pak Pattan. *See also* 1165
Pakistan. *See also* 1238
Peshawar. *See also* 65, 150, 275, 622, 634
Pir Baba (shrine), 458, 460
Punjab. *See also* 159, 747, 1165
Qambar, 516
Ramora, 498
Rawalpindi. *See also* 622
Rome. *See also* 89, 631, 885, 1255
Shangri La. *See also* 876
Swabi. *See also* 622
Swat, 58, 95, 1319. *See also* 609, 656
Takwara, 374
Talash, 498
Taro Jabba, 150
Tirah, 1
Waziristan. *See also* 1058
plains, 58, 213
plant, 593, 1194. *See also* 175, 305
plaster, 367
pleasure, 457, 615, 1116, 1343. *See also* 236, 250, 389, 393, 394, 445, 1181
plot. *See* field
plough. *See* plow
plow, plowing, 518, 1344, 1345
plowman, 1325
plum, 576
pocket, 1280
pod, 200
poetry. *See* proverbs
point, 292, 767. *See also* 223
poison, 617, 1066, 1117
pole, 1009. *See also* 622
politics, political. *See* proverbs
polygamy. *See* wives, multiple
poor man, 164, 971, 972, 973, 974, 978, 981, 983, 990. *See also* 87, 227, 238, 359, 394, 528, 551, 564, 880, 957, 976, 1054, 1312, 1332
poor, poverty, 32, 479, 485, 522, 657, 748, 754, 907, 930, 976, 982, 986, 987, 989, 1029, 1119, 1153, 1170, 1299. *See also* 119, 158, 202, 220, 224, 289, 318, 357, 379, 478, 566,

622, 667, 839, 975, 979, 1119, 1198, 1219, 1325
faqiri. See also 1219
porridge, 100, 244, 245, 246, 968. *See also* 744
portion, 879, 880, 1009. *See also* 70, 317, 980, 1347
pot, 792. *See also* 842
cooking pot, 616, 625, 712, 859
pot for flour, 466
See pitcher
potter, 917, 1325
power, 510, 1006, 1105. *See also* 15, 91, 226, 291, 406, 428, 459, 635, 660, 737, 748, 892, 895, 910, 920, 934, 926, 1104, 1259. *See* strength
powerful man, 695, 1031, 1106, 1135. *See also* 13, 69, 409, 528, 665, 1019, 1107, 1194
powerless man. *See* insignificant
pray, prayer, 420, 480, 1048. *See also* 47, 54, 152, 173, 289, 577, 586, 656, 800, 913, 915, 979, 1006, 1124, 1159, 1181, 1325
bāng, azān, 437, 1029
bismillah, 93
kalima, 96
prayer beads (*tasbəy*), 49
precious, costly, 98. *See also* 31, 52, 201, 447, 544, 712, 766, 1224
grān, 105, 785, 1093
predestination, 276, 286. *See* fate
pregnancy, 1227
pride, proud, 915, 984, 1151, 1158. *See also* 86, 328, 349, 458, 726, 775, 859, 879, 883, 935, 1187
prince. *See also* 6
bāchā, 1021
shahzāda, 1312
princess, 165
profit. *See* gain
promise. *See* word
property, 790, 828
Prophet, 651. *See also* 35, 120, 291, 945, 1313
proposal, 1083
prosperity, 317, 1330. *See also* 174, 726, 747
prosperous man. *See* elder (*khan*). *See* rich

proud man. *See also* 234, 432
proverbs
  blessing. *See also* 301, 501, 652, 667,
    757, 906, 914, 1006, 1281
  contradictory. *See also* 75, 483
  curse, 212. *See also* 1, 24, 47, 129,
    239, 420, 501, 913, 953, 980, 1006,
    1180
  dialogue. *See also* 85, 90, 797, 957,
    1130, 1188, 1199, 1201, 1272
  folk poem. *chārbayta. See also* 275
    ṭappa, lanḍəy. See also 106, 429,
      460, 635, 839, 993, 1159, 1266
  humorous. *See also* 243, 1337
  impolite. *See also* 58, 104, 243, 298,
    321, 381, 409, 423, 757, 858, 1206,
    1319
  ironic, sarcastic. *See also* 6, 68, 103,
    134, 295, 305, 307, 319, 344, 357,
    502, 512, 622, 660, 673, 753, 754,
    781, 816, 817, 827, 869, 892, 907,
    958, 969, 975, 1009, 1014, 1111,
    1115, 1191, 1206, 1215, 1247,
    1289, 1335.
  misogynous. *See also* 873, 1168
  origin. *See also* 65, 83, 454, 473, 521
  poetic. *See also* 75, 106, 597, 1006,
    1185, 1266.
  poetic couplet. *See also* 195, 421, 444
  poetry (*ghazel*). *See also* 1218
  political. *See also* 275, 549, 669, 949,
    1020
  prayer. *See also* 289, 420, 480, 913,
    915, 1006, 1048, 1124, 1181, 1325
  rhyming. *See also* 75, 168, 196, 259,
    301, 725, 746, 826, 969, 1005,
    1012, 1205
  story. *See* story, fable, tale
  variant. *See also* 31, 41, 58, 92, 103,
    208, 216, 237, 243, 305, 394, 406,
    408, 411, 418, 445, 449, 461, 477,
    492, 517, 544, 557, 574, 597, 613,
    617, 645, 668, 702, 708, 746, 762,
    781, 814, 815, 829, 857, 873, 906,
    1069, 1079, 1088, 1159, 1186,
    1187, 1208, 1224, 1266, 1296,
    1306
provisions, 290
prudence, 495
punch, 1210. *See* blow

punishment, discipline, 1325. *See also* 1,
  92, 261, 266, 310, 525, 549, 654, 903,
  928, 1038, 1180, 1210
Punjab. *See also* 159, 747, 1165
pupil. *See* student
pure, 1228. *See also* 173, 178, 562, 1181
purgative, 525
purse, 53. *See* wealth
Qambar, 516
Qamer, 338
Qandahar. *See* Kandahar
qazi. See judge
Qazi Ghulam, 134
quality, qualities, 80, 508, 714, 835. *See*
  also 5, 105, 159, 193, 344, 397, 398,
  462, 499, 507, 520, 640, 816, 928,
  949, 994
quarrel. *See* fight
quilt, 350. *See also* 814, 1009, 1229
quoting behavior. *See also* 106
Qur'an, Holy. *See also* 54, 91, 106, 608,
  635
  khatam, 1014
rabāb, 1302
radish, 414
raft, 1250
Rahman. See God
rain, 44, 46, 272, 511, 685, 712, 754,
  777, 778, 779, 1220. *See also* 122,
  1325
  downpour, 43
rain spout, 272
raisin, 390
ram. *See also* 332
Ramazan. *See also* 76, 332
  See fast (*rozhə*)
Ramora, 498
rat, 735, 1277. *See also* 747
ravine, 973, 1004
Rawalpindi. *See also* 622
reap, 615, 645. *See also* 284, 800
red, 936
redistribution, distribution (*weysh*), 609,
  1285
refuge, 845
  panā, 668
relieve. *See* stools
relieve, ease, urinate, 380, 424, 752, 753

religion. *See also* 89, 738, 1060, 1034

religious law, code, 654. *See also* 152, 415, 562, 828, 979. *See* Islam; lawful

religious leader, teacher, 461. *See also* 85, 459, 460. *See* saint

repay. *See* exchange

repentance, 107, 108, 109, 110, 383, 896. *See also* 389, 539

reputation. *See* honor

resource, 7. *See also* 103, 226, 494, 629, 814, 910, 1017

respect, 724, 1233. *See also* 17, 118, 133, 144, 328, 461 653, 549, 698, 1112, 1136

responsibility, 152. *See also* 32, 42, 104, 155, 259, 266, 346, 625, 650, 758, 810, 1000, 1001, 1012

revenge. *See also* 369, 696, 807 935, 975, 1025, 1063, 1186, 1232
   badal, 247
   See exchange

revenue officer (*tehsildār*), 329

reward, 704, 800. *See also* 14, 491, 659, 810
   sawāb, 945. *See also* 291

rhododendron blossom, 661

rhyming proverbs. *See* proverbs

rice, 157, 1021, 1137, 1329
   palau, 429, 551, 1119
   sangroba, 551

rich man, 50, 164, 1221. *See also* 414, 690, 1238, 1303, 1311

rich, riches, 764, 1170. *See also* 137, 429, 622, 1219, 1238, 1322, 1332
   mari, 989

rider, 15, 19, 582, 982, 1157

ridicule
   tomat, 1050

rival, rivalry. *See also* 115, 198, 449, 629, 684, 933, 1003, 1229
   siyāl, 3, 1259. *See also* 928
   tarbur, 716, 1264

road, 256. *See also* 284, 1226

rob. *See* theft; thief

robin. *See also* 924

rock. *See* boulder

rogue, ill-bred, lowborn man, 132, 136, 138, 141, 142, 599, 1053. *See also* 117, 137, 144, 165, 444, 920, 926, 934, 936

Rome. *See also* 89, 631, 885, 1255

Romeo and Juliet. *See also* 7

roof, 545. *See also* 315, 1009

room, 350, 533
   school room, 133

rooster, 82, 278, 556, 561, 563. *See also* 437, 577. *See* chicken; hen

rose, 1239

rubbish heap. *See* dunghill

rubies, 410

rule, ruler, 37, 163, 385, 831, 986, 1231. *See also* 322, 418, 579, 653, 663, 669, 716, 863, 1020, 1071, 1102, 1222, 1312

rupee, paisa, 22, 31, 117, 220, 258, 1086, 1156, 1349. *See also* 71. *See* money

sacrifice, 476. *See also* 514, 524, 585, 1009, 1060, 1137, 1333

saddle, 27, 34

saddle bag. *See* pannier

saint (*pir*), 142, 458, 459, 460, 461, 462, 653, 881. *See also* 656, 747, 748, 1165

Sali River, 193

salt, 568, 1295

sandal, 788

Satan, (*shaytān*) 299, 311, 314. *See also* 5, 158
   See devil

satisfaction (*nemat*). *See* blessing; bounty

Saul, King. *See also* 726

sawāb (reward), 945

Sayyed Ali Tirmezi. *See also* 460

scabbard, sheath, 449, 1071

scarcity, 820

scarlet, 663

score. *See* twenty

scratch, 515, 680, 731, 942. *See also* 920

scrounger, 161, 162

sea, 262, 358

search, 465, 705, 1280, 1332. *See also* 248, 1118

secret, 76, 117, 590, 1097. *See also* 233, 627, 1111

seed, 354. *See also* 1325
   mustard, 435
   sesame, 520

selfish man, 996. *See also* 112, 472, 699, 866, 937, 1009

September. *See also* 121

servant, 839, 1132. *See also* 266, 409, 615, 917, 930, 1139, 1225
  nokar, 1293
  See menial

service (*khidmat*), 84, 924. *See also* 912, 1165

sesame seed, 520

shade, 80, 867, 1212, 1242, 1246, 1309. *See also* 65, 120, 1212

shadow, 1242

Shah Dawla, 747

Shah Zaman, 569

Shahai. *See also* 504

Shakespeare, William. *See also* 14, 492, 968

shame, 487. *See also* 47, 263, 321, 415, 480, 553, 738, 1108, 1144, 1348
  sharm, 415, 802, 1074, 1141. *See also* 375, 966
  See disgrace; taunts

shameful. *See also* 975, 1078

shameless, 1348. *See also* 1145

Shangri La. *See also* 876

share, 285, 286, 496, 616, 769, 833, 1142, 1285. *See also* 85, 90, 116, 210, 315, 317, 371, 503, 542, 545, 609, 657, 1003, 1017, 1099, 1128, 1215, 1216, 1229, 1306

Shariah. See also 415, 654.
  See religious law

sheep, 437, 1161, 1238. *See also* 396, 1307, 1333

sheet, 812. *See also* 1229
  chadar, tsādor, 814

Sheikh Chili, 1252

Sheikh Farid, 1165

Sheikh Mir, 892

Sheikh Qutbuddin Bakhtiar Kaki. *See also* 1165

shell, 379

shelter, 524, 584. *See also* 650

shepherd. *See* herdsman

shield, 1126

Shiva. *See also* 159

shoe, 788, 1256. *See also* 578.
  See horseshoe

shoemaker, 578

short cut, 340, 342. *See also* 75

shot, 375, 431, 592

shoulder, 8, 152, 328, 938. *See also* 525, 622, 937

shrine. *See also* 458, 459, 460, 656, 747, 795

shroud, 1067

shrubs, 1194

shy, 1074, 1141. *See also* 1108.
  See shame

sick, ill, 1181. *See also* 102, 378, 396, 930, 1054, 1229

sickle, 355, 763

sieve, 817, 1191. *See also* 237

significant man. *See* great

Sikh, 1034, 1158. *See also* 1165

silence, 647, 834, 835, 1088. *See also* 480

sin, sinner. *See also* 94, 668, 723

single, 315, 379, 413, 432, 1071, 1154, 1155, 1344

sister, 2, 3, 4, 84, 343, 387, 825, 997, 1002, 1055, 1170, 1304, 1305, 1348.
  See also 148, 1003, 1216, 1348

sister-in-law. *See* in-laws

Skelton, John. *See also* 398

skewer, 564

skin, 980. *See also* 1102, 1261

sky, heavens, 37, 38, 39, 40, 41, 42, 44, 45, 47, 434, 546, 584, 630, 879, 880, 1128, 1180

slap, 455, 549, 798

slave, 628, 1272, 1335. *See also* 562, 644, 820, 944

slave girl. *See* maidservant

sleep, asleep, 206, 207, 208, 533, 611, 637, 639, 793, 993, 994, 995. *See also* 350, 680, 702, 1281, 1314

sluice, 189, 196

slut, 466

small. *See* insignificant

smallpox, 260

smoke, 1046

snake, 90, 364, 571, 703, 732, 1263, 1264. *See also* 181, 1253

snow, 1054, 1301

soap. *See also* 444

sob. *See* weep

soil, 1061. *See* earth (*khāwra*). *See also* 586

soldier, 977. *See also* 1165

Solomon, King (*Bacha Suliman*). *See also* 54, 310, 315, 659, 705, 726, 835

son, 90, 224, 230, 260, 308, 342, 351, 555, 601, 696, 736, 742, 918, 922, 957, 1092, 1109, 1110, 1121, 1295, 1303, 1312, 1317. *See also* 284, 289, 332, 480, 485, 796, 799, 958, 990, 997, 1003, 1232, 1259

son-in-law. *See* in-laws

sorrow, grief, burden, trouble. *See also* 106, 148, 195, 342, 874, 970, 1218, 1239
  ghəm, 183, 333, 334, 378, 611, 728, 746, 1142, 1192, 1343
  See mourning

soul, souls, 290. *See also* 1181

soup, 87, 281, 816

sour, bitter, 576, 878, 1282

sow, 352, 645. *See also* 123, 284, 800, 1325

spade, 8

spear, 516, 1063

spectator, 497. *See also* 332

spend (money), 116, 361, 381, 441, 805. *See also* 422, 836,1042

spinach, 963, 972

spinning wheel (*tsarkha*). *See also* 58

spiritual guide, 142. *See* religious leader; saint

spoil, spoiled, 143, 310, 979, 1302

spring, 446, 750, 779, 823. *See also* 350

spy, 627

staff. *See also* 54

star, 39

steal. *See* theft

step-father. *See* father

step-mother. *See* mother

stick, 423, 850, 1198. *See also* 613, 713, 939

stomach, belly, 231, 359, 393, 394, 544, 1063, 1311. *See also* 865

stone, 38, 185, 194, 264, 410, 425, 749, 1004, 1025, 1072, 1073. *See also* 196, 425, 489, 945, 1180, 1194 , 1307

storehouse, 778

story, fable, tale, 570, 686, 1114, 1174, 1307. *See also* 83, 85, 91, 152, 204, 480, 540, 553, 576, 577, 608, 622, 637, 1045, 1077, 1109, 1119, 1180, 1181, 1193, 1215, 1229, 1251, 1252, 1277, 1281, 1307, 1312, 1325. *See* myth

stranger, 125, 127. *See also* 128
  praday, 215, 363, 417, 857, 862, 863, 875

straw, 175, 390, 962, 969, 1038

stream, 195, 623, 956, 1209. *See also* 189, 1251, 1314. *See* water

street. *See also* 951
  kutsa, 126, 1227

strength, 13, 270, 490, 612, 695, 915, 1102. *See also* 35, 159, 234, 312, 494, 761, 1077, 1102, 1161, 1187, 1282
  taqat, 1185
  See power

strive, 252, 691, 906. *See also* 553, 672, 701, 931, 978

strong man. *See* powerful man

struck. *See* beat

stubborn, 112, 929. *See also* 935

stubborn man. *See also* 929

student, pupil, 133. *See also* 118

stupid, stupidity, 1206, 1213, 1231. *See also* 83, 907, 1284, 1346. *See* fool

suffer, suffering, 603, 820, 856, 1054, 1144, 1194. *See also* 89, 102, 106, 202, 213, 409, 498, 548, 592, 677, 720, 746, 765, 839, 1327, 1338
  See ghəm

sufficient. *See* enough

Sufi, Sufism. *See also* 291, 461, 747, 1165. *See dhikr*

sugar, 819
  gur, 617, 643, 813, 1066, 1241
  shakari, 388

summer, 1246. *See also* 329

sun, 630, 1212. *See also* 122, 176, 1325
  sunlight, 1054
  sunshine, 1246

Sura. *See also* 91

suspicion, distrust, 1169. *See also* 115, 210

Sutlej River. *See also* 1165

Swabi. *See also* 622

Swat, 58, 95, 1319. *See also* 609, 656, 1314

sweet, 385, 417, 418, 643, 813, 992, 1092, 1114, 1166. *See also* 61, 177, 418, 746, 1081
  khog, 401, 819, 1005, 1282
swim, 172
swine, 735
sword, 120, 149, 449, 508, 509, 510, 513, 626, 663, 678, 1027, 1071, 1126, 1137, 1166. *See also* 106, 289, 385, 1086
syrup, 199, 813. *See* drink
tail, 70, 575, 791, 854, 1045, 1238, 1253
Takwara, 374
Talash, 498
tale. *See* story
talk, 590, 658, 851, 992, 1080. *See also* 442, 451, 467, 492, 524, 815, 849, 889, 951, 991, 1120, 1242, 1348
tamarisk tree, 440
ṭappa, lanḍəy (folk poem). *See also* 106, 429, 460, 635, 839, 993, 1159, 1266
Taro Jabba. *See also* 150
taste, 250
taunts, insults, 1191. *See also* 225, 283, 375, 455, 1044
  shame (*peghor*), 1254
taweez. See amulet
teacher. *See also* 1178
  Akhund. *See also* 85, 89
  mullah, 133. *See also* 1109
  ostāz, 118, 142
tear, 1331. *See also* 148, 683
tease, teased. *See also* 124, 284
teeth, 605, 706, 1015, 1120, 1143
test, tested, 114, 115, 413, 510, 1173. *See also* 1143
theft, 267, 337, 430, 709, 1189, 1323
thief, thieves, 150, 327, 363, 422, 710, 861, 864, 1038, 1189, 1190, 1281, 1288, 1297, 1339. *See also* 282
thirst, 1311
thorn, 145, 1239. *See also* 390
thorn-bush, 533, 1001
threshing, 1197, 1337
thunder, thunderbolt, 43, 318, 522, 584, 685, 1180. *See* sky
thunderstorm, 498

time, times, 81, 195, 308, 391, 426, 443, 519, 752, 753, 877, 1091, 1095, 1138, 1173, 1197, 1321. *See also* 4, 51, 58, 94, 102, 107, 141, 147, 165, 210, 220, 224, 225, 232, 294, 312, 351, 359, 368, 375, 412, 493, 520, 911, 946, 955, 1057, 1102, 1119, 1131, 1137, 1143, 1178, 1212, 1229, 1294, 1312, 1318, 1342
  appointed time, 73. *See also* 72, 501, 603
  appropriate, proper time, 240, 501, 751. *See also* 77, 199, 235, 352, 372, 1306
  multiplication, 228
timid man. *See also* 832
Tirah, 1
tired, 405, 783. *See also* 1314
today, 337, 600, 738, 1291, 1318. *See also* 1230, 1247
Tolstoy, Leo. *See also* 924
tomato(es). *See also* 63
tomorrow, 738, 1291, 1318. *See also* 694
tongue, 383, 385, 418, 499, 641, 804, 815, 882, 968, 1027, 1114, 1120, 1166, 1257. *See also* 216, 401, 834, 835, 1207. *See* mouth
toothbrush, 407, 408
Tor Dalai, 504
Tor Mullah, 507
Tora, 625
Torai, 512
tragedy, 826. *See also* 102, 683, 726
train, training, 143. *See also* 787, 1198, 1247
tranquility, 900. *See* patience
trap, 279, 597. *See also* 1218, 1241
traveler, 1048. *See also* 283, 284, 1314
tree, 533, 1059, 1062, 1309. *See also* 358, 577, 941
  alder. *See also* 941
  castor, 518
  fig. *See also* 1314
  mulberry, 553
  pipal, banyan, 1193
  pine, 1290
  tamarisk, 440
tribe, tribal, 196. *See also* 1, 63, 305, 328, 341, 361, 375, 444, 487, 608, 620, 661, 668, 863, 1119, 1326. *See* Pakhtun tribes
tribulation, 911. *See also* 262, 1313

trouble. *See* calamity; sorrow

trousers, 273, 493, 967

   salwār, shalwār, 329

trouser belt, 770

trumpet, 268

truncheon, 579

trunk (tree), 1290

truth, 89, 688, 894, 899, 1087, 1088. *See also* 76, 173, 232, 340, 645, 650, 671, 678, 705, 726, 850, 857, 1135, 1218, 1252, 1262, 1266, 1298, 1318

turban, 42, 328, 407, 408, 416, 788, 1136, 1158. *See also* 843, 1034, 1081

turn, chance, 1229

turnip. *See also* 425

twenty, 313, 455, 822, 1261. *See also* 1064

   score, 1163

tyrant, 9. *See also* 402

uncle

   maternal (*māmā*), 307, 463, 731, 1003, 1184

   paternal, *akā*, 148

   tru, 898

undisciplined, inexperienced man. *See also* 885

unequal. *See* equal

unfaithful. *See* faithful

unity, 64, 610, 858. *See also* 67, 312, 403, 914, 1032, 1083, 1161

universe, 632

unkind man. *See also* 134

unlawful. *See* forbidden

unscrupulous man. *See* rogue

unworthy. *See* worthy

valley, 1324

variant proverbs. *See* proverbs

vein, 1084

version, 641

village, 89, 150, 432, 552, 615, 671, 673, 688, 713, 714, 715, 737, 809, 933, 979, 1087, 1112, 1124, 1226, 1234. *See also* 210, 275, 339, 374, 609, 620, 668, 903, 1216, 1307

villager, 1075. *See also* 1020, 1081

virtue, virtuous, 326, 1177. *See also* 328, 640, 723

vow. *See also* 119, 747. *See* intention

wages, 316

wait, waiting, 162, 166, 326, 582, 1121

walk, walking, 331, 348, 484, 606, 755, 1127, 1242. *See also* 154, 339, 505, 1348

wall, 77, 367, 1072

walnut. *See also* 421

war. *See also* 120, 275, 513, 863, 889, 1194, 1279

   jang, 529

   See battle; fight

watchman (*chowkidār*), 709

water, 11, 55, 157, 172, 173, 174, 176, 177, 178, 179, 180, 181, 182, 183, 184, 185, 186, 187, 188, 189, 190, 191, 192, 193, 194, 196, 197, 198, 199, 210, 211, 232, 236, 430, 523, 558, 585, 586, 589, 824, 853, 956, 1017, 1025, 1031, 1250, 1251, 1267, 1311. *See also* 195, 374, 553, 739, 858, 875, 941. *See* mud

water buffalo. *See also* 444

water mill. *See* mill

water pitcher. *See* pitcher

way, ways, 631, 673, 740, 903, 914. *See also* 348, 366. *See* custom

Wazir, Waziristan. *See also* 361, 1058

weak. *See* insignificant

wealth, wealthy, 277, 352, 524, 990, 1236. *See also* 50, 53, 55, 620, 622, 660, 708, 726, 805, 1058, 1238, 1332

   dawlat, 360, 664, 871, 1070, 1270

   dunyā, 694, 1037, 1067, 1100, 1322

   māl, 137, 1265, 1266

   See money

wealthy. *See also* 690

wealthy man. *See* rich man

weapon, 1308. *See also* 1027

weaver, 337, 566

wedding, 712. *See also* 77, 378, 615, 1321

weep, weeping, 148, 195, 213, 242, 443, 580, 683, 697, 720, 759, 765, 857, 964, 970, 978, 1113, 1119, 1298, 1310, 1331. *See also* 52, 106

weigh, 1028, 1081

weight, 556, 902. *See also* 42, 54, 1073

weights and measures

   chiṭak, chiṭākəy, 753

   false measure, 719

man, 220, 1028
seer, 413, 749, 1004
weighty. *See also* 556, 902, 1004
well, 203, 456, 597, 1042, 1218. *See also* 1018
Wells, H.G. *See also* 398
weysh. See redistribution
wheat, 5, 518, 695, 711, 821
   wheat bread, 85. *See also* 193
   wheat flour. *See also* 1332
whey, 878. *See also* 1215
whip, 24. *See also* 138
white, 444, 511, 698, 954, 1067, 1136, 1137. *See also* 173
wicked. *See also* 202. *See* bad
wicked deed, 281, 284
wicked man, 142. *See also* 147, 1050, 1210
widow, 44
wife, wives, 629, 1089, 1122, 1280. *See also* 148, 204, 315, 622, 847, 1119, 1167, 1348
   bibi, 836
   wives, multiple, 684, 797. *See also* 3, 1229, 1334
wind, 492, 574, 580, 593, 790, 845. *See also* 41, 1102
wing, 297, 897, 934
winnowing, 548
winnowing basket, 547
winter, 63, 1123, 1246, 1315
wisdom. *See also* 91, 105, 106, 138, 322, 705, 906, 1279
   aql, 110, 538, 871, 1076, 1182, 1183
   hekmat, 831
   poha, 1327
wise man, 1179. *See also* 91, 138, 1138, 1178, 1327
wise, clever, intelligent, 164, 544, 728, 1037, 1067, 1206, 1231, 1260. *See also* 104, 106, 138, 298, 321, 526, 538, 664, 746, 835, 871, 1038, 1212, 1277
wish (*ikhtiyār*), 1272
wolf, 279, 1045, 1161, 1251, 1261
woman, women, 349, 587, 598, 622, 873, 990, 1024, 1136, 1144, 1152, 1167, 1168, 1169, 1209, 1279, 1334. *See also* 58, 77, 83, 106, 143, 148, 266, 289, 389, 466, 473, 540, 635,

684, 775, 814, 836, 975, 1002, 1094, 1101, 1109, 1119, 1159, 1181, 1222, 1348
   Khachana. *See also* 224
   See girl
womb, 538. *See also* 231
wood, 518, 1062, 1247, 1334. *See also* 42, 202, 358, 533, 1302
word, words, 61, 375, 417, 647, 815, 848, 850, 852, 853, 854, 984, 1023, 1079, 1147, 1156. *See also* 1, 82, 138, 160, 205, 405, 645, 746, 855, 1027, 1226, 1257, 1272, 1279
   promise, 285, 387. *See also* 36, 1025, 1215
   See taunts
work, 14, 90, 226, 301, 314, 316, 335, 371, 543, 988, 1205. *See also* 13, 25, 27, 35, 54, 68, 89, 122, 240, 248, 305, 313, 364, 391, 395, 413, 454, 456, 465, 472, 482, 514, 545, 549, 580, 594, 615, 727, 744, 758, 769, 780, 789, 869, 905, 912, 930, 953, 994, 1001, 1040, 1045, 1214, 1277, 1293, 1345
works. *See also* 117, 800
world, 82, 389, 390, 607, 1067, 1128, 1231. *See also* 249, 450, 1203
   watan, 1350
   See country (*watan*); ground; earth
worldly, 694, 1067, 1100, 1322. *See also* 155, 656, 991, 1006
worm. *See also* 54, 829
worry, 805, 930, 1172. *See also* 4, 102, 259, 267, 271, 273, 296, 543, 613, 999, 1228, 1348
   ghəm, 625, 890
   See sorrow
worry beads. *See* prayer beads
worship, 1196. *See also* 91. *See* faith
worthy, unworthy, 741, 918. *See also* 14, 34, 421, 462, 788, 819, 950, 1337
wren, 434, 546, 816
wrestle, 676
yardstick, 1064
Yazid. *See also* 1313
year, 1216, 1254
yeast, 1115. *See also* 259
Yeel Bugh, 1137
yellow, 839

yesterday, 337, 600
young, 547, 633, 755. *See also* 1008
    young buffalo, 446
    young bullock, 777
    young child. *See also* 52, 712, 1181
    young couple. *See also* 479
    young mouse. *See also* 1277
    young person. *See also* 15
    young woman. *See* girl

young man, 90, 108, 149. *See also* 622,
    1058, 1119
youngster (*kasher*), 1040, 1233
Yousafzai, 58. *See also* 305, 609, 1009,
    1180, 1186
youth, 666. *See also* 259, 839, 964.
    See young man
Zarghuna, 1094
Zazi, 512

www.ingramcontent.com/pod-product-compliance
Lightning Source LLC
Chambersburg PA
CBHW070537270326
41926CB00013B/2130